Lifeshocks

Also by Sophie Sabbage:

The Cancer Whisperer

SOPHIE SABBAGE

Lifeshocks

And how to love them

CORONET

First published in Great Britain in 2018 by Coronet
An Imprint of Hodder & Stoughton
An Hachette UK company

This paperback edition published in 2019

1

A CIP catalogue record for this title is available from the British Library

B format ISBN 9781473638020
eBook ISBN 9781473637993

Typeset in Plantin Light 12/15.75 pt by Palimpsest Book Production Limited,
Falkirk, Stirlingshire

Printed and bound in Great Britain by Clays Ltd, Elcograf S.p.A.

Hodder & Stoughton policy is to use papers that are natural,
renewable and recyclable products and made from wood grown in
sustainable forests. The logging and manufacturing processes are expected
to conform to the environmental regulations of the country of origin.

Hodder & Stoughton Ltd
Carmelite House
50 Victoria Embankment
London EC4Y 0DZ

www.hodder.co.uk

For my darling Gabriella.

Just in case.

Foreword

Shoulders of Giants

Talking Sticks have been used as instruments of dialogue and democracy by many tribes for centuries, including the Aboriginals of Australia, the Maoris of New Zealand and indigenous peoples of the Northwest coast of North America. These sticks are passed around at tribal council meetings and important ceremonies, allowing only the person holding the stick to speak. This enables each person to be heard as they express their point of view.

My mentor for sixteen years, Dr K. Bradford Brown, was part Washoe, a Native American tribe of Nevada and California. After the Californian gold rush brought an influx of European-American settlers, Washoe lands were broken up into allotments, and calls for a Washoe reservation, along with compensation for lost resources, were ignored. Instead of retaining precious land in the Pine Nut Mountains, they were left with barren plots that had little access to water. They were finally awarded shockingly modest compensation in 1970.

Brad adapted the use of the Talking Stick for a particular ceremony he held at the end of his advanced courses, using it as an instrument of gratitude, a tradition we maintain to this day. The Talking Stick is placed in the centre of a circle and people take turns to pick it up, bang it three times on the floor in front of someone they feel grateful to and express their thanks.

In essence, this is about recognising those who source us in our lives – the people who touch and awaken us, from whom we learn and grow. Brad was a clinical psychologist, psychotherapist, theologian and Episcopalian priest, but he drew on ancient spiritual traditions from far and wide as well as modern psychological wisdom and practices. Notably, he was a direct student of Viktor Frankl, who survived Auschwitz and went on to write *Man's Search for Meaning*, as well as of the great twentieth-century British philosopher, Alan Watts, who brought Eastern philosophy to the West, and the North American humanistic psychologist, Carl Rogers. Brad was careful to acknowledge them all.

As Brad's student, these are just a few of the giants on whose shoulders I stand. He probably wouldn't like me calling him a 'giant'. He used to say, 'There are no extraordinary people, just ordinary people who do extraordinary things with what they have been given.' Brad was so committed to experiential learning, he never wrote a book describing his work. However, he regretted this in his later years and even outlined the book he wanted to write, but it came too late. And when he was near his end, I promised him I would write it one day. It would not be *his* book, or even follow his outline. It would be mine. It could only be mine, but it would be about his teachings and how I have endeavoured to live by them. As I write, it is now ten years since Brad died in 2007. And I am finally fulfilling that promise.

Throughout these pages, I have acknowledged what he created and taught me. Over the years, my whole being, my very cells have been imbued with his wisdom. Accordingly, on occasion, his words may come out as mine. This is not because I lay false claim to them, but because I have absorbed them like a sponge absorbs water. As such, I own what he has passed down to me and can think of no better way to honour his legacy than this. At the same time, this is *my* story, and in it I am sharing the insights I have come to through my own inner work, some of these picking up where Brad left off. I own these too. I have come too far in my own development not to. In all this, I honour my teacher and my own becoming. I have sought to be as transparent and authentic as I know how to be. Only a few names and dates have been changed out of respect to certain people, a couple of whom I slightly fictionalised to guard their privacy. Some others have given me permission to share intimate parts of their lives, for which I am grateful. And while this is in part my story, my story is not its point. The point is to share the alchemy of fused wisdoms, among them those that came to Brad before I knew him and those that came to me through other channels – including, and especially, lifeshocks.

It is also important to note that some of the insights in this book are 'out there' in other forms, which I acknowledge where I can. Brad developed his work in the 1970s and brought it forward in these particular forms in 1981. As well as the influences they came from, some of these ideas have since morphed into human consciousness on a much greater scale. This may well be an example of the 'hundredth monkey' phenomenon, whereby a sudden shift in consciousness happens when a critical mass point is reached. It is so named because, in 1952, a group of scientists conducted an experiment with a colony of Japanese monkeys on the island of Koshima. They dropped sweet potatoes in the sand for the monkeys to eat. The monkeys liked the taste, but not the sand and dirt. One monkey solved this problem by washing the potatoes in a stream and then taught other monkeys to do the same. After several years, a certain number of monkeys (symbolically estimated at ninety-nine) had *learned* this technique when, suddenly – at the point of the hundredth monkey – *all* the monkeys spontaneously washed their potatoes without needing to be taught. Even more remarkable, this breakthrough in monkey conscious-ness spread to other islands, where monkeys began washing their potatoes too, as if a new field of awareness had been created. This is a fine example of what Rupert Sheldrake later termed (somewhat controversially) 'morphic resonance', a process whereby memory is inherent in nature and 'telepathy-type interconnections between organisms' exist.

I believe something similar has been happening over the past four decades with some of the ideas in these pages – perhaps most notably the understanding that our beliefs drive our behaviour, generate our emotions and can profoundly limit our true potential. Such insights are not unique and, in a world of profound psychological and spiritual suffering, this is cause indeed to rejoice.

Equally, I love Elizabeth Gilbert's notion that ideas are sentient entities, floating around the psychic sphere and beckoning us to bring them into the world. If one person misses it, the idea moves on to the next person until someone lets it in. Personally, I picture them tapping on several shoulders at once and then manifesting in different forms. This may not be a verifiable concept, but somewhere between this and the 'hundredth monkey', universal wisdoms seem to find their way into the world.

At the same time, I have not seen the same cut on how life works as I intend to share in this book by introducing whoever reads it to lifeshocks – their nature, meaning and purpose which, once recognised, may lead us to love the apparently unlovable and forgive the apparently unforgivable. Nor have I come across more powerful methods for personal and collective transformation. May this book serve as a Talking Stick for *life itself*. And may it add something of real value to the evolution of humanity and the world we call home.

Preface

*Have you ever wondered if life is
trying to tell you something?*

This is a book about all the unwanted and unexpected moments of our lives, many of which we don't like and some of which we do. They surprise us. They blindside us. They shock us. They command our attention. These are not once-in-a-while events, but usually a dozen-a-day encounters with what we cannot control, predict or plan. Some bounce off us, some scratch the surface of our lives, others strike deep into our being. These moments are collision points between life as we see it and life as it actually is. They seem so random, so unfairly distributed, so out of the blue.

And yet.

What if these moments are a personalised navigation system helping us chart our way to more authentic, creative and loving lives?

What if there is a pattern to them that may accelerate our development if we could only see it?

And what if life really is trying to tell us something about our own essence and purpose?

If there is as much to these moments as this book

proposes, then they deserve a distinguishing term to help us recognise them more easily: *lifeshocks*. As I will explain, it is, in fact, a term that has been in use since 1981, but has not yet found its way into our culture or common vernacular. It is my sincere hope that one day it will appear in official dictionaries with this definition:

Lifeshock. Noun. *An unwanted or unexpected moment in time, offering an opportunity for personal awakening.*

In these pages I will explain how lifeshocks awaken us. I will illuminate their nature and purpose through the teachings that have been passed down to me, as well as through my own experience of consciously engaging with lifeshocks for more than half my life. Until now, I have taught this material face to face, helping people to dive deep before coming up lighter and freer than they were before. My teacher, Brad Brown, used to say, '*Understanding* (versus experiencing) this is the booby prize.' For this reason, I have offered my deeply personal and erstwhile private story as a vehicle for bringing the theory and teachings to life. I have also included some anonymous stories that clients – as well as a few identified people I know – have kindly allowed me to share. These are a sprinkling of the thousands of stories I could tell.

In particular, I am going to tell you about three kinds of lifeshock we all receive: *limiting lifeshocks*, which challenge our arrogance and appetite for control; *exposing lifeshocks*, which challenge our deceptions and pretences; and *evoking lifeshocks*, which challenge our closed-heartedness. I will also show how these lifeshocks guide us back to the best in ourselves and the possibilities we may have abandoned at the roadside.

Before I met Brad in person, I participated in a course

led by one of his top team, a woman called Sue Oldham. The strength of her backbone was matched by the tenderness of her heart. She had remarkable authority and compassion, neither hard nor soft, but powerful, loving, bold. I didn't really get the teachings at that point. I just wanted to have what she had; to walk through the world as a woman as at home in myself as she was. At one point in her career, she had worked as a school guidance counsellor. One day, a girl came into Sue's office in floods of tears because her parents were splitting up. She believed it would be a disaster for her mother, that she would have to choose between her parents at Christmas and would get caught in the middle of their conflict. Later the same day, another girl skipped into Sue's office smiling because her parents were splitting up. She believed it was an opportunity for her mother to be happy and find a partner who loved her and was excited at the prospect of getting two Christmases every year. These girls were twin sisters.

As I will show, the human mind is highly interpretative. It is capable of generating profound pain, loneliness and self-deception that becomes the bedrock of our lives. It is also capable of remarkable wisdom, resourcefulness and courage, helping us scale heights of wonder and plumb depths of insight beyond any goals we have set out to achieve. The imagination can destroy, and it can create. It can react *against* lifeshocks and it can respond *to* them. It can close to what might be on offer and it can open to extraordinary possibilities even in the darkest of circumstances. We can harness the destructive aspect and liberate the creative aspect. We can treat what life brings us as incidental and haphazard or as deliberate and intimate, mysteriously customised for our evolution as human beings. This book will show you how.

You will find practical 'take-outs' at intervals between the chapters in Part Two. These are the skills and practices I normally guide people through on courses, but I hope readers who resonate with the philosophy I am sharing will feel stirred to navigate life in a similar way. And for anyone who wishes to learn these methods with skilled guides to support them, they will find that information too.

These are largely therapeutic tools that have been repurposed for self-management. One way of looking at them is as 'lifeshock therapy'. Instead of relying on a therapist to help us through challenges, we can rely on ourselves. We can apply these skills to whatever life throws at us. We don't need to have major problems to benefit. We just need to be open to learning and discovering more of what's possible. We can even see life itself as a treatment room and the events of our lives as the encounters that will help us become our best selves. Instead of perceiving life as something to contend with much of the time, we can begin to see it as the teacher of all teachers, with tutorials that uniquely target our individual awakening and expansion.

To this end, my intention is to reveal the remarkably reliable way that lifeshocks can help us find what we most long for, if we only knew how to decipher them: inner strength, connection, belonging, freedom from self-imposed limitations, acceptance of real limitations, integrity, a sense of place and purpose, the power to respond creatively to challenging events, faithfulness, fulfilment, possibility, joy, wonder, expansion, being able to rest in peace *before* we die.

I will show how limiting lifeshocks can restore our natural inner authority and help us glory in our flawed, fallible, beautiful humanness; how exposing lifeshocks can call us back to our authentic selves and a willingness to walk through the world with nothing to prove, but everything we have to offer; and how evoking lifeshocks can bring down the walls around our hearts, ending our loneliness and teaching us not just how to love, but how to *be loved*. This much treasure is at hand.

Life is not what it seems. We are not what we fear we are or believe we have to be. Extraordinariness is not the reserve of the few and the sacred is not confined to other realms. To discern the nature and purpose of lifeshocks is, as my friend Dr Roy Whitten once said, 'one thing that can change everything'. It can place us on our true path and offer passage out of the morass. It can bring us home to ourselves at any moment in any situation on any day.

Contents

Part One

Stillness Moves

What if I should discover that the poorest of the beggars and the most impudent of offenders are all within me; and that I stand in need of the alms of my own kindness, that I, myself, am the enemy who must be loved – what then?

C. G. Jung

I

What If?

I am lying stock-still, my head completely immobilised. It has been bolted into a Gamma Knife radiation machine with a stereotactic metal frame that was drilled on to my skull with four screws – two at the front, just above my temples, and two at the back, in the equivalent position. This ensures the medical team can target each brain tumour with meticulous accuracy while protecting the surrounding tissue.

Multiple tumours pepper both hemispheres, each one measuring between one and five millimetres. The tumours are threatening to take me out piece by neurological piece.

My neuro-oncologist has elected to treat them all in one session and estimates it will take eight hours. Apparently, this is not the norm, but he has decided I am not the norm either. So here I am. Locked in.

The irony is not lost on me. I have been searching for stillness for over thirty years, but have rarely found it.

I cultivated many failed versions of stillness over the years: going on retreats 'to be peaceful'; trying to meditate my way into it (and invariably falling out of it); wandering alone across mountains hoping stillness would bleed through the clouds; practising it like a method;

pursuing it like a destination; chasing it like the end of a rainbow. *If I am just aware enough, diligent enough, conscious enough, loving enough, generous enough and 'spiritual' enough (whatever that means), then surely stillness will be mine.*

But none of this worked, which may be why I have ended up lying inside a giant Polo mint (which is what radiotherapy machines usually look like), fully conscious and unable to move for the best part of a day. I laugh in fractions because the frame won't allow more. I've been living with incurable lung cancer for two years. By the time I received the diagnosis it had spread widely. I was offered whole brain radiation, which indiscriminately targets the brain for the multiple metastases they found at that point, but turned the treatment down. Fortunately, we found other ways to get rid of almost all the tumours and the disease stabilised for a prolonged period. Now they are back, and I am lying in this machine trying to come to terms with this latest development.

At first my mind is as active as my daughter's legs, which were running before she was born. The pregnancy was considered 'high risk' because I conceived her at the age of forty-two and experienced a few complications. Consequently, I had regular ultrasound scans to monitor her wellbeing and her legs were always moving at a gallop. I never saw her sleeping or lying still in the womb. Then, as a baby, she didn't rest her head on my shoulder in that placid way I used to envy other mothers for, and car trips have always been problematic. As a toddler, she couldn't bear being strapped into her child seat for longer than a few minutes, screaming her objections on almost every journey until, aged two, she simply announced (after I'd been driving for ten minutes), 'Mummy, my legs are bored.'

She is six as I write this and it is rare to get through a bedtime story in one sitting. 'Why can't you sit still?' I asked her one night as she did half a dozen head-flips on the bed while I turned the pages of a book. 'Because I am bouncy, Mummy,' she replied, upside down, 'I'm very bouncy.' I set the story aside and watched her for a few minutes, shifting position occasionally to ensure she didn't land on me, and wondering if she would ever love books as I do. She can hardly stand the inertia, whereas I, at the same age, couldn't stand being torn away from whatever I was reading. I never had that kind of physical energy. I wasn't brave like her. I didn't want to climb the highest tree or dive into the deepest part of the river. I never managed a headstand, cartwheel or even a backward roll. My body was tentative and ungainly, unsure of itself in the world. My gym teacher at primary school said I had 'no natural spring' and that was that. I stopped springing.

My energy has been predominantly mental. As I lie here, I observe my mind oscillating between opposing positions like a clock pendulum: *this is a nightmare; this is remarkable; this is the end; this is a new beginning; I don't deserve this; I do deserve this; it's my fault; it's no one's fault; I'm going to die; I'm going to live; I'm out of control; I'm in control; I haven't done enough to heal; I've done all I could to heal; I can't go on with this; I can go on with this; I don't know how to go on; I must go on.* And my mind rolls on and on like a freight train gaining speed, passing each thought like station platforms on both sides of the track, but arriving nowhere. Each shift in perception creates a temporary shift of emotion, my heart closing and opening again like shutters on a camera, momentarily locked in the darkness and then letting in the light. It doesn't make a difference if my mind is being deceptive and destructive or eager and encouraging. Neither brings me to stillness. And I start to realise that however much the mind says, 'I want stillness', the reality of stillness is the last thing it wants because it cannot bear not to exist. Is this why stillness is almost impossible to find?

As my mind runs on, I recall my neuro-oncologist explaining why I need to lie here for eight hours. Initially they found eight tumours at a routine scan, but as soon as the metal frame had been fitted, he scanned my brain with a very fine-cut MRI machine to pick up any others that may have been missed.

'Mrs Sabbage, we found twenty-seven tumours,' he reported in the upbeat tone of a detective who has solved a crime.

Twenty-seven. Twenty-seven. Twenty-seven. The words flash by repeatedly. My mind is trying to evade this hard-to-swallow truth and I keep seeing my daughter, Gabriella, somewhere in a heartbroken future where I am just a memory of the mother she once had.

What if this doesn't work?

What if the tumours resist the radiation and claim dominion? What if they spread like wildfire through a forest until all the trees are down?

What if I don't make it?

What if I don't get to see my girl grow up?

What if I can't guide her through a confused culture that mistakes social media 'likes' for acceptance, position for power and airbrushing for beauty?

What if she learns to measure her worth by her waistline, her success by exam results, her specialness by how favourably she compares to others and her strength by the weight of her pain?

What if she gets lost in the spiritual supermarket where God is peddled in a thousand synthetic packages and stacked up on shelves like a display of competing brands?

What if my time is up?

The conceptual mind is a trickster. It transports us down long, winding corridors with no cheese at the end of them – just damning judgements about our flaws and unsubstantiated suppositions about our futures. I have a mind, but am not my mind. I can bring it to heel or it will bring me to my knees, as it has on many occasions. And what better place to remember this than here, having twenty-seven brain tumours fried?

2

A Reluctant Prayer

The way the conceptual mind tricks us is unavoidable. It is part of the human condition and paradoxically necessary for our evolution.

I grew up in the Christian tradition, saying prayers in school assembly and going to church on Sundays, much of which left me cold. But even in the emotional turmoil of my teenage years, I longed to quieten all the noise in my head: a voice that made me *too ugly, too clever, too weird, too intense, too loud, too privileged, too fat, too emotional, too difficult* and *too damn much.* My friends turned to boys for affirmation. I turned to books. Books were my place of prayer.

I devoured them from the age of three and loved getting English homework. I opened words like sweets with foil wrappers and built tree houses out of sentences I wanted to move into. I tucked my secrets into the paragraphs of favourite pages and kissed them good-night. Some of my sweetest and most vivid childhood memories are of books.

I spent much of my eighth year riding the rollercoaster of cruelties and kindnesses encountered by *Black Beauty*, a horse in Victorian England. I read that book so many times I can still quote whole chunks of it by heart. I was also given a small brown cassette player on my seventh birthday and loved listening to the audio version on long car journeys. My mum tells me I used to fall asleep in the passenger seat next to her, with the cassette player on the floor by my feet where she couldn't reach it, leaving her listening to the sad bits alone. Later, I learned the novel wasn't written to be read by children, but because its author, Anna Sewell, wanted to change the cruel ways horses were treated in those days – and it did, dramatically. That was when I found out that books could change the world.

At the age of ten I read Harper Lee's *To Kill A Mockingbird* in one sitting on a family holiday in New England. We were visiting friends who lived in a white, wooden, ocean-front house at the top of a cliff on the coast of Maine, with a view across the Atlantic Ocean. It was summer. Their garden was in full bloom and the table was laid for a fresh lobster lunch, but I wasn't there. I was in Maycomb, Alabama, with Jem and Scout, as they found gifts in the tree outside Boo Radley's place. I begged to be excused from socialising and was permitted to sit under a tree with my book while our hosts cooked lunch.

Lobsters scream when thrown in boiling water and I cried listening to them. My dad tried to reassure me it was just a release of heated vapours whistling out of the shell joints, but I didn't believe him. Though I wasn't brave enough to save the lobsters, I refused to eat them, which gave me another excuse to keep reading about the complexities of race, class and injustice in the American Deep South of the 1930s. I finished my book under a tree in the summer sunshine, occasionally distracted by the great black-backed gulls laughing over-head, and listening to more lobsters scream.

From then on, I kept company with novelists and poets. I would bring them home after school or university and sit with them in the small hours, inviting them to change me. I wanted to be someone else, to be rewritten; to wake up one day cast as Cleopatra or Anna Karenina – beautiful, revolutionary and epically loved.

By the time I finished university, where I studied English Literature, my large library overflowed with antidotes to my inadequacies. It was hallowed ground. As I packed up my student flat to go home, I bought a roll of black rubbish sacks, filling them with about five hundred books before storing them in the garage at my parents' house in London. These included the beautifully bound collections my godmother had given me as a child, as if she knew in advance how deeply I would fall in love with literature. When I came to pick them up a few weeks later, they had gone. Believing the sacks were full of rubbish, Mrs Yeldham, my mum's cleaner, had thrown them all away. The following morning, I barely registered the degree results that arrived in the post. I was too gutted to take that information in.

There are moments in time when our internal perceptions are confronted by external events, when *what is assumed, wished for* or *imagined* collides with *what actually is*. I would later learn a term for these moments from the man who became my spiritual mentor: *lifeshocks*. This lifeshock – hearing the words, 'I threw them away' from the distraught, abjectly apologetic woman who had worked for my mum for years – forced me to face the unhealthy aspect of my attachment to books. It led me to admit that no number of books could provide permanent refuge from my deepening insecurities and the interminable noise in my head. They were not a temple. They were books. Brilliant, beautiful, mind-bending narratives that often fed my soul when it was hungry, but could not save me from my loneliness, my longing or my shame. I cried all day. I couldn't stop. I kept saying sorry to Mrs Yeldham, who was almost as upset as I was, but the dam had broken – the one I had built with the complete works of Austen and Dickens, Shakespeare and the Brontë sisters, Maya Angelou and Mary Oliver.

Eventually my mum, who was also there that day, got a bottle of wine from the fridge and poured three glasses. And we sat with Mrs Yeldham, getting drunk.

Sometimes we need to lose what we are hiding behind to see that we are hiding. It took the sudden loss of my library to expose the emotional distress beneath my intellectual poise. Without my books, I felt naked. I had written a first-class dissertation about mad women in literature and women who wrote their way out of madness, while my own madness spiralled out of control.

I think that was the day my conscious quest for Something Greater began. I searched far and wide, often on life's fringes because that's where the New Age Movement could be found in those days. After university, when I worked as a copywriter for the BBC, I spent most of my spare time and much of my income immersed in psychological and spiritual development, signing up for as many courses and experiences as I could find: psychotherapy, astrology, meditation, rebirthing, sweat lodges, acupuncture, angel cards, spirit guides, worry beads, fire walking, psychic readings, flower remedies, past life regression and strange encounters with channelled beings from other worlds. Some of it made a difference, opening my eyes to versions of the divine from beyond the confines of my conservative upbringing and, at times, opening me up to myself. Some of it made no difference at all.

I knew I didn't want to spend all day meditating or praying. I didn't even want to eat lentils and drink herbal tea. I wanted to walk the streets of London, where I had lived most of my life, and find the divine in the paving cracks. I wanted to grasp life's nettles to see what I, and they, were made of.

One day, in my early twenties, I was at a very low ebb. I was on holiday on the Greek island of Lesvos with two girlfriends from one of the courses I had taken at university. Lesvos was where, as a seventeen-year-old on holiday with my parents, I had first fallen in love and begun to believe I was more lovable than I had thought, though little evidence to that effect had surfaced since. I knew I was clever and interesting, up to a point, but was usually cast aside for someone thinner and prettier and less *intense*. Which was fair. I was intense. Apparently deep-and-meaningful was not an attractive quality to the few twenty-something men who thought I was hot and wanted to jump my bones. Invariably, they tired and moved on.

There was a central street in the seaside village where we were staying, lined with bars and tavernas on both sides. Every evening the Greeks strutted up and down in their best attire, apparently as a way of meeting each other in a strictly controlled social culture. I sat in a taverna with my girlfriends, Suzy and Anna, eating calamari and watching people while we made up stories about their lives. We gave them names, jobs and passions, as if we were writing a soap opera, spinning the next episode about regular characters night after night. We ate at the same taverna each evening because I fancied the waiter, but when Suzy and Anna got bored of the menu they urged me to ask him out. Two glasses of wine later I had a date.

It was fun and purely physical, adding some spice to the sunshine and some credits to my self-esteem. I saw him when I wanted and skipped it when I didn't. It was a bona-fide holiday fling. My real interest lay in deepening my friendships with Suzy and Anna – especially Suzy, who had a soft-skinned, full-lipped, unassuming beauty I appreciated more than envied, a wicked sense of humour and a quiet, self-possessed confidence that I wanted for myself. When she invited me to join them on holiday, I had felt like the school nerd who was being befriended by the coolest girl in class.

The night before we flew back to England I got blind drunk on tequila shots that you down in one before licking some salt off your hand and biting into a slice of lemon – a new experience. I didn't mean it to get so out of control. I just didn't know my limits when it came to tequila. But then my Greek fling walked into the bar. He was very attractive, dark and swarthy, straight off the pages of a Mills and Boon novel. I remember him offering me a lift back to the cheap apartment rooms where we were staying and climbing on to his yellow motorbike with high handle bars. After consulting Suzy and Anna, who wanted to stay up a bit longer, I told him I was too drunk for any shenanigans, but yes please. I needed to crash out.

I don't remember what happened after that, but I

woke up face down, half naked, uncovered, blood on the sheets, bruises on my thighs and shoulders, and very sore inside. He was long gone. 'Date rape' wasn't even a term back then and it took me many years to really call it what it was. The fact of the assault was overshadowed by my shame for losing control and consciousness, the belief that I had invited it. *I probably deserved it. I had been stupid and reckless. I had abused my own body long before someone else did, so what should I expect?* I didn't feel angry. Instead, I shrivelled into a familiar feeling of mortifying embarrassment, brought on by a brutal disregard of my body's value. I locked the experience away with all the other self-harming secrets I had hoarded before that day.

What I did do, on the last morning of our holiday, was go to the beach, place my feet in the salt water lapping over the rocks I perched on, and pray. My prayer was more reluctant than reverent, but it was honest. It sprang from that hollowed-out place inside where there is nothing to hold on to and no one to turn to. It was one of the loneliest moments of my life. The prayer went something like this:

I don't know what to call you and that's the problem. I don't want to talk to the clouds or the carved image of a man dying on a cross above a stone cold altar. I want a flesh-and-blood spiritual teacher – someone worldly, fallible and wise. I want a human being I can look up to and speak to directly, who will give me clear-cut answers to deeply felt questions in the here-and-now.

Please, grant me access to a human teacher; a guide, not a guru; a Western master, not an Eastern mystic. I want someone who has mined the mysteries in a context similar

to mine; who has learned to be in the world, but not of it;
whose language I speak, whose heart I trust and whose feet
still stumble upon this earth.

I didn't say 'Amen', but I ended the prayer on my
knees in the salty Mediterranean ocean, which washed
the dried blood from between my legs and the self-pity
from between my toes.

Within days of returning home to London, another
girlfriend gave me a small hardback book with a white
cover called *Touchstones for Awakening*. Inside were glossy
pages with short sayings like, 'Other people's criticisms
are never so cruel as those we level against ourselves'
and 'Aloneness is not so much about being separate
from others as being separate from ourselves.' Each one
chimed with my inner experience until I found a small,
black-and-white photo of the author on the inside flap:
Dr K. Bradford Brown. He looked about sixty with white
hair, twinkling eyes and deep grooves of living on his
brow. I recognised him at once. My teacher.

It would be a couple more years before I met him in
person. During that time, I took some of his courses,
learnt his methodology for 'personal growth' and
immersed myself in the educational programme he had
founded in 1981 – which was called The Life Training
at that time. I also discovered more about him. A clinical
psychologist, theologian and psychotherapist, Dr Brown
had started out as an Episcopalian priest in California,
but stopped serving in a parish after some years. Not
long after he was ordained he had taken to interrupting
his droning congregation in the middle of a hymn and
bellowing, 'You are singing for the love of God, for
GOD'S SAKE!' His bishop did not approve. Devoted

as he was to his chosen faith (he remained in the priest-hood until he died), a white collar could not bridle him. He was a spiritual troublemaker.

As I mentioned in the preface, Dr Brown had been a direct student of three great twentieth-century influences: the Auschwitz survivor, Viktor Frankl, author of *Man's Search for Meaning*; the American humanist psychologist, Carl Rogers; and the British philosopher, Alan Watts, who brought Eastern philosophy to the West. Brown often marked the margins of his books about spirituality and psychology with three letters, YBH: 'Yes, But How?' *How* do we repent? *How* do we forgive? *How* do we love neighbours who drop bombs on our cities or honour the fathers and mothers who have beaten and raped their children? *How* does the truth set us free? *How* do we live in the light? *How* do we access the unconscious mind? *How* do we heal divisions and mend our broken spirits when the whole world seems to be at war? Answering these '*hows*' became his life's mission.

Two years after my post-rape prayer on a Greek beach in Lesvos, I finally met the man who would become my spiritual mentor for the next sixteen years. I loved his work so much I wanted to do it full time, but the educational programme he founded was not-for-profit and couldn't provide an adequate income. After some persuasion, a wonderful entrepreneur called Janet Jones convinced him to set up a company that would take his methods into large blue-chip organisations and I joined them within a year. It was called Interaction, grew into a successful business and I continued to lead it until my cancer diagnosis in 2014. In this capacity Brad was my business partner, and he often acknowledged me for evolving his work in ways he hadn't considered when serving in these contexts. But above all, I was his apprentice and he was my teacher. There was never a hint of attraction or romance between us, but a few months before he died – leaving a tribe of other apprentices he had also raised into leaders – he clasped my hands in his and said, 'Dearest Sophie, you could have done many things with your life. Thank you for choosing this path and being my wife in the work I created.' He had not achieved enlightenment; far from it. He was flawed and fallible and, lest someone mistake him for a 'guru', wore his faults openly. But he was the perfect answer to my reluctant prayer.

3

Just In Case

As the radiation strikes, the hours replenish themselves. I am no longer judging this experience one way or the other. It is what it is and I am *in* it. Letting go. I have entrusted my beautiful brain to a team of strangers who are monitoring it every second to ensure I am still Sophie at the end of the procedure. And as I recognise this reality, gratitude dawns and spreads across my chest. This is what cancer does. It repeatedly brings my need for control to its knees.

All my life I have encountered Something Greater in the ebb more than the flow. From early on, I needed to march *into* the world not away from it, to find the sacred in the slime and grace in loss and peace on the other side of pain. I have never encountered the divine by going to a church or temple. I find it in those 'lifeshock' moments when what is really so confronts what I believe is so – until all the bullshit is shaken loose.

This is what Dr Brown, whom I knew as 'Brad' and will refer to as Brad from now on, taught me: to look for specifics in a shit-storm; to pick one crest of one wave out of the rolling surf, the one that picks me by catching my attention more than the others; to hone in on a precise moment within the whole cascading experience. Not cancer, but 'twenty-seven brain tumours'; not the loss of my books but the words, 'I threw them away'; not date rape, but the bruises on my thighs after a night I couldn't remember; not Gamma Knife radiotherapy, but the sight of a metal helmet screwed to my head like a vice when I looked in the mirror.

This is a lifeshock: *a moment in time when something happens that you didn't want or expect.*

The specificity of these moments is very important. The mind loves to analyse events retrospectively, inter-preting what happened by looking back on them and drawing conclusions. This is why some people spend years in counselling, trying to figure out the causes of their pain (which is a great way of not *feeling* the pain). Analysis does not reliably access the unconscious mind, which mostly remains hidden because that's where it likes to stay.

When Brad was a practising therapist, he realised that taking people back to a specific lifeshock moment, and asking them to *re-experience* it, instantly unlocked their emotions and unconscious 'mindtalk' (what we tell ourselves about any given thing). It is like opening a file on a hard drive. This is because the thoughts and feelings we had at the time, which went unnoticed, *are sealed in the memory of a single instant.* You may have observed those occasions when you tell someone a story about something that happened in your life and, as you speak about the particulars, your feelings surface again, some-times with great force. What I am describing is a way to invite emotions and mindtalk to surface very deliber-ately so that we see them in the clear light of day. This is a way to access the unconscious *at will.*

We get dozens of lifeshocks a day, some more signifi-cant than others. We allow many to bounce off us, unnoticed. We perceive them through our senses: we hear, see, smell, taste and touch them. They are external to us, appearing as empirical data and colliding with our internal expectations of how things should be. They are out of our control. Through lifeshocks, factual reality knocks on the door of personal reality, inviting us to realign with it, like sailors responding to sudden changes in the wind direction by adjusting their sails. Discovering how to do so on a daily basis, while awakening and evolving in the process, is one of the primary purposes of this book.

Sometimes lifeshocks need to get very loud before we hear them. Sometimes we need to look death in the eye to realise what we want to make of living. Sometimes we don't keep our promises until it is nearly too late. We think we have time. We get distracted. We doubt we can live up to our self-imposed standards. Until now, I haven't known how to write about what Brad taught me and do it justice. He didn't even do that himself. I've tried a few times and came closest in my first book, *The Cancer Whisperer*. But that didn't express its true essence, just as it didn't express the most sacred aspects of my relationship with cancer.

Lying in this machine is a thundering wake-up call to remind me I am ready. I don't need to write the book he might have written or attempt to emulate him in the process. There is a story to tell that integrates various wisdoms I have collected along the way, including my own. I have found my own voice.

My mind quietens and something stirs in the stillness. I breathe. I listen. I wait.

Out runs Gabriella, at high speed. She fills my consciousness in the same way she fills our home with somersaults. She is north to my south and high to my low. Where I was awkward, she is at ease. Where I excel, she struggles and where I struggle, she excels. She is so like her daddy.

The universe is a tease and, suddenly, I get the joke. In the autumn of my long search for stillness the universe gave me a child who can't stop moving, even in her sleep. I start laughing again, still in fractions because my head can't move. When I am as physically still as I have ever been, I realise that stillness *moves*. It opens its doors at the place where searching ceases. When I enter it, it enters me – not as something passive and silent, but as something animate and *lived*. Like rejoicing in my daughter's relentless cartwheels instead of resisting them. Like finding a rapturous *yes* to my head being locked into a machine for eight hours while parts of my brain are being burnt away.

Gabriella is everywhere now, filling my consciousness as the treatment moves into its final hour. When she is twenty-eight and the last burnishes of youth yield to a definite, if still wide-eyed adulthood, I want to ask her how it was to grow up with the cancer that moved in with us, like a fourth member of the family, when she was just four years old: accompanying us everywhere; competing for her mum and dad's attention; taking up room in our suitcases; pressing its face against car windows; crawling into our bed in the small hours and waking us up like a terrible dream.

Will she be able to forgive the tensions that boiled over in her direction and my long absences from home when I was receiving medical treatment instead of reading her stories or teaching her how to write? Would she release the fear that drove her into my arms, more than once, crying, 'Mummy, Mummy, I'm scared you're going to be deaded', and the anger she once told 'God' she would feel towards Him *forever* if He took me to heaven instead of letting me stay here with her? Will I have done okay? Was I right to tell her the truth instead of hiding my illness and pretending things were normal for our family, whatever 'normal' is supposed to be? Was it enough truth or too much truth? Hard-to-bear or set-you-free truth? Will she duck life's curve balls because of these beginnings, or catch them and run with them, as she does with Frisbees in our garden, tracking their unpredictable path through the air before leaping to grab them in full flight?

This is what I want for her. To leap at life, whatever it throws at her. To find beauty in how she rises to each challenge and success in what she becomes as a result. To join the birds as they sing after a storm.

And now I know what this book wants to be. It wants to offer my daughter – and anyone who seeks to catch curve balls in full flight – another road to riches, another light to shine and another way to pray. The chapter headings enter my consciousness like instructions: *Beauty. Privilege. Success. Power. Love. Loss. Forgiveness. Grace.* I recognise them as developmental chapters of my life.

I like that cancer doesn't get its own chapter. This feels like progress. It will feature, certainly, not just because it is still such a central force in my life, but because living with it is the most powerful spiritual practice I have known. Cancer will find its place in a bigger story of my search for bliss in the bustle of living and a stillness that moves through it all.

Three months from now I will be told that the Gamma Knife radiation, combined with natural treatments I chose to enhance its efficacy, has worked. I will sit in my neuro-oncologist's office at London Bridge Hospital as he tells me the brain lesions have all but gone and I should 'go home and be normal for a while.' I will cry at the prospect because I haven't relaxed into normality since this whole thing started and I don't realise how deeply I miss it until he holds it out to me, almost casually. Then I will celebrate with my husband by drinking two glasses of Prosecco on a small patch of sun-drenched grass outside the Tate Modern on the South Bank, a twenty-minute walk from the hospital, and lean into tomorrow again.

Gabriella is very good at sharing, except when it comes to her mum. Even Daddy is pushed aside furiously if she catches him hugging me without being in on the action. I hope she will forgive me for sharing this book with strangers and making this love letter to her so public. It is not *instead of* what I want to teach her in person. It is *as well as*. I aim to stick around long enough to ask her, as an adult, to assess how I did with what is in these pages – where I hit the mark and where I missed it along the way. I will do both. I already have. My actions will inevitably fall short of my highest intentions. I hope Gabriella will learn that this is okay too. As Brad often said,

'*Seven times down, eight times up*: the warrior's way.'

I am equally aware that the future, which once seemed to roll out like a certainty, is far too tenuous for promises. The risks to my health are grave indeed and I am way past assuring my child it will all turn out fine. I am as fearful as I am faithful, half-dark and half-light, fully and finally human. Accordingly, as the Arab proverb reminds me, I will 'tie up my camel' by putting this all down on paper. Just in case.

Part Two

Life Speaks

There is no event through which Life itself is not trying to awaken you to your most authentic, loving and human self.

K. Bradford Brown

4

Beauty

Whatever it is that pulls the pin, that hurls you past the boundaries of your own life into a brief and total beauty, even for a moment, it is enough.

Jeannette Winterson

Pizza Face

It has taken me time to recover from zapping my brain tumours, but the treatment has proven effective so far. Now I am in India, on retreat. This is not an escape from reality. It's an escape from my cluttered mind and busy life.

This year has been epic. As well as the medical challenges, I have been responding to a gathering storm of 'cancer whisperers' – patients from around the world who have read *The Cancer Whisperer* and want to integrate its principles into the way they deal with their disease. I didn't see any of this coming. I am doing my best to meet a real need in the cancer community without cooking my still tender goose. I am walking a familiar line between serving others where called and taking care of my own wellbeing. I need to be engaged, creative, evolving – meeting life head-on to feel fully alive, but I still get carried away sometimes. I forget my limited mortality, even when cancer is shoving it in my face.

So, India it is. I need to leave my worldly responsibilities behind me and go inside; reintroduce myself to myself. But I also want to pause long enough to give thanks for all that has led me to this point.

I will be here for three weeks. My darling John is looking after Gabriella and they are counting 'how many sleeps' until Mummy comes home, which makes me as important as Father Christmas. I will return in time to see her perform in her school nativity play – her first with actual lines to say. She is the Star of Bethlehem. Of course.

It's very simple here. I sleep in a narrow single bed with a thin mattress and an almost-pillow. There is no Internet. The shower is a tap with a bucket, and bathing is restricted to one bucket every other day to save water. My towel is a small, thin sheet of chequered cloth. The food is vegetarian and delicious, if I avoid the really spicy dishes. My room looks out over a courtyard with cobbled pathways crisscrossing between banyan trees and bountiful bougainvillea. There are no formal activities here, like meditation or yoga. No health spa or massage suite. A dusty old library provides ample entertainment and it feels incongruous to be typing on my MacBook Pro. Mostly, there is a deep, bellowing silence.

It took me about twenty-four hours to shake off my Western privileged need for readily available toilet paper and a phone signal. Driving through Mumbai on the way here, I encountered a stream of lifeshocks that highlighted the extreme poverty so many people in India endure: barefoot kids walking through piles of stinking rubbish on the roadsides; row upon row of corrugated steel huts, with no electricity or sanitation; makeshift plastic tents with women crouched over brass pots on open fires; even my charming taxi driver charging me less than a thirty-minute fee in a London black cab for a seven-hour journey from the airport (having driven seven hours from his home near the retreat to get me). The roads roll out against an immense ochre landscape. Lanes are meaningless. Cars just squeeze into the nearest available space, weaving in and out of each other, their horns beeping constantly to avoid collisions. It is thrilling in a way, a chaotic meeting of recklessness and faithfulness, as if risk-taking is calculated against good odds of divine intervention. After a while, I relaxed and went with this flow.

There is an overwhelming radiance that shines through the heat, fumes and dirt. Not just the luminous colours of women's saris or the kaleidoscope of market stalls in the villages, but a mayhem of life in all its extremes. This is why I came.

It's hot, but we dress in long sleeves and loose trousers. This is a relief. I gained weight this summer on post-radiation steroids, which alleviated the pain of my severely burnt brain, but bloated my body and triggered cravings for carbs that I failed to control until I stopped taking the pills. I have tried to be gentle with myself about it: understanding, forgiving, patient; true to the peace I made with my body when I was first diagnosed with cancer. But it's not working now. I am on edge again. I've been off the steroids and back on my mainly vegetarian diet for a while now, but the weight is shifting very slowly and despair lurks in the corner.

My discomfort with my weight is almost as old as I am. It bores me. And yet it keeps gate-crashing my story. It isn't my personal struggle alone that matters, just as it wasn't merely my personal struggle that mattered when I wrote *The Cancer Whisperer*. My story was the story of millions of people living and dying from that disease. I wasn't a stand-out, beat-the-odds miracle case but a just-like, one-of-many who happened to find the words to say what some other cancer patients were wishing would be said.

And so it is with my pilgrimage to self-acceptance. It is the same pilgrimage that many millions of women and burgeoning young girls are trying to make in a glossy, airbrushed culture that demands they conform to impossible standards of beauty and shames them when they don't. My perspective is female, but these demands are not exclusive to women. Men are facing a parallel onslaught of expectations about physical perfection, more so now than when I was growing up. Eating disorders in men and boys are on the rise as they struggle to find self-acceptance too. This acceptance is a far cry from the quick fixes of pseudo-self-esteem we experience when we live up to those demands – that fleeting freedom from judgement when men's muscles tighten and women's stomachs flatten or our thighs stop touching at the top. Rather it is that deep, enduring ease in one's own body that arises from an authentic contentment with one's unique being. I glimpse it in the Indian women who clean our rooms. They walk around the building in purple and lilac saris, the exposed rolls of their brown bellies adding folds to the fabric in a mutually enhancing design. Perhaps I am projecting my own wishes, but they seem to wear their flesh as I long to – as if this is what women are supposed to look like; as if these soft curves are nature's inspiration and intent.

One of the brown-bellied women in a purple sari comes to clean my room as I am writing. She has a severely scarred face. The skin is taut with creases on both sides, as if it's been badly ironed, and the lower part of her nose is missing. *Lifeshock*. It is clear she has been badly burnt and I wonder if she is the victim of an acid attack, which is all too common in India. She looks up at me as she enters and I almost flinch – not with disgust, but with the memory of being gravely ill and then being offered a possible reprieve in the form of a targeted chemo drug. My relief had been immense, but didn't last. Within a few days the drug had destroyed the mucous membranes in my mouth and throat, rendering me unable to swallow anything except the smallest sips of water, while blistering my face so badly I didn't want to step outside the house. As if my vulnerability hadn't already reached its nadir, now I was ugly and disfigured too. I called it my 'pizza face'.

Until then my illness had been invisible. I could get on a train or go to the shops without anyone noticing the almost-dead woman walking. I could step out into the world and feign normality, if only to leave my terror in abeyance for a while. Now there was nowhere to hide. My plight was as apparent as leprosy.

I tried to be rational and keep it in perspective, but I was more traumatised by this ugliness than the fact that I couldn't eat. It was one of two occasions when death looked preferable to living. The ugliness cut deeper than reason. It returned me to the adolescent years of

self-destructive behaviour that perhaps sowed seeds for
cancer to flourish in my cells. The starving. The laxatives.
The smoking behind bike sheds. The lacerating judgements I levelled at my own reflection because I didn't
conform to the skinny, delicate rendition of beauty that
infiltrated my upbringing.

The cleaner holds her head up high and smiles. Her
scars, far more severe than mine were, are permanent.
Mine have long gone. I remember the stares when I did
go out and wonder how she walks with so much dignity
and grace. I can't say she has accepted what happened
to her, but she is accepted in this place and works diligently, sweeping the floor proudly and smiling broadly
at me when she is finished, as if to say, 'I survived and
I am here and I do my work well.'

Formative Lifeshocks

My search for Something Greater began with my search
for beauty. Naturally, we seek what we lack, or believe
we lack, oblivious to the deeper longing that may reveal
itself later if we are paying enough attention.

Two key things determined this pursuit: the context
I grew up in and the early lifeshocks I received.

Lifeshocks begin when we begin. They make up the
fabric of daily life – every moment we didn't expect or
plan. They are external moments in time that grab our
attention and invite us to turn that attention inwards.
Some we like, some we don't, and many we pass off as
the stuff of everyday existence. Normality. The traffic
jam we drive into on the way to work, the printer breaking
down, the rainbow arching over the fields, the baby

dropping food on the floor, the kids waking us up before we want to be woken, reading our exam results, a first kiss. (These are typical kinds of lifeshock but, as I have explained, the real value of a lifeshock lies in its specificity.)

My first kiss was at fourteen. He was called Christian and towered over me, which few boys did at that age. It was at a teenage birthday party in 1980. The Moody Blues song, 'Knights in White Satin', came on. I was wearing slightly flared red velvet trousers and a frilly white 'Spandau Ballet' shirt. He pulled me close, bent down and pressed his lips on my lips before opening them with his tongue. That was the lifeshock moment, one I didn't expect but liked. I went mushy inside and decided my ugliness was over. It wasn't. But I tasted redemption for a few delicious minutes and a truth was seeded that would later grow to counter all the lies that darkened my mirror: *I am beautiful to some.*

Early lifeshocks are formative. Our unconscious reactions to them shape our lives for years and decades to come. They strike deep from an early age. Some children grow up in brutal contexts with lifeshocks that pound and bellow day by day, but they become some kind of normality too. I have worked with clients who were assaulted so frequently by a family member that they couldn't distinguish one assault from another, let alone identify which ones were the most formative. But no one is exempt from lifeshocks or from the mind's reaction to them – which is where the invisible and unnecessary suffering begins.

Of course, I can only speak from my experience. And if I do so it is more to reveal the process at work than to simply share my personal story. But my story matters, just as all our stories matter. Authentically told, our stories can reflect and awaken our joys and griefs, loves and fears, dreams and disappointments.[1] This is my purpose here: to make my engagement with lifeshocks over the past twenty-seven years an open book for anyone wondering if life is trying to tell them something. Because it *is*.

Naturally, I had many formative lifeshocks in my family context, but I don't intend to hang their laundry out with mine. My brother has always been very handsome and acutely intelligent; my sister is tall, lean, athletic and pretty; and I was sandwiched in the middle of this double dose of beauty wondering what had gone wrong. I am certain their memories of childhood are very different from mine, just as I am certain my parents do not need a public display of their parenting from my subjective perspective. There were some very difficult times. There were some very wonderful times. But a description of events is less relevant than the interpretation of events I carried forwards into adulthood. Of these I can write.

I can't recall exactly when I started overeating, but I know why. I was the child who threw embarrassing tantrums in the supermarket and raged uncontrollably when I wasn't understood or didn't get my way. 'No' was my favourite word. I felt things deeply, but I didn't know how to channel what I was feeling or express my

---

1 By 'stories' I mean the unfolding narrative of our lives rather than the noise inside our heads. This word is sometimes used to describe what I am calling 'mindtalk'.

inner world to other people. I was also uncommonly empathetic, a gift I later learned to make good use of, but in my early years I assumed everything I was feeling was mine. It was overwhelming. All I knew to do was explode by throwing a tantrum or screaming at whoever was in front of me, usually my mother. I didn't mean to cause trouble – to exasperate Mum when she was carrying in the shopping bags or lash out at my siblings. But I didn't know where to put my frustration, my fear and my fury. I was a cauldron without a lid.

I recall one lifeshock which I took as a sign that I must learn to control myself emotionally, whatever way I could. Every year a group of families who knew each other well would get together on New Year's Eve and play 'family charades'. A new topic was chosen each year and announced in advance so we could all prepare. On that particular occasion, when I was about nine years old, the theme was 'Another Family': we had to enact one of the families in the room until everyone guessed which family it was. In reality, what was supposed to be funny was in fact a set-up for mutual mockery, overt judgement and passive aggression. When New Year's Eve arrived the host-family was the third to go. I can't remember the scene they enacted or how much time elapsed before one of their daughters, close to my age, lay on the floor, thrashing her legs in the air and started screaming, 'No, I won't! No, I won't!' in a full-blown dramatic tantrum: at which the whole room cried in unison, 'That's Sophie!' and fell about laughing. *Lifeshock*. At first I froze, mortified with embarrassment, hurt by my own family guffawing in solidarity with my ridiculers, but seconds later I pretended to laugh too.

I have to laugh, I told myself. *I have to take the joke. If I show what I'm really feeling they'll laugh more and say I'm too sensitive. That's how they all think of me – behaving like that – but they don't ask why. I'm not normal. I'm too emotional. I'm out of control and it has to stop. They think I'm crazy. There's something wrong with me. I'm too much. I have to control my feelings. I have to stop this happening again. I have to protect myself and rise above it. I have to be like them.*

This is how the mind reacts to something it doesn't like. It coats the lifeshock in a layer of assumptions (*they'll laugh more*), beliefs (*I'm crazy/too much*), demands (*I have to control my feelings*) and decisions (*it has to stop*), which then drive our behaviour going forwards. In this case, from then onwards, when feelings arose that I couldn't control, I would eat. That was my solution. I would raid the kitchen cupboards and steal money from Mum's purse to buy chocolate on the walk home from school. I used food not to feel.

This kind of reaction to lifeshocks tends to be unconscious when they actually happen, especially at that age. Only when I was much older did I return to this, and many other formative moments, to unlock the various meanings I construed at the time. The mind is a meaning-making machine. It interprets lifeshocks at lightning speed and, before we know it, our behaviour and emotional life have changed. This 'mindtalk' is very powerful and frequently false (no matter how deeply we hold it to be true). It defines our relationship with ourselves, others and the contexts in which we move. It becomes our worldview. It is more commonly known as 'self-talk', but it isn't the 'self' that is talking. It is the mind. There is a big difference.

When 'mindtalk' goes unnoticed and unchallenged it shapes our 'personality', which we then think of as 'who I am'. It is not who we are. It is a dramatised way of behaving based on unnoticed and unchallenged beliefs that create a *false self*. The false self envelops the authentic self until our innate qualities of being get concealed and forgotten. But those qualities have not disappeared. They remain retrievable when we wake up and reach inside to resurrect them.

At the New Year's Eve charades, it wasn't the lifeshock that changed me, which in retrospect was relatively harmless piss-taking. It was what I made it mean: *I'm too intense, too emotional, too much.* I did that to me. Of course, someone was bound to get hurt or take offence that evening. At the same time, this experience gave me a glimpse of how I came across to other people and what I was doing that made it so hard for them to understand me. I wanted to be heard. I wanted to be heard so desperately I would scream, wail and gnash my teeth to attract attention. I was trying to say, 'Listen! I'm flooded with feelings and don't know what to do with them! Help!' Instead, from that point on, I silenced my innate sensitivities as best I could for nearly two decades. And I ate.

Pre-mature

My periods started when I was ten. It was the school holidays and I didn't know what to think, except that it must be bad. For three days I hid it successfully, carefully folding sheets of toilet paper into makeshift pads and putting them in the lining of my knickers. Almost hourly,

I flushed these down the toilet on the half-landing at home. In between I carried on as normal, quashing my fear and not saying a word. I was meticulously careful to prevent leakage and put clean, unstained underwear into the laundry. Failing that, I stuffed it in a plastic bag before cramming the bag into the rubbish bin where it wouldn't be noticed. This was all consuming – pretending to be fine when I wasn't; trying to manage it without being found out; hiding my defects lest the outside world confirm them.

On the fourth day, the toilet got blocked. I knew my number was up. I was mute with shame. Only when my dad laid down some tarpaulin in the bathroom and unscrewed the piping did the evidence finally materialise. I was sitting halfway down the stairs at the time, biting my fingernails and waiting for a grenade to blow.

It didn't.

'Oh Sophie,' Mum exclaimed sympathetically and slightly wounded, as if I had withheld something momentous. 'You got your first period! Why on earth didn't you tell me?'

'What's a period?' I responded sheepishly, utterly relieved that something normal was taking place.

Dad was stellar. He gave me a quick, slightly awkward hug, as if to say, 'well done darling', and quietly fixed the toilet while Mum took me to her room to explain. It had happened so early. She wasn't expecting it. She hadn't thought to tell me yet. Then she got practical, which is her strong suit in such situations, explaining the mechanics of it all. As I listened, my relief turned to sadness. My body didn't seem to be my own any more. I was maturing faster than I could compute.

Before I reached eleven I was five feet six inches tall, the same height as I am now. I was wearing a DD cup bra, which I loathed, and had to take ID on public transport to prove I was younger than sixteen. I was literally a foot taller than Annabel, my best friend at my next school, who remains one of my dearest friends to this day. At this school, I found myself in a class of petite, flat-chested, rosy-cheeked girls, upon whom the shadow of self-consciousness was yet to fall. I would watch them in the open changing rooms before sports lessons, chatting and laughing as they stripped off effortlessly, their childhoods still intact. Initially, I would wait until the room had cleared to start changing, even if it meant being told off for being late, but I soon learnt to pull my sports shirt over the one I was removing before wrestling the latter through the sleeves of the former. *If I can just hide my defects then no one will notice them*, I reasoned, though I drew more attention to them in the process.

At the beginning and end of each term we were weighed and measured. Although this was probably designed to prevent eating disorders, it provoked mine instead. I was twelve the first time it happened. The process was military in its precision. We lined up in a corridor outside an open door to a room next to the gym, where our sports teacher, Miss Muirhead, stood by the scales. On the other side of the room a selected classmate sat behind a desk with her pen poised over an alphabetical list of our names. As each girl stood on the scales, Miss Muirhead barked their weight across the room to be recorded, loudly enough for everyone to *hear* and *know*: ninety-four pounds; ninety-nine pounds; eighty-seven pounds; one hundred and six pounds (occasionally); ninety-two pounds. All 'normal' weights for twelve-year-old girls.

Each number was a lifeshock, a confirmation that I was bigger, heavier – and therefore *uglier* – than them all. I was also several inches taller, but that didn't compute. I was rigid with resistance by the time I stood on the scales. As the line shortened I had deployed all my don't-cry missiles and left my body. I was pretending to be somewhere else.

'One hundred and twenty-six pounds,' barked Miss Muirhead, and my disgrace was complete.

First dance

Until the age of sixteen I was taller than most boys. Their eyes tended to meet my boobs when we were introduced. Mostly they would step back awkwardly, shake my hand and move on as quickly as possible. They rarely asked me to dance and the ones who did were accused of 'practising their weight-lifting' by some of my brother's meaner friends. I learnt to head their judgements off at the pass by beating them to it with jokes at my own expense. 'Here are my boobs, the rest of me is coming tomorrow!' I announced frequently. It broke the ice and enhanced my popularity. It also left a few cracks in my dignity. Because of all this, I secretly dreaded parties.

I attended my first proper 'dance' at fourteen, a charity do with 1000 tickets and pretty good odds of finding someone to dance with. There were bound to be some boys who were taller than me or old enough to actually like breasts. Mum bought me a deep pink chiffon dress and a brand-new bra. I had been wearing one for four years by then, but still stared upwards when I clipped it on every morning, as if looking away would erase my breasts. And a flat-chested skinny girl, who lived in the ceiling, stared back.

The invitation was on thick white card with a black font. Embossed. It requested 'the pleasure of your company', as if it was a private party for an honoured few, instead of an indiscriminate shindig with expensive tickets. The words glared at me for weeks from the living-room mantelpiece, where Mum had placed it, just left of centre. I kept catching it out of the corner of my eye while I ate salad, counted calories and sucked in my stomach when walking past the mirror. As the day drew near, my anxiety intensified. I started eating chocolate faster than I could taste it, to make myself immune. I couldn't do it. I didn't want to do it. There had to be a way to get out of it. But I couldn't find a way out without admitting my anxiety – and 'the pleasure of your company' sounded like something I would really like to know. I hadn't taken much pleasure in it yet.

I loved my dress and blended in well. I drank a glass of wine and chatted to girlfriends who hadn't been snapped up by the most handsome boys on arrival. I played it nonchalant and cool, hoping no one would catch me looking around every so often and that some tall young man would notice the private, but passionate heart I was wearing on my deep pink chiffon sleeve. Far sooner than anticipated, a tall, dark-haired sixteen-year-old boy, who looked as awkward in his height as I felt in mine, asked me to dance. I tried to maintain my composure as we walked on to the dance floor, but was too excited and skipped. It didn't matter what song was playing or what my partner's name was. It didn't matter if this was my only dance of the night. All that mattered was that he had noticed me and asked; that I would have something to tell my friends about later; that I would feel beautiful for a few brief minutes.

Suddenly strobe lighting illuminated whatever was white on the dance floor and cloaked everything else in darkness. I felt brave (being invisible) and began to relax. The music moved into my hips and pulled me into my skin, spinning me into existence. My self-consciousness lifted and, for the first time since my periods started and my breasts arrived, I felt normal and attractive and free.

It can only have been a couple of minutes before I looked down and noticed my brand-new white bra blazing like neon through my transparent chiffon dress. My breasts were luminous and my partner several 'I'm not with her' feet away. This lifeshock stopped me dead in my dancing shoes. Then I slipped off the dance floor quietly, leaving 'normal' and 'attractive' behind me, certain of my partner's relief.

Weighing in

I tolerated weighing and measuring at school for four more years (six times a year), during which time I mastered the art of crash diets and vomiting after meals for the last few weeks of each term. At sixteen I embarked on studying for three A levels and S level English Literature, wherein I continued to find solace from self-reproach and the comfort of alternate worlds where my too much-ness – physical and emotional – found belonging. By then some of my friends were the same height as me and a few were taller. They all wore bras, though none as large as mine, and some weighed 126 pounds or so too. The playing field had levelled and I had developed an intellectual confidence that carried me most of the time. But being weighed still loomed.

Accordingly, in the first weigh-in of sixth form, I didn't show up. I was done. I didn't care about the consequences. It just had to stop. I wasn't brave enough to confront it though. Instead, Miss Muirhead found me crouched on the floor of a school cupboard, in among the brooms, demanding to know why I had missed it.

'Because you have tormented me with those scales long enough,' I replied, rising to my feet and my stature. 'From the start, I was the biggest, and to date I'm the bustiest. My weight is private information. You have no right to ask for it and even less right to publicise it. If you want to weigh me ever again you will have to pick me up, carry me and drop me on the scales yourself.'

Tears burnt my eyes as I spoke, but I didn't let them fall, and I braced myself for a blasting that didn't come. Miss Muirhead got it, instantly. She said she had no idea it was so difficult for me and gave me a permanent exemption for the remaining two years of school. That was that. The weighing stopped. But the mindtalk didn't. Mindtalk doesn't. Not until you realise how it holds you back and pins you down. Not until you learn how to grab it by its tail and curb its lying tongue and put yourself back into perspective again. Now aged fifty-one, I am still five feet six inches tall (with F-cup boobs). And 126 pounds is my ideal weight.

Mindtalk

We have many formative lifeshocks from childhood through adolescence, often pressing on a particular theme that continues to run through our lives. These are shaped by family contexts and social forces. Although my background was privileged in many ways, it wasn't exempt from a wider social fixation to look good. There was no Internet then but, like most adolescent girls in Western cultures, I was subject to glossy magazine images of impossibly skinny women, many of whom were later revealed to be anorexic in an industry where the disease is rife. 'Plus Size' models were not yet on the map and there were no alternative versions of beauty to consider. The pressure to be petite, pert, pretty and perfect was intense. This pressure was magnified at a private girls' school where we flicked through the pages of *Vogue* in awe and colluded in extreme weight-loss plans to make us more 'marryable' – which, despite our educational advantages, was the definitive goal.

This was the late 1970s and early 1980s. The feminist movement that arose at the start of the 1970s through the likes of Germaine Greer (author of *The Female Eunuch*) and Kate Millett (author of *Sexual Politics*) had still not reached our school shores. Margaret Thatcher was elected prime minister in 1979, but she did little to further the cause of women's liberation in any broader sense. Indeed, she was widely criticised for hindering women's chances of success, with economic and social policies that were often detrimental to their advancement as a social group. As the journalist, Hadley Freeman, observed in an article about Thatcher in 2013, 'Far from "smashing the glass ceiling", she was . . . the one who got through and then pulled the ladder up right after her.'

We had 'career talks' with teachers, but framed our professional ambitions with 'ifs', 'wants' and 'love-tos': 'I want to be a teacher . . . if I become a writer . . . I'd love to be an actress one day.' We hoped more than aimed. The outcome was optional. A nice-to-have. But marriage was a 'when'. It was as taken for granted as the sun rising in the morning, and we forecast having children just as we anticipated stars shining at night: 'When I get married . . . when I have kids . . . when I walk up the aisle . . .' This was how we spoke about relationships and children: in certainties.

I played along, partly to keep my fate at arm's length for as long as possible, but mainly to save face. 'When' didn't apply to me. I knew that. The writing was already on the wall. In need of a back-up plan, which was really my primary plan, I continued to submerge myself in books. *If I can't be thin, I'll be informed,* I told myself. *And if I can't be beautiful, I'll be bright.* I worked hard. I rewrote my English essays if I got a grade 'B' to prove I could have got an 'A' – even if it was the 'B' that went on record. I debated for the school. I won a national public speaking competition out of thousands of entrants. I took fourth term entrance exams to Cambridge University. I binged on poetry instead of chocolate. I ate as little as possible. I smoked behind the bike sheds. I ran from my body as fast as I could.

As it turned out, our expensive education didn't live up to its price tag. I think I was the only girl in my largely intelligent and promising class who scraped into a degree course (but not at Cambridge, as was the plan for me). I don't think the school was entirely to blame, though. I have since learnt the true power of intention. Here, intention manifested husbands for most of my friends by their early twenties. By the time I began my degree course, I was severely bulimic, sustaining an addiction to laxatives for several years in an ongoing attempt to carve myself in beauty's image while furthering my education. I manifested my underlying intentions too.

These outcomes were in direct alignment with my reactions to formative lifeshocks relating to my appearance. Along with many others on the same theme, they accumulated over the years until I was encrusted in the dispiriting conclusions I had come to: *I'm too emotional, too womanly, too big, too ugly, too intense* and *too much*. While I was certainly on the receiving end of other people's judgements at times, no one wrote this script but me.

This is how the mind works. It talks to us, relentlessly. At its best, it sees a situation for what it is, without judging it one way or another, and responds accordingly. But as we have seen, we imagine, project and interpret events until a foundation of *core beliefs* has formed in the psyche: *I'm selfish; I'm out of control; I'm weird; I'm worthless; I'm crazy; I'm invisible; I'm unlovable,* to name a few very common ones. Unable to tolerate the pain these cause, the reactive mind demands that we be a certain way and do certain things in order to prove we're not what we have already decided we are: *I have to please others; I have to control myself; I have to act normal; I have to stand out; I have to rebel; I have to hide my weakness (at all times).* For example.

I saw myself as *too emotional* and *too much*. As such *I had to control myself* and *hide my feelings (by eating)*. I saw myself as *too big* and *too ugly*. As such *I had to be thin and intelligent (to compensate)*. I saw myself as *unlovable*. As such *I had to be bright and admirable* instead.

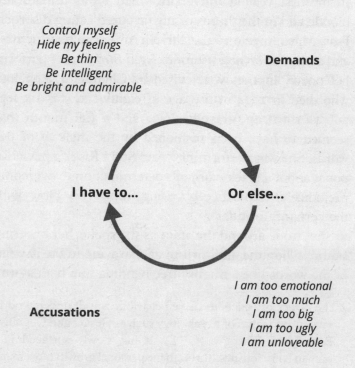

Control myself
Hide my feelings
Be thin
Be intelligent
Be bright and admirable

Demands

I have to...   **Or else...**

Accusations

I am too emotional
I am too much
I am too big
I am too ugly
I am unloveable

This explanation is a bit more simplistic than the nuanced workings of our mindtalk, but it demonstrates how one damning accusation about yourself sets up a demand about how you must behave as a result. Mostly, the accusations go underground, becoming unconscious, while the demands form 'my character'. Many people are aware of how they think they should act in life, but don't consider what underlying fears and self-accusations that script is based on, let alone if any of it is true.[2]

Turning Points

In my first year at university, when I was unnaturally blonde and in the throes of my favoured eating disorder, I saw Maya Angelou – the African American poet, activist and author of *I Know Why the Caged Bird Sings* – perform her poetry in a show televised by Channel 4. Angelou, who died in 2014 at the age of eighty-six, was six feet tall with a deep, gravelly voice and a full mouth that seemed to have been fashioned by the majesty of her words. She was performing, 'And Still I Rise', a powerful poem about a black woman's determination to overcome prejudice and injustice by rising from every blow 'with the certainty of tides'.

She strode around the stage as she spoke, her towering stature filling the auditorium and swaying to the rhythm of the words like a mighty tree bending in a high storm.

2 The power of beliefs to drive behaviour is well understood in several modalities of psychology such as Gestalt and Cognitive Behavioural Therapy (CBT). It has slowly surfaced into human consciousness through the personal growth movement, emerging in the work of people like the author and researcher, Brené Brown, who calls it 'the story we live out'. Transforming 'core beliefs' is also a central tenet of CBT, which is increasingly popular. This understanding of the mind is liberating more and more people from profoundly limiting belief systems, even though we still have a long way to go. But I learnt about how the mind works from Brad Brown who founded his educational programme in 1981, when such knowledge was less accessible.

She occupied her curvaceous hips like a throne. Her body spoke the poem. It was the poem. I was transfixed, laughing and crying all at once as I felt my entire construct of beauty collapse.

A torrent of jaw-dropping, heart-opening lifeshocks streamed through each sentence and movement. I savoured her words like fat drops of water from a giant leaf in the rainforest. It wasn't just her physical beauty that stunned me. It was the majesty of her presence, her unequivocal self-regard. Not a cell in her body apologised for its existence, which was what made her flawless. *She recognised her worth; therefore, she was beautiful.* And I had believed it was the other way around.

This is the message that women – and to an increasing extent, men – receive, both blatantly and insidiously: the greater your physical beauty, the greater your worth. It doesn't seem to have changed since I was young, though there is more protest perhaps and a little more awareness of its dangers. Even so, eating disorders are now more common than ever before and are responsible for more loss of life than any other form of psychological illness. Our definitions of what is attractive have become so narrow that millions of people are making themselves ill and putting themselves under the surgeon's knife to change how they look, sometimes with dire consequences. This is the world my daughter is growing up in. This is the beauty lie.

Even the women who qualify as 'beautiful' in society are not exempt from the pain this lie inflicts. I discovered this in my thirties when I was leading a workshop in the More To Life programme that Brad co-founded, one I had delivered many times. One of the tools of the course is a set of 'disciplines' that participants are asked to commit to for its duration: no alcohol, speaking in a voice loud enough to be heard, being exactly on time for each session, to name a few. Most people react against these, perceiving them as 'rules' and attempts to control them. Some become defiant and others compliant, which directly reflects how they react against the unwanted events of their life. The true purpose of the disciplines is to help participants start noticing these automatic reactions: how they feel, behave and think in other situations. This becomes the vehicle for their awakening and transformation as the experience unfolds.

It is an intense course and it's easy to nod off – especially when the subject matter is pressing on painful issues that participants unconsciously seek to avoid. One of the disciplines is to go to the side of the room if you feel sleepy and stretch your body at some white tape marks that have been laid down on the floor for this purpose.

At the start of each session, the group is asked which disciplines they have broken, and the learning begins. By the second day I noticed that one woman in her late twenties had persistently neglected the discipline of going to the side of the room to stretch when she felt sleepy. She admitted it each time, but nothing changed. As I listened to her explain that she just kept 'forgetting', I was struck by her physical beauty: tall, slim, long blonde hair, fine facial features, huge blue eyes; the kind of beauty I had often envied and assumed was effortless to wear. She could have walked off a page of *Vogue*. But this time I was sensing a deep sorrow just beneath her stunning surface.

'What's it like to be as beautiful as you?' I asked, with all the compassion I could summon.

Her eyes welled up with tears. 'Don't call me that,' she answered.

'But you are beautiful,' I pressed, trusting my instincts. 'How many people here agree?' I added, turning to the rest of the group for confirmation.

When all their hands went up, the lifeshock hit her chest and tears streamed down her cheeks. She had no words.

'If you stood at the side of the room, you would be more visible, wouldn't you?' I continued.

She nodded, head bowed, body trembling.

'And what do people see when you are that visible?' I persisted.

'My beauty,' she responded, very quietly. 'But they don't see *me*.'

Until this conversation, it hadn't crossed my mind. I had been so blinded by my envy of women who didn't have to work for their physical beauty, I didn't understand that they might believe they were invisible too – objects of other people's fantasies, desires, projections and imaginings. And, yes, objects of envy like mine. In the absence of such obvious beauty, the rest of us need to show up in other ways – with wit, quirkiness, intelligence, character or kindness. We are more easily seen for what is beneath the surface, which is where our essence resides. But this woman had to bring those qualities forwards with far more force if she was to be recognised as more than a pretty face. And part of her had given up. Her exterior had overshadowed her interior for too long. Now she resorted to hiding out, keeping her head down, trying to lose herself in the crowd.

I worked with her for a while to help bring her inner

self to the outer world. I brought her to the front of the room to be seen, not for what she looked like but for who she really was. At first, I asked her to just stand, without words, and experience the whole group's eyes on her. Initially she was scared and shifted from foot to foot, averting their gaze. I encouraged her to breathe into her abdomen and keep bringing her attention to the group instead of listening to her mindtalk. Before long, she was standing still, making eye contact and really seeing what was there: soft eyes, some full of empathetic tears, others bright with light, all focused on her.

'What do you see?' I asked her.

'Kind faces,' she answered. 'Loving eyes.'

'Are you willing to hear what they see in you?' I pressed, moving a little closer to let her know I had her back.

She looked terrified and her breathing grew more shallow as she shifted from foot to foot again. I was taking her to the edge of her fear, but I was certain this is what she came for: to reveal the depths beneath her surface and become visible again.

'You can do this,' I assured her. 'It is time.'

'Okay,' she responded tentatively as I helped her steady her feet again.

'Are you ready?' I checked before calling on the raised hands. She nodded. 'Are you sure?' She nodded again.

Then, for a few minutes, I invited the group to say what they saw beyond the surface. 'Keep it real,' I added. 'No pleasing or embellishing or making things up.'

'I see your courage,' someone began as she stood there with shaking knees. 'I see your honesty'; 'I see your strength'; 'I see your vulnerability'; 'I see your resilience';

'I see your tenacity'; 'I see the kindness in your eyes.' I see you. I see you. I see you.

There is a Zulu greeting, '*Sawubona*', which means 'I see you' and the response, '*Ngikhona*' means 'I am here'. In other words, *I exist because you see me – your seeing brings me into being.* I have worked with thousands of adults over the years and it is rare indeed that we don't unearth some version of 'I'm invisible' at the bottom of their loneliness and fear or their bluster and bravado. Our hearts need to know we are visible to others as acutely as our bodies need food, water and rest. The Zulus understand this. We Westerners, with our eyes increasingly glued to the screens on our various devices, do not. We have created a culture where some simple recognition falls like water on a desert, as it did with this woman.

Her discomfort persisted at first, but before long a new beauty emerged from deep within as tears of gratitude rolled down her stunning face: a light that radiates when we stop guarding what we believe is wrong with us and start claiming what we know is right; when we wear humanity on our sleeves instead of foundation cream on our faces; when we rise 'like dust', as Maya Angelou did, and let our souls shine.

When I knew she had slotted back into herself, I joined her – not as the course leader, but as another woman who had wanted to crawl out of her skin (for antithetical reasons). We both longed to be loved for what was on the inside instead of being judged for what was on the outside. In this pursuit, we were no different. We were one. And there we stood, silent, open, grateful – she, coming to terms with her physical appearance and me, coming to terms with mine.

Beauty Is a Verb, Not a Noun

All the time I was chasing beauty I was running away from myself. I bought the lie.

I wasn't *too emotional*. I was a deep feeler in a context where depth of feeling had no language. I wasn't *too big and too ugly*. I was a fully developed, healthy-sized woman – with a significantly larger than average bosom, for sure – before I was mentally ready to be one. I wasn't *weird and crazy*. I was a bright, flawed, passionate human being who loved literature and poetry and encounters that touched my soul. I wasn't *unlovable*. I was loved by many, but didn't love myself enough to see it or let it in.

It isn't truth we need to seek to be free. *It is lies*. We need to spot them, track them, hunt them down – the demands, judgements and accusations that veil us from what is really so. We are the walking blind, buying the myths, living the stories, perpetuating the pain. But when we peel false beliefs like scales from our eyes, then 'truth' is what remains.

This is the return to authenticity. The road back may be as long as the road we walked away from it, but the incline is downhill. It can be reclaimed at high speed as soon as we start dismantling our judgements. I had a lot of reclaiming and an awful lot of dismantling to do. Perhaps that's why it took so long for me to find my husband, John.

I met him on a leadership course, three months after Brad's death. I was heartbroken and nearly bailed at the eleventh hour, but the course leader was lovingly persuasive and assigned me the task of facilitating the first evening of the course – a role that was passed around for the ensuing three days. I took it on, but there was no stemming my sorrow. Consequently, I wore my snotty, unkempt, grief-stained loss on my sleeve without a care for how I looked or what anyone thought of me. I was entirely myself that day, without apology or shame.

John approached me in the garden afterwards. He meant to say, 'That was amazing facilitation and leadership.' But 'you're beautiful' came out instead. He was embarrassed and genuinely surprised, glancing over his shoulder as if someone else had said it. 'I'm not hitting on you!' he added quickly, 'But you are. Beautiful, that is.'

He had me from that moment because I knew he had really seen me, from the inside out. That was the beauty John acknowledged and the beauty I later acknowledged in him: a simple quality of being that blooms in the authentic expression of unguarded hearts. It was what I had held out for when every previous relationship ended. By the time I met John, I had pretty much given up on finding a 'soul mate'. I certainly wasn't looking any more. I had nearly married someone in my late twenties and someone else in my mid-thirties, but ultimately kept choosing to be alone rather than to be half-seen and half-loved.

In our ten years of marriage, John has rarely noticed what I'm wearing (unless I'm dressed up all glam) or what size I happen to be (which certainly varies). It doesn't matter. It's not that he's unobservant. He doesn't see it because he sees something else, something behind and beyond, something more permanent and permeable. Even when the chemo drug ravished my face, John neither placated me with disingenuous reassurances nor judged it as unattractive. He saw pain, not ugliness, and held my essence in his protective grip as I felt it slip through my fingers. At one point, in my despondency, I apologised for my appearance and asked why he didn't wince when looking at me.

'Because, my darling,' he replied, 'I don't know anyone whose beauty is more congruent with their soul.'

As if this wasn't enough for my world to right itself, four-year-old Gabriella then ran into the living room after pre-school to find me sitting by the log fire, which had been laid and tended by John. She straddled her legs across my lap and looked at my damaged face without speaking. I wanted to turn away from her, to spare her this ugliness, but stayed still, determined not to airbrush my flaws or pass on the toxic version of beauty I had bought into for so many years. I wanted her to grow up knowing what it took me decades to learn and to be loved one day as I am loved by her daddy – for who she is, not what the world demands of her or how it expects her to look. I also knew it was not my job to protect her from what was happening to her mum, but to help her meet it on her own terms. So, I sat still, waiting, until she cupped my face in her little hands and asked,

'Does it hurt, beautiful Mummy? Shall I kiss it better?'

Beautiful Mummy. This was a lifeshock too. I let her kiss my burning cheek before she wiped away the tears that silently escaped like soft spring rain. The wind changed direction. I forgave my face its ugliness and all the ugliness I had seen in it for as long as I could remember. I began to feel grateful for what the chemo drug, Afatinib, had done to me. My 'pizza face' exposed residues of the judgements I had put in place decades ago and gave me the chance to dissolve them in the bosom of my loving family. This is what lifeshocks do. They reveal us to ourselves. And this is what love does. It listens and sees and remembers who we are, even as our faces scar and faculties fail. It doesn't try to fix things that are broken. It holds our brokenness to the sun so that light may find its way through the fissures. This is how it earns its keep.

Beauty is a consequence of love, not a precursor or prerequisite. It is the sap that rises when we are finally free to be ourselves without pretence or pretension: a *way of being*, not of looking. This is what I want my daughter, and all the daughters of a culture obsessed with appearances, to learn. Because this is what she and her dad taught me that day. A few weeks later, having corrected the dosage, my face healed without leaving any permanent damage and my vitality returned.

But a deeper healing occurred before the physical one, another laying to rest of self-condemnation along with my worn-out need to be beautiful and acceptable by superficial standards. In the lifeshocking reflection of my blistered face and horrified eyes, I saw love's true nature. Not the passionate, adoring, flattering kind, but the kind that begins where judgement ends, the kind that kneads and pummels until we see the truth of things, the kind that will never lie and will stop at nothing to crack our protective casing so that beauty many enter again.

The Reactive Mind

Throughout this book, I will be referring to 'the reactive mind'. This is a state of self-deception in which we react *against* lifeshocks. We separate from what is happening, turning away from the specifics because it seems too painful to face them. In doing so we also separate from the authentic self by walling it off in the name of self-protection. Similarly, we disconnect from others in both subtle and blatant ways. We are driven by fears (*I'll fail, be rejected, die*); judgements (*I'm less than, more than, undeserving, entitled, an insider, an outsider, a winner, a failure, a useless, worthless nobody*); demands (*I have to be perfect, other people should respect me, life should be fair*), and false beliefs (*I am worthless, other people are cruel, life's a bitch*). Some of these beliefs are decisions we make early in our lives. This state is *below the line*.

Above the line is 'the creative mind'. This does not mean 'artistic' (though it may include artistic qualities). It is about our creative responses to lifeshocks. This is a connecting state of being in which we are aligned with our authentic selves, our care for others and to life's creative possibilities. I will be illuminating this state, and how to access it, as the book unfolds.

The 'I Am' Structure

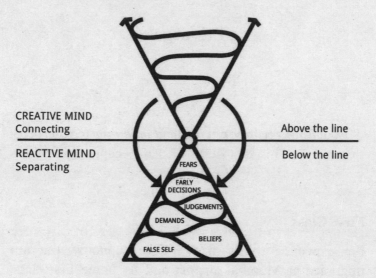

CREATIVE MIND
Connecting
Above the line

REACTIVE MIND
Separating
Below the line

FEARS

EARLY DECISIONS

JUDGEMENTS

DEMANDS

BELIEFS

FALSE SELF

5

Privilege

The difference between privilege and entitlement is gratitude.

Brené Brown

First Class

I'm expecting to sit in premium economy, but am upgraded at Mumbai airport and fly home first class. Apparently, economy has been oversold and business class is full, so when the kind check-in agent notices I have ordered a wheelchair, she moves me to the front. This is the second time I have had this experience: boarding ahead of all the other passengers; being offered champagne and pyjamas as I find my seat-cum-bed for the night flight back to England; plugging my phone in to charge while I am sleeping; lying flat under a crisp, white, cotton duvet for most of the trip and waking up rested as the plane approaches Heathrow Airport after eleven hours' flying; prefacing each request of the cabin crew with 'sorry but can I . . .' for fear of appearing entitled; pushing through several contractions of discomfort with the fortunate position in which I find myself. Again.

Across the aisle, in the middle front row, is an elegant

blonde woman in her thirties who knows the ropes. She hangs her jacket in the personal closet I've yet to notice in my private 'suite'. She was probably the first to board because she is already in her pyjamas and her champagne glass is half empty. She wants slippers and requests them impatiently, even though the male crew member is serving another passenger. Her self-importance is airtight. Her husband is in the suite next to her. He intervenes to get her what she wants quickly, ensuring she has her glass filled and is perusing her dinner menu while the rest of us wait our turn. The crew member complies politely, apologising to the other passenger and promising to return to him soon. I feel embarrassed, as if I am the one behaving that way and need to atone for her conceit. Part of me relishes the luxury after hours on dusty roads, but I am also uneasy in this cabin and wonder why there are travel classes at all. I get the economics. I was a consultant to British Airways for several years. They make their money from business and first, which keeps economy prices down. But this also reflects a class system that has done untold damage in differentiating people's worth.

I am conscious still of the Indian children who pressed their dusty noses to the windows of stationary cars in the Mumbai rush hour, when the log-jammed lanes of heaving traffic – six across in each direction – made it impossible to ignore their desperate eyes and pleading hands. It is hard not to wonder what put me here and them there.

Today I have been sandwiched between both extremes. This is how life works. It becomes more insistent until we notice the masks we wear, games we play and lies we live. I am privileged in many ways, but I haven't worn it well. I am white, relatively well off and well educated. I live in a free democracy where women are legally, if not yet literally, equal to men. I have always found meaningful work. I have almost always earned money. I married a man of my choosing. I have travelled to around twenty-five countries. My life has not been exempt from trauma, but I have wanted for little materially, socially and politically.

My fear of adopting airs and graces, had led me into guilt and apology instead. And this experience on the plane is peeling back another layer of awkward disquiet about the circles I have moved in and the skin I wear. There is a disquiet that feels different from guilt and embarrassment, as if it is trying to rise above those feelings and make some important truths known. I can feel the lifeshocks accumulating and commanding my attention.

When we land at Heathrow Terminal 5, I am aware of my relief to be home, to see roofs on all the houses as we approach the runway and cars that indicate before changing lanes. I feel well enough to walk instead of using a wheelchair and let the crew know. We exit through the doors behind our seats, which means I leave before the front-row passenger I noticed before, but she soon rushes past me as if addicted to being ahead of the pack. She chooses the lift down to the trains that transport us between gates and I choose the escalator. I am waiting at the train doors by the time she arrives and hear her scold her husband for choosing the slower route. Part of me wants to get ahead just to piss her off, but I let her find the best position for a rapid exit when we arrive at the main terminal. I cruise through passport control because I'm near the front and find the right baggage belt, expecting the first-class bags to appear before all the others, but they don't. This is fine with me because it levels the playing field if only for ten minutes, and I am one-among instead of one-apart. As the economy passengers load their trolleys and head for customs, she starts pacing furiously, her race-winning tactics and sense of superiority thwarted. I am watching little lifeshocks pelt her like a scattergun, but I'm confident she doesn't recognise them for what they are. However, I do recognise my own fear of being like her and my need to distance myself from what she reflects back to me about myself. And suddenly I feel some empathy towards her. I remember it's a fear of being less-than that drives the desire to be better-than. This is a thirst of the psyche that a thousand won races cannot quench, and she is in its grip.

As I emerge through the double doors at the other side of the 'Nothing to Declare' lane, my darling daughter hurtles towards me and leaps into my arms as John takes pictures. I am returning to a post-Brexit-vote Britain, in which racist attacks are on the rise and people with a different accent or skin colour are more afraid than they were before the referendum. Donald Trump has been elected president of the United States, *#blacklivesmatter* is giving expression to another Civil Rights movement and Facebook is awash with fearful posts about the rise of white supremacy.

These are lifeshocks which challenge the collective. The issue of privilege is in the forefront again and we need to take heed. I need to take heed. Something is pressing on me to examine this again, to examine myself again, to learn how to raise my daughter in a world of such profound disparity that even a wealthy white woman who travels first class is racing towards the only place where she can be sure of her value: the front of the line.

A Political Heritage

I didn't know I was privileged – 'a right, advantage or immunity granted to a person or body of persons beyond the common advantages of others' – until my teens. My world was what it was and I knew no other. If anything, I thought I was significantly worse off than my friends, several of whom lived on vast country estates or in the grandest of houses in London's Belgravia. A few had both. My family had nowhere near that kind of wealth, but I did grow up in three homes for a few years, of which my parents owned one. This started out as a ruined water mill in the heart of the Black Mountains, which my father converted into a cottage with the help of his best friend. We spent many weekends there, camping in the garden while the two of them laid the Welsh stones and roof tiles. It was a DIY job from top to toe until he had it extended some years later.

The second home was in London. My parents took a short lease on a tall, thin house in Chelsea so Dad could go to the House of Commons for work, and eventually they bought a home in Battersea where they live to this day. The third was a small bungalow we rented in Pembrokeshire, the westernmost tip of Wales, which was my father's political constituency from 1970 to 1989. My mum hated running three homes to support Dad's career and would have greatly preferred to have one place where she could put down permanent roots and become queen of her domain.

My relationships with privilege and politics are inextricably linked. I was far more conscious of the latter than the former. I was four years old when Dad was first elected as a Conservative MP in a constituency that had been a Labour stronghold for decades. His majority was very slim, but he stood in Wales because he was Welsh and deeply proud of it. He had descended from a family of notable Welsh Anglicans, including the first Archbishop of Wales, and did his national service with the Royal Welch Fusiliers. From that point on, I spent a lot of time in cars, travelling from east to west and back again in the back of a blue Volvo estate with my two siblings and our three spaniels.

Far from thinking myself fortunate, I disliked it. I have extreme motion sickness, even now, and spent most of those journeys vomiting out of the car window. I didn't like leaving my friends in London and I dreaded being paraded around Pembrokeshire like a political mascot, especially during election campaigns, when I was expected to go from door to door with political leaflets and ask complete strangers to vote for a party about which I was completely ignorant. While I loved the rented bungalow in St David's and the huge sandy beaches nearby, I soon developed asthma when we spent time there. Mum thought it was caused by mould in the walls. I thought it was an allergy to being the local MP's daughter. Either way, I never got asthma anywhere else.

In 1979, when Margaret Thatcher became Prime Minister, Dad joined her Cabinet as Secretary of State for Wales – a position he remained in, despite being offered 'bigger' jobs, for eight years. I was thirteen. That was the year my political lifeshocks intensified. At first, I felt very proud of him. I was at school with the daughter of a more senior Cabinet minister and all our friends seemed to think it was cool. Our fathers had power and influence. They appeared on television. They were in the 'right' party, according to the majority of fee-paying parents, and this enhanced our popularity. What was not to like?

But my unease surfaced slowly. I recall a series of lifeshocks at our home in the Black Mountains during his first year in office: protestors marching with banners outside our gate on weekends, when I wanted to play in the garden but was made to stay inside; eggs and tomatoes being pelted at our car windows when we drove out of the gate (a frequent occurrence that year); coming home to dead rabbits on the lawn; protestors lying down in the middle of the road to stop us passing; watching a news report about 'second homes' belonging to English people being burnt down by angry Welsh locals; someone in the nearby town telling me I was only Welsh if I spoke Welsh, which I didn't.

Up until then Dad had just been Dad. Suddenly he was an object of hatred and resentment – a 'privileged Englishman' (despite his deep-rooted Welshness), who worked for a 'wicked' woman and was likely to use the Welsh Office as a stepping-stone for his personal ambitions (which is often what happens). Naturally this bothered and, at times, frightened me, but I didn't realise how deep the hatred ran until one summer weekend when my granny came to look after us in Wales while my parents attended a party in London. Granny was my mother's mother and I adored her. My brother, who is two years older than me, slept in a ground-floor bedroom at the front of the house. My sister, nearly five years my junior, slept in the bedroom opposite mine at the top of the converted mill under slanting ceilings and original wooden beams. When we went to sleep that night, there was nothing untoward.

The next thing I knew, Granny was standing over my bed and pushing my shoulder with some urgency. It was very dark outside. 'Wake up darling,' she said in a calm, almost cheerful voice. 'It's two in the morning and there's a bomb in the house.' She was so matter-of-fact about it I didn't feel remotely scared. Nor did I take it seriously. It wasn't the first time we had received a bomb threat. But I did get up quickly, just in case.

'How do you know?' I asked her as she scooped up my sister and chivvied us down the stairs, where my brother was waiting with a policeman at the bottom. The front door was open. Outside I could see blue lights, a big red fire engine and an ambulance. *Lifeshock, lifeshock, lifeshock.* Maybe this was for real.

As the policeman ushered us into the back of a police car, he explained they'd received a tip-off about the bomb and needed to sweep the house to look for it. I relaxed. Another empty threat, most likely. So, there we all were in the back of a police car at 2a.m. in our pyjamas, while the supposed terrorist's real target danced the night away in London. At this point, my nose started bleeding heavily, which it often did when I was young, while my brother bemoaned the impending loss of his tickets to a Clash concert, which were in his bedroom.

Granny got the giggles. We all got the giggles. Perhaps it was displaced anxiety or our confidence that they wouldn't find anything, but it simply felt like a big adventure we could share with our friends when the sun had risen in the sky and we had some breakfast in our bellies.

However, it was no hoax. We soon learned that a petrol bomb was indeed in the house, pushed through my brother's half-open bedroom window on the ground floor. It was sitting on the windowsill behind closed curtains, six inches above his head. We were driven to a friend's house to spend the night there while the bomb squad dealt with it and the house was swept for other devices. We called Dad to tell him. Naturally, he was horrified. And many things changed after that.

For the next few years we had metal blinds inside all our windows. We had to pull them down and lock them tight every evening, like bars. Red panic buttons were installed in different parts of the house, including our bedrooms, and outside there was twenty-four-hour police protection. Any packages larger than a letter were opened for us, even at Christmas. We carried on as normally as possible, determined not to be intimidated, but the context was a political landscape that put us in danger. The result was to smash my naivety and challenge my social and political illiteracy, laying the ground for a far greater cognisance of the society I was living in, beyond my barred windows and ivory walls.

I didn't feel fear; I felt guilt. *Surely there are good reasons for people wanting to kill us. Surely, we deserve it or represent something that does.* I wanted to know why. I wanted to understand what Thatcher's government was up to and to understand the people its policies alienated. I wanted to wise up. Thus, my rebellion against my social and political inheritance began. But the lifeshock I remember reacting to most – even more than a policeman saying, 'We found the bomb' – came from my headmistress during the General Election of 1983.

By now I was studying for my A levels, one of which was Politics, and the headmistress had decided to run a parallel mock election at school. Earlier that year, I'd won a national competition, which was reported in *The Times* as 'Cabinet Minister's Daughter Triumphs at Public Speaking'. The headline was another lifeshock, one I reacted to resentfully, believing: *I have no identity of my own. I am just my father's daughter. I will always be seen as that. I have to get out from under his shadow. I have to be seen as Sophie. I have to prove I'm not him.* My headmistress threw fuel on this fire by calling me to her office and saying, 'I want you to stand as the Conservative candidate in the school election.' I was livid. It was as if all the preceding lifeshocks on this theme crashed into my body at once, like a pile-up on the motorway. I'd had enough.

'No,' I responded defiantly. 'I will stand as the Labour Candidate. And I will win.'

I did win – by a landslide majority. I won in a context of predominantly right-wing entitlement. I made the case. I made my fellow students laugh. I shocked them into voting against the grain. I appealed to their social consciences. I proved I wasn't my dad.

The Bill, Please

Alongside my guilt at the privilege I was born into, this desire to prove I had a mind of my own continued to deepen. Around the same age as my school election victory, I also became aware of the privilege of my whiteness. About a year earlier, at the age of sixteen, I had made my first black friend, Michael. We had met in London's King's Road where he worked in a men's clothes shop. We fancied each other and flirted outrageously, becoming on-off lovers for several years and lifelong friends from that moment on. He had grown up in Jamaica. His parents and grandmother were black, but his grandfather had been white – the owner of a large estate who had had 'an affair' with his maid. As a child, this earned Michael a stream of derogatory abuse for being the illegitimate offspring of a deeply resented man and for not being fully black. He was an easy target, ostracised by his community until he moved with his large family to Leicester, in the UK Midlands, at the age of eight. He came down to London as a young adult, where he lived on a council estate in Battersea, not far from my first flat. Yet what divided us materially never estranged us psychologically or spiritually. We just clicked.

The first time I became fully aware of our 'difference' was one afternoon when we were heading back to Battersea from the King's Road in Chelsea. Something I have always loved about London is how diverse and multicultural it is. I knew there were areas where specific cultures or religions were concentrated, like Jewish communities in Golders Green and Finchley or Indian communities in Croydon and Tooting. But in most places, you could just walk down the street or sit on the tube and witness ethnic diversity – even in Chelsea's toff infested King's Road. It was raining hard that day so I suggested we get a taxi and started hailing black cabs with their lights on. None of them stopped. At first, I couldn't understand it. It had never happened to me before.

'They won't stop for me, Soph,' said Michael in the first of three short lifeshocking sentences. 'I'm a black man with dreadlocks. They never stop.'

'Fuck that!' I retorted. 'That's fucking outrageous! Wait here.'

I marched on ahead of him and hailed the next cab, which stopped immediately. Then I called him to catch up and jump in. I noticed the taxi driver's indignant scowl, but didn't care or consider whether I might be patronising my friend. I simply exercised my taken-for-granted white privilege – the privilege that meant taxis stopped for me, restaurants let me in without question, police didn't stop and search me for drugs without provocation (which they might well have found in those days), shop staff didn't hover around me to make sure I wouldn't steal something. My whole notion of 'advantage' was toppled that day. It became an utterly inadequate understatement of the gulf that suddenly opened between my black friend and me. I hadn't noticed it before. I had worn my white skin without consciousness or conscience. I had been sleepwalking through this city of diversity, imagining a parity that did not exist.

Michael wasn't angry, but I was. He wasn't resigned either. He told me how proud he was to be British, how there were few places in the world a black man could enjoy the freedoms London gave him, that he experienced less racism here than when he was a child in Jamaica. 'It will change,' he tried to reassure me. 'We have come a long way.'

But the guilt I had been harbouring about my social and educational privileges now extended to the pigment of my skin. It moved into my cells like a toxin, concentrated by beliefs about the necessity of overcompensating which I had already put in place: *life is unfair; I don't deserve what I've been given; I'm unworthy; it's too much; I'm too much* (my favourite); *I have to make amends; I have to make it fair; I have to give away what I've been given; I have to pay the bill for other people's poverty and injustice and pain.*

These beliefs would later be compounded by a six-month experience of living in New Orleans during my gap year before university – further evidence of my privileged existence. Known as 'The Big Uneasy', which felt like a perfect term for my own growing disquiet in racially divided contexts, the city had a majority black population and bore the worst scars of slavery, just as it carried one of the brightest torches of freedom. I was eighteen years old when I arrived and it was the first place I lived independently. It was where Southern kindness dissipated my fresh-out-of-private-school shyness and wild flowers sprung up in my landscaped garden. It was jazz, raw oysters, White Russian cocktails, Mardi Gras, marijuana, big hair and gay pride. New Orleans blew my narrow mind.

While I was there, the Brighton hotel bomb exploded at the Conservative Party Conference, killing five people and leaving several more seriously disabled. It was an IRA assassination attempt against the highest tier of the British government. The news reported that 'the entire Cabinet was staying there' so I assumed my parents were involved. This time fear struck my heart. Not just the fear that they might be dead or injured, but also the recognition that my siblings, grandmother and I might indeed have been killed just a few years prior as we slept in our own home. Current lifeshocks often awaken past lifeshocks and open the door to whatever we unconsciously feared, believed and decided at the time. As it happened, my parents weren't even there.

By the time I arrived at university on my return to England, I was more aware of my privilege than ever: I had a British passport and white skin; I had grown up in more than one home and been given a private education; I had material advantages; I was a woman who could make my own choices without fear of recrimination; I knew people of enormous wealth and influence. Margaret and Denis Thatcher had been to dinner in our London home and once spent a weekend with us in Wales, where she climbed a mountain in high-heeled shoes and lacquered hair. Her bodyguard slept in my bedroom while I was relegated to sharing a room with my brother. This was my context. This was what I had been given by my birth. It also made me a target – not just of political venom and violence, but of personal envy and resentment too. As I was about to find out.

My degree course was in Humanities – English Literature and Psychology – at Bristol Polytechnic (now the University of the West of England). Bristol Poly had a very socialist bias and very few students who had attended private school. This delighted me. I wanted to continue extending my social and political horizons as well as educational ones. I felt shy on the first day, but eager and open. I was ripe for renewal.

In some ways, it surpassed my hopes. One of my tutors was Dr Rosie Jackson, a brilliant academic and talented writer, who led a seminar on feminist literature. I found myself in a predominantly working-class group of intelligent, passionate women who had more grist in their mills than I had silver in my spoon. Some had overcome significant hardships to be there and all of them had attended co-educational state schools. I particularly recall Carol, a mature student with dark curly hair and rough energetic edges. She was openly gay (this was the early 1980s), very outspoken and brazenly herself. I was in awe.

I also knew my posh accent stood out and felt very out of my depth. In New Orleans, my accent had been deliciously British and people kept asking me to repeat things so they could hear it again. Here it jarred. I heard it jar, but couldn't do anything about it. It was how I spoke. I didn't want to curb my tongue in a class that was all about the power of female expression, and I was too in love with the feminist syllabus to withhold my questions. In one of the first seminars, Rosie asked us to talk about the contexts in which we had grown up and how these had influenced our relationship with literature. A number of students explained how few books were in their homes as children, how they had relied on local libraries and what obstacles they had faced to become literate. It was sobering and humbling. When my turn came, I told the truth without really thinking about the impression it would make. I grew up with books: hundreds of them. We had bookshelves in almost every room and my mother had frequently caught me trying to climb them as a toddler to reach the higher shelves. I began reading at the age of three.

From that point, though I tried to ignore it, I sensed

I was in a hostile environment. Little digs. Discounts. Ignoring me when I spoke. When Rosie tried to include me, I assumed she was just doing her job, but I was suspicious that she too was complicit in various ways. I believed I was being scapegoated. At the time, I was living in a tiny bedsit in a shared house with a group of students from other courses who ignored me too. The single bed almost filled the room so it served as my table and desk as well. Sometimes I treasured this 'room of my own', this place where I could finally discover my own mind and speak it. I loved sitting on the bed with the likes of Adrienne Rich, Alice Walker and Zora Neale Hurston, who drew back my horizons like curtains and revealed entire universes beyond – just as Harper Lee had done when I was ten. Other times it was like an isolation cell, a place where I was forced to confront an aloneness I'd never known before, one shaped by my birth and accent and the privilege of growing up with books. I felt angry more than hurt by their rejection. I wanted to evolve. I wanted to be more than my context. I wanted to be like them.

Things came to a head (by which I mean the lifeshocks got louder) towards the end of the first term, when we were studying George Orwell, who was required reading on the syllabus (not Rosie's choice). Orwell's inclination to present his female characters as inferior to men revealed a disparaging attitude towards women that drew considerable criticism from our group of student feminists. The discussion became more and more heated until someone concluded, 'Well what do you expect? He went to Eton.'

I had been silent up to that lifeshock, choosing my

shots as I had learned to do, believing they wouldn't listen anyway. And when Rosie turned to me, perhaps genuinely valuing my voice, to ask what I thought, I felt the weight of privilege rest on my shoulders like concrete, as if it had fallen to me to atone for the sins of entitled Etonians and all their kind. *I'm being set up*, I thought. *I'm under attack. Whatever I say will be wrong.*

'You're right about private schools,' I replied, carefully. 'They are full of snobbery and prejudice and entitlement. I've seen it all. But I haven't encountered the level of snobbery that I have experienced in this room. It's just the inverted, begrudging, chip-on-the-shoulder kind. You have all judged me for *how* rather than *what* I communicate. That is all I have to say.'

As I stood up and left the class, my sense of defeat lifted for a few moments. I felt relieved. Even if I didn't return the following term, a likelihood at that point, I had stood up for myself. I had also tasted a wee morsel of prejudice, the kind that discounts your humanity and submerges your identity if you let it, the kind that my friend Michael experiences every day. It was summer. I sat on the grass in the university grounds and let this realisation seep into my cells. It was almost more than I could contemplate or bear – the sheer scale of it in the world. I felt the toxic tendrils of white privilege, British colonialism and the deeply divisive class system twining around my bones like ivy. I took them into me as if they belonged to me. And I wept with shame.

Before long the mature student, Carol, came and sat down next to me on the grass. She put an arm around my shoulder and apologised for how she had treated me. I assured her that wasn't why I was crying, but it didn't matter. She was truly sorry and implored me to return to the class to give them another chance. I melted into her accepting arms and wept some more as the waters of our common humanity levelled between us. And I did return.

Before the term ended, Rosie asked us to hand in the journals she had asked us to write since the first week – reflections on what we were studying, our own writing, anything we were wanting to say in her seminars but were withholding. After many weeks of biting my posh tongue, my journal was full. She returned it a few days later with a note apologising for any way she had misjudged me, and admitting how much she had envied my privileges when she heard I had grown up with books. The message was very touching and concluded, 'You have shown me that before and beyond all our differences, we have more important things in common – like a love of literature and the search for truth.' These commonalities have, in spite of our disparate backgrounds, kept us in touch over the years. Rosie has taught me about the pain of poverty and the triumph of the human spirit in the face of adversity. She remains a close friend to this day.

But the effect of these experiences was not so easily erased. Despite the turnarounds, my reactive mind had me in its grip and made a deep, unconscious commitment: to pretend to be what I wasn't (by toning down my accent and hiding my background) and to pay for what I feared I was (by picking up the tab for other people's lack).

I have to make amends for it all somehow, I told myself, quite unconsciously. *I have to prove I am not what they think I am. I have to hide my background. I have to make myself seem normal. I have to be a giver, not a taker. I have to share my privileges and spread them around. I have to stand with the 'have nots' and against the 'haves'. I must pay for my advantages. I must always pick up the tab. 'The bill please.'*

This mindtalk ran aspects of my life for a very long time. By the time I graduated, I had changed my accent, accumulated debt, denied my dad so many times he (affectionately) nicknamed me 'Peter', and the ivy had fused with my bones.

A Psychological Honey Pot

It isn't the lifeshocks that cause us to react. It is what we make them mean. In my reaction to lifeshocks relating to my privileges, I opted for guilt, pretence and reparation. I took it upon myself to apologise for entitled white people everywhere, while trying to prove I wasn't one of them. I created a *false self* to hide my background and atone for it in largely unconscious ways.

Our first versions of the false self are often firmly formed by the time we are nine. Sometimes Brad called these ways of being 'dramas', because they are costumes we wear on a stage of pretence; dramatic expressions of who we think we have to be that conceal who we really are.

We can see this at school – the good kids in the front of the classroom, the rebels at the back; the ones who always put their hands up and the ones who keep them down; the bullies in the playground and their victims; even the heroes who stand up for underdogs and rescue

others from harm. Enough lifeshocks have occurred by
now for our little minds to assign false meanings to
ourselves: *I'm different, I'm not good enough, I'm superior,
I'm right, I'm wrong, I'm good, I'm bad, I'm unpopular,
I'm unworthy, I'm alone.* We may not be aware of it, but
we all do it. This is the nature of the reactive mind. Some
of us take a 'less than' position by judging ourselves;
others take a 'better than' position by judging others
(and thereby deferring the pain of self-criticism). These
'core beliefs' then generate demands about how we have
to be when presenting ourselves to other people: *be smart,
be good, be nice, fit in, please others, blame others, go along
with, rebel against, be the joker, look good, hide out, be the
best, control feelings* and *prove, prove, prove my worth.*[3]

In this instance, my unconscious 'the bill, please' drama
was insidious and rife. It led me to pay the bill for others
whenever possible, giving away what I had been given
(my ideas and talents as well as my earnings), striving
to fix other people's pain and avoiding talking about my
political heritage. For example:

- My first job after graduating was as a copywriter at
  the BBC. I loved working there, but resigned on a
  whim within a year of being promoted to low-level
  management (better paid but less creative) with no
  other job to go to. I ended up on welfare and got to
  be a have-not for a while. To their credit, my parents
  refused to help me out and left me to get on with
  finding another job, which I eventually did. That was
  the only year in my life when I struggled to buy milk.

3 Core beliefs are the opposite of core values. The former are
  false, the latter are true.

- I turned my back on almost all my school friends and the whole social package they were part of. Over the next ten years I dated an electrician, an ex-con, a decorator, an alternative healer, a Greek barman and an aspiring actor subsidising his income as a plumber. They taught me about what I called 'real life' and shook me into greater social awareness, which I will always be grateful for. I genuinely cared for each in turn. But, in ways I didn't recognise, part of me was unconsciously using them to 'normalise' me socially. To my shame, they were part of my scheme to shed all things posh.

- When it came to money, I offered to pay in restaurants as soon as the bill came, if not at the start of the meal (except with wealthy white people and sometimes even then). I didn't claim expenses in business. I called back to foot the phone bill when worse-off friends called me. When I became the sole owner of my business I *gave* a large number of shares to a new director because she believed previous employers had taken advantage of her (which was up to me to make up for, of course). Then, when the economic recession sent my business into a downturn, I used accrued profits to keep staff on for several very lean years instead of making redundancies and withdrawing a significant sum as security for my family. And I liked myself for it. I still like the underlying intention, but the dramatic win was proving I wasn't an entitled 'have'.

The truth is that, although I do have a genuinely generous spirit, I was often being run by my 'the bill, please' mindtalk. While this was the case, I put out a vibe of 'what's mine is yours' and became a psychological honey pot attracting lots of needy bees. My behaviour wasn't just benevolent. It was irresponsible and unharnessed. My generosity haemorrhaged into almost every area of my life. I gave myself away sexually and emotionally as much as materially. I had flimsy boundaries. I set myself up to be taken from and used. It turned me into a living apology: sorry for my education; sorry for my skin colour; sorry for earning money; sorry for being well educated; sorry for my talents; sorry for breathing; 'here, let me pay for that'.

Mindtalk is that powerful. It runs in every area of our lives and the more unaware of it we are, the more power it has. We all have blind spots and this has been one of my biggest. It's easy to miss the 'do-good' dramas that give us regular fixes of self-vindication and pseudo-nobility, as this one has given me. The payoffs for all this behaviour were juicy enough to keep me ignorant. I got to be needed, useful and magnanimous. I got to knock blocks off my guilt.

Just for Show

I would like to say I've dismantled my 'the bill, please' drama completely, but I haven't. It has been a slow awakening with incremental shifts along the way. It didn't beg my attention the way my distorted and palpably painful perceptions of beauty did. I couldn't see the ugliness of what I was doing. I still saw my dramatised generosity as a redeeming feature, not a flaw. However, personal growth is usually an incremental process, a layer-by-layer peeling back of all that removes us from our authentic selves. I peel as I write.

I recall a moment in my twenties, when I was participating in a course created by Brad called 'Making Money Count', when something important shifted in my relationship with money. I had been dismantling my resistance to being an entitled 'have' and to pursuing material wealth at the expense of spiritual wealth, when I became aware of a simple personal truth that offered a viable solution: *making money is not my purpose in life. It can follow my purpose in life, which is to play my part in creating an inheritable world.* This was a game-changer for me, liberating me from having to choose between earning well and giving to society through charitable or public-sector service. That choice seemed so either/or in our society, and remains so in many ways. Now I could make money by serving. I just needed to find a way. Before long, I had co-founded a business with Brad that took his work into companies in the private and public sectors. I also became a leader and trainer in the educational foundation he co-created. All this allowed me to serve people's growth and awakening, earn good money from lucrative clients and contribute to service organisations with thin resources.

Another shift came in my thirties, during a conflict with one of my business partners. We were attempting to get to the bottom of our increasing disagreements by expressing what each of us meant by, and expected from, 'partnership'. When I asked why she wanted to put our company name instead of mine on 'inspirational quotes' I had written for our website, she explained, 'Because in a partnership, what's yours is mine.' *Lifeshock.* 'What's yours is mine.' There it was, my own belief (*what's mine is yours, theirs, anyone's*) reflected right back at me. I objected to it from the bottom of my being – not because it was her belief, but because it had long been my own and I could suddenly see what it had cost me. Putting my name on what I created for our company was new behaviour and it was now clear why I was fighting for it. I hadn't just been trying to apologise for the privileges I had been born *into*. I had also been trying to apologise for the talents I was born *with*.

Perhaps the most significant break from 'the bill, please' resulted from lifeshocks in a personal relationship, also in my thirties. I got involved with someone charming, skint and, as it turned out, very needy. Before long, he moved into my flat from the bedsit he had been living in since a breakup with his long-term partner. He didn't pay rent and I didn't ask him to. He ate my food while charming me and bared his emotional scars while adoring me. I became his counsellor as well as his girlfriend, a receptacle for his lifelong depression and rage. I was seduced by all of it. Here was someone whose life I could fix and whose pain I could pay for as if I had caused it myself.

Soon enough it began to drain me and, despite periods of relative joy, I couldn't seem to dent his depression. Nor could I tolerate his intensifying jealousy and possessiveness. Finally, but tentatively, I ended it, while agreeing to let him stay in my flat until he found somewhere else to live. Of course, this didn't happen and, still pinned to my guilt cross, I was a sucker for every excuse he came up with for not moving out. Being taken advantage of lessened the burden of being advantaged in the first place and of breaking his dysfunctional heart.

One night I went out on a date and didn't tell him. I just went. When I returned home around midnight I noticed the door to my office was open. The first lifeshock was seeing folders of private papers strewn across the floor, with my personal journal open in the middle. The second lifeshock was seeing the email in which I had arranged the date open on my computer screen. *So, he knows.* The third was standing at the living room door and seeing him out cold on the sofa with two empty bottles of wine on the floor next to him and – biggest lifeshock moment – an empty bottle of pills.

I stood there stunned and angry. Not guilty. Angry. This was new. I had lost a dear friend to suicide a few months earlier and could see this for what it was: a manipulation. I knew I was not responsible. I knew I was not at fault. And I knew he was not dead. This clarity of knowing dissolved my anger. Suddenly, I felt calm and light-hearted, as if a stone had been rolled back off my chest and the air had rushed in. I checked his pulse and called an ambulance. Then I called a friend who didn't do 'all that touchy-feely nonsense' to keep me company. I needed someone practical and funny. We took care of my ex-boyfriend, ensuring he was taken to hospital and verifying that it wasn't as dramatic as it looked when the paramedics came. 'Some are just for show,' one of them said, before taking him away. While he was in hospital I put a deposit down on a room in a shared London flat, left his bags there and changed the locks on my door. This time I wasn't footing the bill for his pain, but for my freedom. I was investing in my personal boundaries. I never attracted that kind of relationship again.

Paid in Full

While I was in India I read *The Glass Mother*, a beautiful and heart-rending memoir by Rosie Jackson, who had been my tutor at university. It is as brave a book as I have read because it chronicles the excruciating story of how and why she left her son at a young age, how her own mother was absent, even when present, and what it took to heal her relationship with her boy. In one chapter, she mentions our friendship, which grew from its unlikely origins of social difference in that English seminar. She describes me as 'Sophie Sabbage, the daughter of. . .' who had taken some heat in her seminar for being acquainted with Margaret Thatcher. It was simple, accurate and sympathetic. But those last three words were also a lifeshock. I felt instantly irritated and defensive. There it was in black and white. The author of *The Cancer Whisperer* was the daughter of a Thatcherite politician. I had been exposed.

This is what lifeshocks do. They knock on the doors of our pretences and invite us to walk authentically through the world. Those three words convinced me to write this chapter. It was as though life had answered my reservations directly by putting it out there in a deeply vulnerable memoir that must have been far harder to publish than my angst about privilege. I had not wanted to include this part of my life in this book and most of my readers would be none the wiser if I had skipped it. I almost convinced myself to do so. *No one will notice. Who will miss a chapter that isn't there? Why draw attention to my privilege and advantages? What if I fuck it up, offend people, set my work up to be discounted because of where I came from (which has happened several times)? What if it stops people learning about lifeshocks? What if it diminishes the value of my voice?*

But this is why it must be written. Because marginalised communities live with such fear every day. Because their value is disregarded and their voices silenced as a result of where they come from, what colour their skin is and who they choose to love. Because, however empathetic I am, I believe there are moccasins I cannot walk in, the ones that will never fit my privileged feet.

Material privilege alone protects us from one of life's great hardships – poverty. Apart from that year on welfare in my twenties, I cannot claim to know this struggle directly. I have my dad's work ethic and am proud that any money in my account has been a result of that effort since I was twenty (until I raised funds for cancer treatments). I have not seen my father relax into the kind of wealth his friends enjoy. In fact, I've seen him fret about money and work himself to the bone for it. I work as hard as he does, but wish I had inherited more of his integrity with finances. He has known lack, you see. He was a war child who grew up on rations. As such, he does not fritter or waste. But nor does he hoard or deceive. Once, he lost his camera and claimed for it on his insurance. When he found it several months later, he wrote the insurance company a return cheque that day. Another time, he got on a train without a ticket, but no ticket collector was on board to charge him. He could have gone home without paying, but didn't. He went out of his way to pay for it at the other end. I believe his attitude is rare and exemplary. He has no sense of material entitlement, of laying false claims to what is not his.

I rejected entitlement in favour of guilt – neither of which was necessary, or a reflection of my true values. I ran so fast from taking my privileges for granted and claiming them as a right that I ended up paying for what *I had already been given*. This was a form of ingratitude; a waste of grace.

In part, this chapter is my confession. Not because privilege is a sin, but because that's what I mistakenly believed it to be. And I denied, lied, hid and withheld because of that belief. I made amends for what I had not done and apologised for what was not my fault. Somehow, I find this more excruciatingly exposing to admit than being bulimic or taking drugs or being raped. Nor indeed is privilege a virtue. The virtue is in what we do with it and how we channel that into the world.

Even the Welsh 'left' forgave my dad before I did. The protests outside our house stopped after two years because they began to see he was committed to their interests: preserving the Welsh language by ensuring it was taught in all Welsh schools; transforming Cardiff Bay into a thriving hub of international business; and, ultimately, staying in his post for two full terms of Parliament to make a lasting difference in the land of his fathers. This was unprecedented and has not been repeated since. I vividly recall sitting next to the Labour chairman of Cardiff County Council, one of Dad's fiercest political opponents, during a rugby match at Cardiff Arms Park, shortly after Dad had announced his resignation. At half-time, the chairman leaned over and, in lilting Welsh tones, whispered in my ear, 'Don't tell your old man this, but we're all sorry to see him go. Best Secretary of State we've ever had.'

Dad is eighty-three years old as I write and dealing with lung cancer. We are quite the pair. He goes straight from radiotherapy to the House of Lords to sit on another committee. He will do what he believes is right, not what the Tory Party expects of him. Even when I stood as the Labour candidate in my school election, he would proudly introduce me to his parliamentary opponents with, 'This is my daughter. She is one of yours.' If anyone has taught me about using advantages for public service, it is him.

Privilege is a responsibility, not a debt. Whatever talents we are born with, social and material privilege can put us at a huge advantage. As such, the moral responsibility to give a shit falls to people like me.

The Power of Pure Shame

This moral responsibility extends to gender privilege, religious privilege, sexuality privilege and race privilege. Recently, I read a blog post by a white, male, American student of Brad's called Bruce Mulkey. It was entitled, 'I am a Recovering Racist'. He had grown up in the American South and was raised by white, liberal parents, who supported Martin Luther King and the Civil Rights Movement. Nonetheless, he 'unconsciously took on common beliefs and attitudes prevalent in the dominant cultural paradigm about people whose skin was darker than mine. "White people are smarter." "Black people are better athletes." Etcetera. And though I have become conscious of those beliefs, I have not rooted them all out and doubt I ever will.'

In early 2000, Bruce took a race bias test which flashed

words and photos of black faces and white faces on his computer screen. He had to quickly categorise them as 'good' or 'bad'. Because he had little time to think about his responses, his unconscious beliefs surfaced and his test results delivered a significant lifeshock by revealing he had 'a strong preference for white'. He felt devastated by this revelation, saying, 'I felt nauseous. I felt a sharp pain in my heart, extremely sorrowful and went to lie down in bed. My wife, Shonnie, came in to see what was wrong. I drew her close to me and held on to her for dear life.' Later, he went to work on the lifeshock, as he had been taught to do, uncovering this mindtalk:

> *I am a racist.*
> *I'm not who I thought I was.*
> *I'm just like those I've been judging.*
> *There's nothing I can do about it.*
> *I've just got to live with it.*
> *I'll be like this forever.*
> *I'm a miserable piece of shit.*
> *It's hopeless.*
> *I'm hopeless.*

As I will explain in more detail, all mindtalk can be challenged until we can distinguish facts from falsehoods, responsibility from blame and realisations from ignorance. This is what Bruce did and this is what he came to:

'*I do have some racist beliefs that I took on very early in my life: "White people are smarter . . . people of colour could raise themselves up if they really wanted to . . . young black men are scary etc." While I have been indoctrinated by the white supremacy on which this country is founded and still operates, I can and will let go of these beliefs and acknow-ledge there is only one race: the human race.'*

As a result, he decided to seek out and connect with people of colour, to invite them to meals, to talk honestly about racism and what he could do to help eradicate it. He began the systematic work needed to eliminate his own racist beliefs and to acknowledge how he benefits from white privilege. He and his wife, Shonnie, also got involved with Building Bridges, whose mission is to dismantle racism by fostering relationships that respect diversity, seek understanding and encourage action, He is currently the co-chair of the racial equality leadership team at his daughter's school.

He also started blogging publicly about the issue. He was willing to expose himself in order to encourage others to confront their racist beliefs. In 'I Am a Recovering Racist', he takes ownership of the deep, inherited racism he is committed to challenging on an ongoing basis in himself and his country, calling on his fellow Americans to 'come to grips with our sordid past' by asking forgiveness and making reparations with those they had abused, from slaves to Native Americans. It was an example of accountability without guilt or blame; personal and systemic responsibility without denying or pretending, justifying or defending. It was also an example of how engaging with a lifeshock and chal-lenging the false beliefs that lifeshocks confront can transform someone's mindset. As the election of Trump to the presidency brings white supremacists out of the woodwork, and the Brexit vote in the UK emboldens racism, the privileged among us need to own it and challenge it in a similar way.

Part of what Bruce felt when he received those race bias test results was shame. This is different to the kind of guilt I carried, which is unhelpful because it focuses on oneself more than others. It turned other people's lack into a burden I had to carry, which is unsustainable. Pure shame is different.[4] Guilt has been a heavy burden for me, rooted in the beliefs that I am wrong and undeserving. Shame – feeling ashamed – has been the opposite. There is a moment, just before the 'reactive mind' lays anger, regret and judgement on top of it, which makes the shame toxic, when you see what you have done with lucid clarity and feel true remorse, true grief and true humility. The cost to ourselves, others and the world becomes apparent. The ego surrenders and something inside says, 'No more. I will not do this again.' The heart opens rather than closes. Creative and healing possibilities emerge. For me, it is that moment when we pass through the eye of the needle from a reactive to a responsive way of being, as Bruce did. It is the moment we wake up and become instantly capable of response-ability. This is when we can play our part in the health, wealth and evolution of the world.

It was a terminal cancer diagnosis that handed me the final bill for the meal I had made of privilege by shouldering guilt. It occurred a few months after my business went into the red for the very first time. John,

4 As I write this, I'm aware that the brilliant researcher and author, Brené Brown, has the opposite view of this. She sees guilt as helpful and adaptive, and shame as a consequence of believing we are flawed. Perhaps this is just semantics, but I can only write from my personal experience.

Gabriella and I had been living in a rented barn in Kent for just over a year with the intention of buying our forever home when we were sure we wanted to stay. But now I was too ill to work and the 'terminal' label made me ineligible for a mortgage, which we couldn't get on my husband's modest income alone. After working hard and earning well for the best part of my adult life, I now had precious little to leave my little girl. This was sobering indeed. But it also showed me what my guilt had held me back from doing, the potential it had stopped me tapping and the advantages I'd failed to put to good use: the writer I had wanted to be, the doctorate I had wanted to do about the nature and purpose of lifeshocks, even the progressive politician I might have become.

Pure shame delivered me to what guilt didn't, the awareness of an indiscriminate inheritance that is available to all: the simple truth that no one is worth more than another. It also enabled me to stand, gratefully, on the speak-up, face-into-it, give-a-damn side of contrition.

Being 'privileged' is not all that it seems. It does not mean we skip suffering, which is often how it is perceived. We are not exempt from loss, grief, broken-heartedness, depression, disease, abuse, addiction and loneliness; nor, indeed, from the pain imposed by our own self-critical and judgemental minds. It does give us additional buffers, though: more ways to self-medicate (like shopping and going on luxury holidays); steelier buttresses to avoid the truth of our loneliness or despair, like the illusion of power and conviction of having 'made it' that privilege can bestow – and, in some cases, a feather-padded psyche to keep us from ourselves all our days. And this is its curse. The lifeshocks don't always strike deep enough to awaken people to who they really are. This is a spiritual poverty. It is what social and material privilege can cost us: personal awakening, profound self-awareness, an evolution of the soul.

No more apologising. No more defending. No more wasting what I have been given on self-indulgent penance. Whatever debt I imagined I owed has been paid in full. This frees me to be who I was created to be – someone empathetic, generous, morally and socially responsible – however privileged, faulty and blessed. And I am deeply blessed. Blessed by my talents and fallibilities; by the service I render and the failures I learn from; by all the lifeshocks I have recognised and all the grist in my advantaged mill.

The First Practice: Noticing

The liberally dispensed term 'self-awareness' is open to very broad interpretation, but what does it really mean and *how* do we achieve it? The simplest way to answer this is to identify precisely what we need to become aware of and start *noticing* those things as often as possible. If we can become aware of lifeshocks, mindtalk and feelings (and distinguish them), we will begin the process of awakening and freeing ourselves from our reactive minds.

What follows is how I train people, which you can practise, step by step, beginning with this:

Noticing Lifeshocks

As I have explained, lifeshocks are *moments in time that we do not want or expect, offering opportunities for awakening.* They are external to us and we experience them through sensory data: sight, sound, smell, taste, touch.

Some seem small, some seem big, all are *very specific*. These are not simply life events. They are specific *moments* in time: the woman at roadside rescue on a dark and stormy night saying, 'Someone will be with you in an hour'; seeing blood on sheets one morning;

the first touch of a new baby's skin on your skin; a daughter saying, 'Beautiful Mummy'; a doctor saying, 'incurable cancer'; a six-foot African American woman saying, 'Still I rise!' as her broad hips sway from side to side.

For the reasons I have already stated, the specificity is extremely important: re-experiencing the precise moment unlocks the often unconscious beliefs we put in place and the feelings they caused.

Practise noticing lifeshocks

1. Watch out for them during your day, however big or small.
2. When you feel your emotions change (you got out of bed in a good mood and suddenly you feel pissed off), you can be certain you had a lifeshock in between. Ask yourself what happened. *Notice* the moment when your feelings changed.
3. Buy a journal and write down three lifeshocks before you go to bed every night.
4. If possible, choose one you liked (e.g. my daughter responding to me calling her a smart cookie with, 'And you're a beautiful soup') and two you didn't (e.g. seeing the exact amount of my tax bill this year).
5. The more you do this, the more easily you will spot them. This is a skill and practice in and of itself.

Noticing Feelings

Feelings and thoughts are frequently confused. It is very important to recognise the difference for two key reasons: first, feelings are always true and thoughts are frequently false; second, reactive feelings *are caused by* false thoughts.

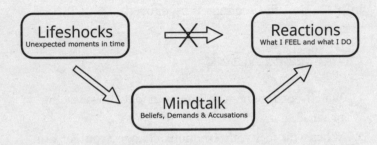

© *K. Bradford Brown PhD. 1983.*

We tend to blame lifeshocks for how we react. This is because our reactions occur at lightning speed and because both lifeshocks and reactions are *visible,* if not always conscious. Mindtalk, however, is largely invisible and unconscious. Many of us don't hear it easily. Of course, lifeshocks have an impact, but we also interpret *every* one and *this* is what causes our reaction.

In other words, when I *think* I'm being betrayed, I *feel* angry. When I *think* I'm *ugly*, I *feel* anxious. When I *think* I'm dying, I *feel* scared. When I *think* I'm a failure, I *feel* embarrassed, even depressed. When I *think* I'm unworthy, I *feel* despair.

Watch out for 'I feel *that*. . .', after which a strongly held belief almost invariably follows: 'I feel that I'm alone' is a belief, not an emotion. It means, 'I so deeply believe I am alone I have turned the belief into a feeling (to prove it's true).' *But deeply believing something does not make it so.*

Feelings are physical. We experience them in the body as sensations: heavy or light, closed or open, relaxed or tense, trembling or still. Some are *separating*, born of the reactive mind. Other are connecting, born of the 'creative mind'. All are integral to our humanity and serve some purpose. For example, our fear alerts us to real danger as well as imagined danger. Anger sometimes arises from deeply held values and issues we *truly* object to. It also arises from deeply held self-righteousness. We need to know the difference. We need to challenge judgements (which have us *react* in anger) and pull out the objections (upon which we can stand and with which we can *respond*).

To assist you in recognising emotions, this is a fairly comprehensive list of human emotions and where they sit above and below the line. That said, we need to do more than 'notice' to access many of the connecting feelings (such as awe and ecstasy). These will follow.

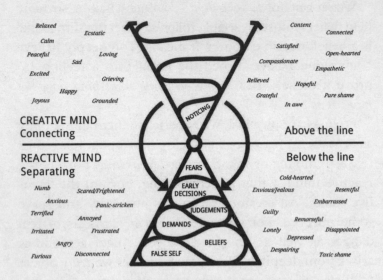

Copyright © K Bradford Brown 1984.

Practise noticing feelings

1. Choose a lifeshock from your list (one with a strong charge, but not necessarily the strongest when you are starting out). Write it at the top of a clean page.

2. Close your eyes and go back to that moment *as if it is happening now.* Do not look back on it. Be there again. See what you see. Hear what you hear. Feel what you feel.

3. Often the feelings will just arise. We often stop breathing properly to keep them at bay. Instead, *breathe into them and let them expand.*

4. Notice the physical sensations (tightness in your chest, heat, heaviness, openness). Trust this and

put a hand on the part of your body where you feel it. Keep breathing.

5. Ask yourself, *if this sensation had a name what would it be?* Anxiety? Excitement? Fear? Irritation? Anger? Joy? Love? Jealousy? Despair.

6. Write this feeling underneath the lifeshock.

For example

A woman called Elizabeth (whose name I have changed) had been a student of Brad's work for some years. She had raised two children – one of whom had been born extremely prematurely and whose twin died – and had been married for thirty-two years. Three months before their daughter's wedding, her husband disclosed he had been having an affair for nine months. This was the lifeshock that stood out to her:

Lifeshock: 'Sitting in the kitchen, my husband opposite in an armchair, elbows on knees, head bowed, says with a quiet but clear voice, "She feels wonderful in my arms."'

Physical sensations: 'Fat head, pressure, tight pain in upper back and chest, ice-cold hands, hollow dropping stomach, hard to breathe.'

Emotions: 'Shock, high levels of anxiety, heartache, outrage.'

This is very simple, but not necessarily easy. It is worth asking someone you trust to help you with it at first. Again, the more you practise, the more adept you will become.

It is also challenging because it takes you back to painful emotions. As you practise these steps, breathe right into the emotions (which is usually counter-intuitive). Breath literally *dissipates* these feelings. Holding our breath inten-sifies them.

NB: Some people numb out and find it hard to get past the numbness. This is okay. Remember numbness is also a *feeling*. If this happens, breathe fully, down into your belly until you feel your diaphragm come out. If there is a sensation in your body, however subtle, place your hand on it, press gently and breathe right into that place.

The rest of Elizabeth's process will follow in this and in later 'how to' sections. I felt some outrage for her when I heard this and sensed some profound grief lurking underneath.

Noticing Mindtalk

When you re-experience the lifeshock, you are likely to notice your thoughts about what happened racing through your mind. This is *mindtalk*. This is often uncon-scious but re-experiencing the lifeshock brings it back up to the surface. At first, you may just hear a few sentences, a commentary about what happened, the other person involved and/or yourself. Just tune in to this. It will come out in short, complete sentences, which you can write down.

Practising noticing mindtalk

1. As already described, re-experience the lifeshock moment.
2. Feel your feelings.
3. Listen to what your mind is saying.
4. Write it down in complete sentences.

For example

When Elizabeth re-experienced this lifeshock and listened to what her mind was saying, this is what she heard:

Mindtalk:
I'm left behind
I'm abandoned
I'm helpless and isolated
I can't survive this
I'll never stop crying
I'll never trust again
No one loves me just as I am
I will never be safe again
I will never stop feeling lonely
No one will ever find me sexy
I am ugly
I am being violated by my husband and his lover
He is a spineless coward
I am unsafe, at risk, in danger
The only choice is between acceptance and madness
I have to protect myself
Go to war
Or else I will crumble, disappear and die
I can't do it
It's too much grief, too much pain
My heart can't take it
I won't ever recover
I am broken
So I have to stay small and keep quiet
I have to try and save our marriage

If you hear this much mindtalk the first time you do it, you are already flying. If you get six or eight lines, that's a good start. Later, I will tell you how to access more and reach deeper levels, as Elizabeth did. Don't turn this into another thing to demand of yourself or criticise yourself for. You are confronting something that does not want to be confronted. Take. Your. Time.

Noticing is the beginning of self-awareness. . .

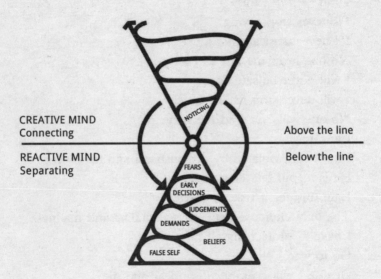

CREATIVE MIND
Connecting
                                                    Above the line

NOTICING

REACTIVE MIND
Separating
                                                    Below the line

FEARS

EARLY DECISIONS

JUDGEMENTS

DEMANDS

BELIEFS

FALSE SELF

Copyright © K Bradford Brown 1984.

6

Success

Exposing Lifeshocks

Many of the 'lifeshocks' I have written about in 'Privilege' are *exposing* lifeshocks. This is one of three primary manifestations of lifeshock. Exposing lifeshocks challenge us when we are *pretending to be something we are not*. We are obeying the demands of the 'reactive mind' about how we have to be: nice, powerful, in control, out of the way, self-effacing, better than others, successful, unique, special, rebellious, compliant, defiant, good, protective, a winner. Take your pick. The demand defines the false self (or drama). 'I have to pay the bill for other people's pain' becomes a 'pay the bill' drama. 'I have to be thin' becomes a 'look good' drama. 'I have to be perfect' becomes a 'perfection' drama. 'I have to dominate or control' becomes a bullying drama. 'I have to hide' becomes an invisible drama. And so on. These can be very hard to see because we think that this way of behaving is our 'nature' or 'character'. Sometimes, this is because the demand is something we truly value and would *choose* to be, like being kind or loving or successful. But 'I have to be kind, loving or successful' turns our values into *fear-based demands* that leave us no *choice* at all. This may also explain why we get defensive if these 'characteristics' are challenged. 'But that's just me! It's who I am!' Except it isn't. It really isn't.

Behaviour is the fourth key aspect we need to notice (in addition to lifeshocks, mindtalk and feelings). For some people it is easier to notice feelings and for others behaviour is more apparent. Our behaviour is a direct expression of the false or authentic self. To identify our false selves – our dramatic ways of being – the following list of reactive default positions might be useful. In part, this is what *exposing* lifeshocks draw our attention to. They are all versions of the 'false self'.

Blaming	Pleasing	Controlling
Fixing	Avoiding	Self-indulging
Victim/Poor me	Martyr	Superiority
Perfection	Self-effacing	Proving
Good girl/boy	Rebel	Bullying
Enlightened	Saviour	Rescuer
Persecutor	Long-suffering	Calculating
Stiff upper lip	Pay the bill	Guilty as charged

As has been explained in several branches of psychology, including by one of Brad's teachers, Carl Rogers, a 'feared self' begins to replace the 'authentic self' when the reactive mind starts running the show. In turn, these versions of the 'false self' form a protective crust around the 'feared self' to numb the pain and regain a sense of control.

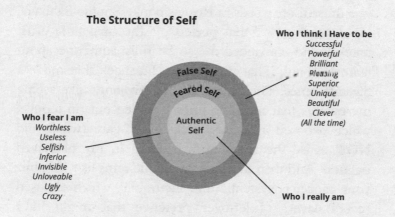

The Structure of Self

Who I think I Have to be
Successful
Powerful
Brilliant
Pleasing
Superior
Unique
Beautiful
Clever
(All the time)

False Self

Feared Self

Authentic
Self

Who I fear I am
Worthless
Useless
Selfish
Inferior
Invisible
Unloveable
Ugly
Crazy

Who I really am

© *K. Bradford Brown PhD. 1983.*

Once the false self is formed, it thickens like a tree trunk. The feared self becomes less visible and the authentic self gets lost. We literally forget ourselves. This runs deeper than the way I denied my dad and hid my background in certain situations. We become what we believe and *what we believe is often profoundly false.* Consequently, we get many *exposing lifeshocks*, whereby reality holds up many mirrors to reveal the masks we are wearing. Still, we look in the mirror, see the false self and think we are seeing ourselves. Why wouldn't we? We are more familiar with it that any other 'self' we may have known. But the lifeshocks continue to come knocking, as if to say, 'Pay attention. Look closely! You are not what you seem!'

I had many exposing lifeshocks about the way I was denying my privilege. Some, like Dad calling me 'Peter', didn't get through at all. Over time, others did. But it was those three words in Rosie's book, 'Sophie Sabbage, *the daughter of. . .*' that peeled off the final little crust patches and convinced me to be fully authentic about it in this book. That was a small lifeshock that made a big difference. Then there are the big ones, like seeing my bruises that morning after I passed out on tequila, which exposed a reckless lack of self-care (which did NOT cause the rape) and, beneath it, my perceived ugliness. And then there are hydraulic rams like, 'Sophie, your cancer is systemic and incurable', which exposed several layers of leftover pretence that might have prevented me being fully Sophie in whatever time I had left.

In all these ways, exposing lifeshocks penetrate our demands and reveal the fearful beliefs that they cover over, which form 'the feared self': *life is unfair, I'm not enough, I'm too much, I'm ugly, I'm unlovable, I'm a failure, I'm a loser, I'm average, I'm weak.*

First, the lifeshocks expose how we think we have to be. Then they expose who we fear we are. At that point, we often resort back to the drama again, flipping back and forth between these two false selves for years on end, even entire lifetimes. Eventually, for some people, a momentous lifeshock comes that penetrates the feared self as well. This can seem random and accidental. Many of us may recall 'that moment' when everything changed. This usually indicates that many other lifeshock 'moments' have bounced off our false selves, unnoticed. But once we become aware of lifeshocks, and of the mindtalk they confront, it becomes easier and easier to let them *in* and *all the way through*. We can literally leverage them for our growth, awakening and authentic living *at will*, every single day. Imagine!

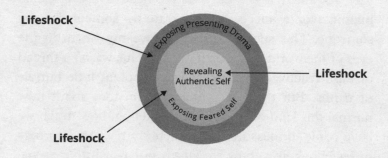

© *K. Bradford Brown PhD. 1983.*

After my first book came out, it was auctioned in the USA, and various promotional activities were initiated after I chose my publisher. Someone I know in the States generously offered to help me out too, because she operates in a market that my book might appeal to. She wrote an email to her subscribers to raise awareness of the book and my story. It was very well written, impressively pitched and packed with bold, US-style sale speak, which is usually more brazen than the way we Brits promote things. Big promises and exaggerated descriptions seem to be the norm. A few lines into the email, came this: 'Sophie went from being nobody with nothing to. . .'

An exposing lifeshock.

I was confident her intention was to say, 'Sophie wasn't a public figure and had a small social media following', or something of that nature. Instead, 'nobody with nothing'. I didn't hear it as a truth. I have done enough work on myself to know I am somebody with many somethings, but it still troubled me. I felt indignant. I wanted her to take it back instead of painting me that way. I wanted to shout, 'I don't need a social media platform or a successful book to be someone! I *am* someone. This success doesn't prove my worth in the eyes of the world. My worth just is!' This wasn't a thread of false reactive mindtalk. It was a potent little bundle of truths. But there was anger there, too, about how normal this kind of thing is in marketing, how much we have come to measure our somebody-ness by numbers of Facebook likes, how we attach our worth to material wealth and professional success, how we lose ourselves in the seductiveness of it all. Lifeshocks don't just expose personal pretence. They expose the lies that run the whole world and the issues we most need to address.

Ink Stains

I had a strong rebel drama by the age of ten. It wasn't one lifeshock in particular that my reactive mind had latched on to. It was many, over time. These are the day-to-day events that shape our world as we're growing up and, as I say, it is how our minds interpret these events that determines how we behave. In part, my rebellion was a way of dealing with being 'over-emotional', as was *exposed* to me at the New Year's Eve charades. In part, it was my way of being seen and heard as the middle child in a noisy family with two siblings who seemed so much more lovable than me. And, perhaps more than anything, it was a way of making my behaviour more visible than my appearance, as if defiance would make me less plain. Somewhere along the line I decided there was something *wrong with me* and that I had to prove there wasn't. In primary school that meant puffing myself up in public and eating chocolate in secret at home, being 'cool' with my school friends and obnoxious to my teachers, being tough on the outside and tender on the inside. And when it came to my emotions, it meant doing whatever I could to numb them out.

Of course, I wasn't conscious of all this. And my numbing strategies were rarely successful for long. I just stuffed anxiety down until I couldn't hold it any more and then I would lash out, throw a tantrum, scream at my mother, be mean to my sister or reject a friend. Somewhere, deep inside me, a river of fear ran through.

Many of us have grown up in intellectually literate, but emotionally illiterate contexts. Happily, this has been changing since the dawn of the Human Potential and New Age movements. These began in the 1960s and 1970s and have been expanding ever since. The personal growth market in Western society is now flooded with philosophies and methodologies that give permission to feel and teach people how. I first engaged with it in my twenties, but none of it had touched my childhood. Not that this is a complaint about how I was raised. I received very real love. But it *is* a statement about the context in which my parents were raised and the stiff-upper-lip exercise of great emotional restraint in the face of adversity that had typified British stoicism through two world wars. When I was receiving targeted radiotherapy to my brain for eight hours, my mother – who has painful arthritis – happened to be seeing her own doctor that day. She told him where I was and admitted, 'I don't know how to cry, but all my bones ache.' I think this poignantly said it all. Add to this expected emotional restraint an advantaged life in which complaining seemed 'spoilt' and a 'count your blessings' expectation wagged like an accusatory finger, and I had no idea where to put the intense feelings that crashed through me every day.

Don't get me wrong. Many days were happy. I was popular at school. I celebrated life with my friends. I had a childhood. But even in my private primary school in London, which seemed to promise a good education, a place at a great secondary school, a job, a marriage, a Volvo and a future in which suffering would not enter, I had already failed. Suffering *had* entered. And I fought for my right to feel pain.

The problem was I loved learning. I wanted to do well, excel even, but I didn't want to dent my rebellious image. I learned to walk a line between compliance and defiance: attending classes diligently while pretending to look bored; always completing my homework, but never carefully enough to achieve the highest marks; making myself average wherever possible. I was frequently rude to my teachers while longing to ask questions about subjects that enthralled me. Instead, I tended to forgo that pleasure in favour of quick fixes of bravado in front of my friends. Of course, the fixes were fleeting and, when the fuss died down, there was Saturday morning detention and a clammy loneliness that carpeted my world. Believing I was 'different' and that different was 'bad', I often sought refuge by walking through the back of my wardrobe into Narnia or riding Black Beauty through the night.

It was then that I started writing stories in which I could conjure a land where the sun lay on the low hills and wild horses roamed the ridges while long trails of ants went home. I could howl at the wind in twilight shadows because happiness wasn't mandatory and loneliness had a dozen names. I never spoke of this place nor opened its doors to another. I kept my stories secret and, for a time, they were the most fertile place in my life.

All this remained hidden until an English teacher assigned us a story to write for homework one week. She entitled it 'SILENCE', chalking the word across a blackboard in capital letters. I was stumped. The teacher had coarse blonde hair falling in waves round her bony shoulders and wore blue, plastic, 1970s National Health glasses with pointed corners above the outer edge of each eyebrow. I judged her as dull and ugly (because judging was what I did to feel better about myself) and defied her at every opportunity lest she tarnish me with her favour. I believed I was popular because I was trouble and therefore had a reputation to keep. But I loved writing stories more than I relished rebellion. And sometimes lifeshocks are written in large letters on blackboards to ensure we don't miss them.

'SILENCE' reached down from the front of the classroom to *expose* the story-writer behind the rebel, the girl whose heart broke when Black Beauty was mistreated and was holding her heartbreak inside. I knew what silence was. I had been tongue-tied with shyness in many social situations. I had squeezed shame into the back of my

throat when the changing room taunting began. I had
kept my love of words quiet in the classroom. I knew
silence was a sound that rang like a bell when I was
awkward or awesome. And being awesome was as scary
as being unremarkable – perhaps more so. Being a *nobody*
seemed far safer than being a *somebody*, which would
surely *break my cover and put me on the outside, looking in*.
All this was suddenly laid bare, if only to myself. A single-
word lifeshock had dared me to break my own silence,
to risk not being part of the gang and, worse, to risk
discovering that my inner life was unremarkable after all.

I was trembling when I finished the story with my
special Parker pen. I reached for a ruler to underline the
title and spilt blue ink on the pages, quite accidentally.
I minded for a moment, but decided it didn't matter,
dabbed them with tissue so you could still read my
writing and handed them in that way.

A few days later my teacher returned it with a big red
'B' in the top left-hand corner just above the underlined
title. 'B' for bitch. 'B' for bad. 'B' for baffled, beaten and
bottomless disappointment. I wanted her to take it back,
read it again and recognise my art. Mostly, I wanted to
smash her glasses, rip the pages and retreat to the silence
I should never have spoken out loud.

'This was a brilliant, A-grade story, young lady,' she
added as an afterthought. 'The ink stains got you that B.'

All lifeshocks are 'defining moments', if we recognise
them and know how to listen to them. I didn't know
this, but I felt something shift inside that day, something
that meant I was never quite the same. I had been exposed
again: by a B that could have been an A, by an unwitting
act of self-sabotage and by a dim realisation that what

I believed was *terribly wrong with me* might perhaps be *terribly right*.

At my next school, I sustained my rebel drama as best I could, but left it at the door in English classes from then on. I was shameless in my passion for literature and blatant in my desire to be top of the class. One of my English teachers, Miss Carrdus, noticed this, and encouraged me in many ways, especially after I got tearful in a Shakespeare class, aged fourteen. We were studying *Antony and Cleopatra*, taking turns to read ye olde dialogue, when Antony's loyal servant, Enobarbus, died on the battlefield. He was in deep remorse for having crossed sides to support Caesar in the war. I was inside his armour when he fell, fatally wounded, and cried out to Antony for forgiveness while conceding the world should 'rank me in register a master-leaver and a fugitive.' It was heartbreaking.

Miss Carrdus, who had short, light brown hair and a husky voice, fed my hunger in the years after his passing. She slipped poems into my mailbox on winter mornings, which soothed the sting of seeing friends who had acquired boyfriends read the love letters that I never received. She watered my desert with Yeats, Blake, Whitman and Larkin. She taught me S level English in private tutorials. She even predicted I would screw up my English A level by warning me in advance that I wouldn't get top marks unless I reined in my passion long enough to pull off four full essays in a three-hour exam. She tried to restrain me from answering questions to higher standards than the curriculum could accommodate, apologising for this and calling it a 'temporary freeze'. It didn't work. As Enobarbus lay dying in my third essay I was way over time and a fourth was out of the question. So, I buried him with full military honours and an epitaph that read, 'Here lies a loyal soldier who served his master well.'

Afterwards I walked to the woods to smoke cigarettes and kick myself. I had done myself an injustice. I wanted top marks. I needed them to secure my conditional place at Cambridge University (and my *worth*, for fuck's sake). I had blown it. I'd sabotaged my future and secured my own tragic ending. In my privileged context it seemed I had smudged my whole life.

At the same time, I had honoured the part of me that felt Enobarbus's grief and came alive in writings where I didn't need to hide. This was a victory of my spirit over my self-critical mind, of *being* rather than *doing*. Externally, I had 'failed'. But internally, I had won. I had yielded to the deeply feeling child I had been and the deep-hearted woman I wanted to become. My A level results arrived later that summer, among them 'English Literature: Grade B'.

The Not Enough Train

As a result of this, I left school knowing I was *somebody* rather than *nobody*. But my mind was in a bind. On one hand, I believed I had to prove I was still smart, having failed to get into Cambridge – or any other leading university, for that matter. I got a D for Politics, which exposed how resentful I had become on that subject. On the other hand, I believed I had to be careful not to put the 'somebodyness' these lifeshocks at school had introduced me to on too much display.

While I had owned my 'somebodyness' in English

classes, the rebel in me remained alive and well up to the age of sixteen. By then, I had been caught smoking behind bike sheds several times and did my best to be disapproved of by teachers. This was intended to secure my sense of belonging, but it didn't work. My headmistress took a particular shine to me, which was irritating for some of my classmates and got me into hot water on a few occasions. This was compounded when I won the National Public Speaking competition, after which one of my best friends said, 'I don't think I can be your friend any more. You have gone beyond me.' I concluded that *whatever makes me special will make me unpopular too.*

It is important to register these kinds of lifeshocks. In many ways, they are the run-of-the-mill stuff of first-world life, not earth-shattering traumas. But that's the point: *the stuff of life.* This is how LIFE comes to us and speaks to us, moment by moment, day by day. This is where the reality in our heads meets the reality in the world, each moment an invitation to examine our own thinking and align it with *what is so.* We don't need to wait for huge lifeshocks to get the message. We need to pay attention here and now. I firmly believed it was not okay to be special, that standing out would attract envy and hostility, and that I'd better not get carried away. So, what did Life give me? Opportunities to stand out and get carried away.

Not standing out is a very British attitude. Unlike in the USA, where the successful are mostly appreciated, we have long suffered from 'tall poppy syndrome', a social phenomenon whereby showing off success is viewed as crass and vulgar (something I need to get past

every time I mention an achievement in these pages).
Tall poppies are resented, criticised and cut down –
especially by our press, who often praise them as they
grow to full height and then mercilessly hack them back
or stamp on any petals that fall.

I don't know how many potential successes all this
chipped off my life over the years. I know I dumbed
myself down. But it didn't run my life, especially after
I discovered Brad's work in my twenties. He gave me
the chisel to start sculpting my own clay. I learned to
notice my lifeshocks and verify my mindtalk. *Everything*
we believe can be *challenged* and *evaluated* as 'true', 'false'
or 'I don't know'. Everything.

I am very aware of the widely held perception that
'there is no truth', but let's begin with ascertaining what
is incorrect and therefore *false* or *don't know*.

These were strong beliefs that I needed to challenge
during this period of my life:

1. I am ugly.
    False. Any statement this absolute is false. It makes
    us fundamentally ugly, stupid, worthless, etc., which
    we are not.

2. I am too much.
    False. This is also too absolute, and who is in
    charge of measuring our much-ness anyway?

3. There is something wrong with me.
    False, in that whatever is wrong is fundamental and
    permanent. But I am certainly flawed and do things
    wrong at times. There are also things very right
    with me.

4. I am weird.
   False as an absolute statement and a judgement.
   This reminds me of a postcard I saw where a little
   girl asks her mum, 'What is normal?' and the mum
   replies, 'A setting on the dryer, darling.'

5. I have to hide my background.
   False. Excellent as I was at this, it was never true.
   'I have to' is *never true*. It always comes with an
   'or else'. 'Or else I won't be seen as Sophie . . .
   which makes me invisible . . . and just a daughter
   of . . .'. And on runs another stream of false
   beliefs.

6. I have to hide my talents.
   False. For the same reasons. 'Or else I will be
   unpopular . . . resented . . . lonely.' All *false* because
   so definitive and *don't know* because we *never* know
   the future or what other people think of us unless
   they tell us.

7. It is not okay to be special.
   False. And what if I am in some ways? And what if
   I want to be? And aren't we all? But more importantly, claiming my uniqueness is an act of
   authenticity, which is what I am about.

8. I have to play small.
   False. And what a waste of myself if I do.

9. If I stand out, people will resent me.
   I don't know. Some may, some may not. This is out
   of my control and no reason to lurk in the shadows
   all my life.

10. If I fail, I will be a nobody.
    False. If I fail, I fail. No more or less. And nobody
    is a nobody.

11. Which means I have to stand out after all.
    False. I can choose not to if I prefer. I don't need
    to prove I'm not nobody.

12. Which means I'm damned if I do and damned if
    I don't.
    False. I'm not 'damned' either way.

But I swung between hiding and standing out for years
because of that mindtalk. Notice how I replace the falsehoods with more accurate statements. This creates the
shift in perception. Over time I have learned that I can't
control what I attract when I am true to myself. Nor do
I wish to. Sometimes I have attracted envy. But more
often, I have attracted other people who wanted to teach
me and learn from me, people who want to share their
light and bask in some of mine.

I also attracted Brad. Not sexually, but spiritually. He
was drawn to me, just as I was drawn to him. At that
time, he was the vibrant charismatic leader of The Life
Training (now More to Life), a global, not-for-for-profit
organisation dedicated to teaching people how to harness
the transformational power of lifeshocks. I am very
proud to have been one of its leaders and senior trainers
for over twenty years. As soon as I tasted its wares at the
age of twenty-five, I was in for the long haul – partly
because of the difference it made to me personally, but
also because it wasn't about the personal *per se*. I have
already acknowledged that the Human Development

movement has brought a lot of good to the world, but there are times when the *personal* in 'personal growth' means self-centred and ego-based. The fact that it often stands alone as a genre, unconnected to others or the world, is indicative of this problem. Over the years I have participated in various courses that taught pseudo-enlightened, false mindtalk as essential truths: 'You are not responsible for other people's pain'; 'You need to love yourself before you can love others'; 'You need to follow your feelings, not what other people expect of you.' Once I met a course participant who actually said, 'I have released the horrors of Rwanda to a higher power.'

These lifeshocks became signposts for me on my path to my own path, telling me where not to go. It may well be true that the pain of others is not my direct responsibility, but it lies within my 'response-ability' to offer support within my limits and wherever I can.

And it was bullshit that I couldn't love others until I loved myself. I could. I did. I think I had all my life, without knowing that I hardly loved myself at all. I would have preferred to be in on the act, but loving others taught me what love is and how I would recognise it when it was channelled my way. Equally, as someone whose emotions had run away with me for much of my life, 'following my feelings' seemed foolhardy. I wanted to experience and take charge of them, not let them take charge of me. Mostly, I objected to people abdicating the world's horrors on their path to 'enlightenment', as if they could just take their anger about the homeless woman on the street to therapy and then walk past her on the pavement, guilt-free. To my ears, 'self-help' sounded like social suicide.

Brad's approach was different. It was about 'mastery of self *in service* to others and *in response* to personal and global lifeshocks.' After sampling many 'self-help' teachings, this came as a great relief. It also answered my longing to be *in* the world, to get my feet muddy mindfully. After a few years of participating in his programme, which was akin to strengthening my spiritual muscles in a gym, I told Brad I wanted to take his material into the workplace. There was very little material like this being offered in business back then. Now the market is flooded with consultants offering 'mindset change' and 'transformational leadership' programmes in business, but it was quite unusual – even daring – when we started out in the early 1990s.

With the help of our third business-savvy partner, Janet Jones, our company took off. In part, we saw how to help clients achieve more success by noticing their corporate lifeshocks (sales results, market data, customer feedback), verifying their reactive mindtalk and responding with greater clarity and insight about what was happening. Our diagnostic research process began with identifying lifeshocks, personal and shared, that were flying around the business. And we took it from there.

During this time, I came to witness the profound levels of fear that generate success in the Western world: fear of failing, underperforming, losing jobs, not being able to feed families, being overlooked for promotion, not being able to keep up with colleagues, dealing with angry customers, ending up sleeping under the arches and, for many high-achieving leaders in senior positions, being exposed as 'intruders' or 'frauds'.

At the bottom of it all was this: *not enough*. I'm not

enough. We're not enough. It's not enough. *It's never, ever enough.* Of course, a business needs to continue setting new targets and moving forwards, just as an individual does, but this hooks into and feeds off our deeply held, predominantly unconscious need to *prove our own worth* (as if it needs to be proven). Most of us have experienced this. We set a personal goal, achieve it, perhaps enjoy a brief fix of satisfaction, then set another goal in order to experience more. *If I get this promotion . . . drive this car . . . buy this house . . . get married . . . have kids . . . become a leader . . . get the best sales results . . . lose twenty pounds . . . then I will be happy . . . then I will be satisfied . . .* **then I will be enough.** Although that last piece of mindtalk is often invisible rather than highlighted in bold. It stays lurking in the silent shadows where we can't spot it and grab it by its nasty tail.

However much we achieve, it is never enough. It's never enough because we haven't noticed the 'not enough' mindtalk that is running the whole show. In simple terms:

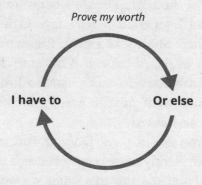

© *K. Bradford Brown PhD. 1983.*

I estimate that this 'Deception Generator' runs in the minds of millions. It yields considerable 'success' at a considerable price. In business alone, 'stress management' is a huge industry, and many of the services in this area still fail to address this fundamental source of stress. I have also seen 'I'm not enough' mistaken for a *feeling* by many life coaches and therapists. Recently, I read a Facebook post entitled, 'How to stop feeling not good enough forever!' When I respectfully challenged this, explaining that when we *believe* we're not good enough, we *feel* anything from anxiety to despair, my comment was deleted and I was blocked from his page. Being accurate about this matters hugely, because for many individuals this generator leads to sickness, depression, addiction, even suicide. It also goes a long way to explaining why so many 'successful' people do not find lasting joy.

Recently, a woman in her thirties attended a workshop I was leading. She had clearly been struggling with what we were doing all morning so, after the lunch break, I asked why. She said she couldn't concentrate because something had happened a few days earlier that was 'consuming' her. She looked pale, frightened, and her eyes were almost glazed over, as if her spirit had cut and run. It was clearly hard for her to talk so I moved closer to her and stood right next to her. I matched her quiet tone of voice and asked,

'I can see you are in pain. Do you want some help?'

She nodded silently as tears pricked her eyes – small signs of life. I warned her that what we were about to do would be a vulnerable experience, but that I had her back and would not leave her in this pain. She seemed to trust me and agreed, even though she didn't really know what she was agreeing to. It began with me asking her what had happened.

'I have been ill for five years and my partner just left me.'

We had all been identifying lifeshocks before lunch, so I asked her to close her eyes and hone in on some specific moments, which she did: her partner saying, 'I can't do this any more . . . I'm unhappy . . . I want to leave.' She could have engaged with any of these lifeshocks, but she had also asked him, 'Are you sure?' His one-word answer was the lifeshock that hit her hardest: 'Yes.'

I asked her to freeze-frame that moment in her mind's eye and re-experience it as if it was happening now. Immediately, her fear and grief rose to the surface. I helped her focus on the fear until she could hear her mindtalk:

> *I had to give up my career when I got ill*
> *I was successful and now I'm not*
> *My life isn't worth living*
> *I don't have a job*
> *I don't have a partner*
> *I don't even have a cat*
> *I have nothing*
> *I am nothing*
> *There is not enough for me to live for*
> *I am not enough to live for*
> *My life has no worth*
> *I have no worth*
> *I am worthless*
> *I can't go on*
> *I may as well just give up*

This is what despair looks like. There are no 'I have tos' in despair, just 'I can't', followed by a deep resignation to your perceived lot. Piece by piece, she challenged her mindtalk in front of everyone else on the course. They were all rooting for her and I made sure she knew that. This gave her courage. By the end of this process, there were only three true statements:

> *I don't have a job*
> *I don't have a partner*
> *I don't even have a cat* (but we took out the 'even' and its implied patheticness)

By now, the despair had lifted and a glimmer of light had appeared in her eyes. But her sorrow still ran deep and a sense of bewilderment set in. What next? Where to go from here?

'When did you decide you were only enough if you were successful or in a relationship or had a pet?' I asked. 'When did you attach your worth to having these things?'

'I don't know,' she answered. 'But I can't remember not feeling that way.'

'Well, it seems it is time to change that,' I told her.

'Yes, but how?' she asked me.

This time I leaned in close to her again and, in a whisper that carried through my microphone, asked,

'What do you think life might do to help you understand that you are enough just as you are, that your worth does not depend on all the things you have acquired or achieved?'

She looked up at me, curious, but silent. Then, after a minute, she said, 'I don't know, what?'

'TAKE IT ALL AWAY,' I responded, still whispering, but my tone emphatic.

She gasped and some of the group gasped with her. The glaze in her eyes melted and the light in them started to blaze. She smiled, as if in wonder, then laughed just a little. Relief seemed to soften all her muscles as those four words opened her up to possibility again, to the hope that she could value herself as she never had before.

'I see that,' she finally answered. 'That makes sense to me. Being enough is all I have ever wanted. Do you think I can really find that now?'

'You are already finding it,' I assured her. 'What do you notice has happened to your despair?'

'It has lifted.'

'And your grief?'

'Still there.'

'Yes, grief is connecting and healing. There is much grief for you to feel, but you just took hold of the fears that have long had a hold on you. You are already on new ground. You have already won far more than you believe you lost when he left you.'

By now, her posture was changing. Her shoulders had come down. Her back had straightened. Somebody was home.

Finally, she made some choices: to feel her grief, to accept his decision, to do more work with her mindtalk, to join one of my groups for more support and *to live her life because it was worth living after all*.

Her relationship with her partner had failed, but she had begun to win back her relationship with herself.

The Banks of Fear and Desire

Of course, being human, I had my own version of this too. I wanted to prove my worth to Brad. I wanted to prove to my family I hadn't wandered down a weird and unworldly path. I wanted to prove I wasn't self-serving and entitled. I wanted to prove I had value, even though I wasn't married or raising kids like so many of my friends. I wanted to prove my generosity and buffer my loneliness by being brilliant. And, all the while, I wanted to keep making amends for my privileges. So I drove myself hard. I won big contracts and achieved big things. I spent many years on the road running programmes in hotels and training centres. We had diverse international clients, from start-ups like last-minute.com to established brands like British Airways and Unilever. I co-led a programme that won a management consulting award for the 'Best Culture Change Programme' one year. I ran hundreds of courses for thousands of people. I made a real difference. I also burnt myself out.

I want. It seems so innocent. And sitting on the page as two simple words, it is. When applying the *principle of veracity* (true, false, don't know), 'I want' is true. It is normal and appropriate to want things. What we want gives us purpose and direction, and some of our biggest wants spring from our deepest longings. These wants need to be honoured and expressed – the way small children do when they announce, 'I want' a hundred times a day as naturally as breathing. During that intense period of hard work, I wasn't always trying to prove something. Much of the time I was following a deeper longing – to be of service and to make a difference in the world.

But it took me some time to notice that other motivating forces were also at work within me. We tend to see 'motivation' as a good thing, acknowledging people for being 'so motivated' and building an industry of 'motivational speakers' to get us all fired up. Simply defined, *motiv-ation* means our *motive* for *action*. The relevant question is not, 'Are you motivated?', but 'What are you motivated *by*?' An amoeba is motivated. So was Bin Laden. So are white supremacists and IS fighters. And, in those cases, you can be certain they are *highly* motivated – by fear, resentment and hate.

Increasingly, fear-based work cultures are being acknowledged as problematic, but we have a long way to go. In the first decade of this century I was a consultant to a highly successful retailer in the UK that was dominating its market while experiencing 40 per cent staff turnover each year. When we were brought in to change this we found, unsurprisingly, very low morale, in a culture of fear with a bullying leadership style. I will never forget giving feedback to the board of the business about why it was important to empower people rather than scare them. 'You mean you want us to get rid of *fear*?' the CEO asked, almost incredulous. 'No. We need people to be scared. It gets things done.'

The personal growth industry, including a number of management consultants, *is* working hard to change this. Fear is slowly being recognised as an undermining motivational force for which we ultimately pay a price. It is gradually being dismantled in favour of vision and purpose, by focusing on what we *want* rather than what we *fear*. This has real value, but it also casts a shadow that too many of us are not noticing. 'I want' is not as innocent as it seems. There is an insistent kind of wanting that is easily missed. Indeed, it is highly lauded in our culture. It is a magnetic, internal source of motivation that is best described as 'desire'.

This is not 'desire' as we commonly understand it: love, passion, rapture. Nor am I referring to our 'heart's desires' which, for the sake of clarity, I will call 'true longings'. The 'desire' I am talking about is an attitudinal state that runs most of the Western World. This state *feels* exciting, *seems* dedicated, *generates* adrenalin and *attaches* our worth to outcomes (which is the part we don't notice). It tricks us by twisting an innocent 'I want' into 'I have to have' when we're not looking. It drives us harder and harder, fuelled by little shots of fleeting satisfaction, before driving us on again in pursuit of our enough-ness. And thus the ego licks its lips and survives another day.

This kind of 'desire' looks like fear's opposite because it's on the other side of the riverbank. By clinging to the bank of 'desire', we convince ourselves we are free: free from fear because it's *over there*. We believe we are free-willed; free-spirited; free to pursue our dreams and achieve them; free to fly. Provided its path is not impeded, this feels pleasurable, even thrilling. We don't feel our muscles ache or our nails starting to bleed. We don't notice the force of the river rushing past us towards something lasting and eternal. We pride ourselves on holding on instead of jumping in, believing we are in charge of our destinies. We hail it as the source of our success.

For a period, I was sucked into this state without noticing. Ironically, it was while I was helping that retail business dismantle the fear at the heart of its culture. An important personal relationship had come to an end for good, if painful, reasons, and I was longing to have a child. Being a mum was beginning to seem impossible and my loneliness grew intense enough for me to elope with other aspirations. *If I can't succeed at love, I want to succeed at work. I want to win respect. I want to make a difference. I want to awaken organisations to what is possible. I want to create a systemic shift in society. I want to rock this corporate corner of the world. I want to excel at this. I want to succeed big.* This didn't seem 'reactive' to me at all. It seemed normal, even noble. Consequently, I worked my butt off and ticked off what I regarded as each 'achievement' along the way. For a while, it was a buzz and I was on a roll, winning more clients, generating more income and increasing the credibility of our brand. I was also making people's lives at work better. To this day, I sometimes hear from people I trained in business to thank me for what we taught them. But underneath, my stress levels were rising and the band eventually began to snap. My 'passion' for my work started cavorting across the prairie like a horse on the loose, dragging me behind it.

After a couple of years, I became impatient and unreliable. I had taken on too many commitments. I began erupting with my colleagues like I erupted as a child. I arrived late at meetings. I became increasingly exhausted. Nothing was good enough, however hard I tried. I hadn't noticed 'desire' snapping at my heels, insisting I prove myself over and over again. I thought I was making 'a success of things', and that feeling stressed was just part of the necessary cost.

Desire is actually a *fear-based* state of being that attaches our value to results, setting us up to run headlong into our inadequacies whenever we miss the mark. Masked by 'I want, I *really* want' is this kind of mindtalk: *I have to get more, have more, be more, own more, possess, control, prove, win happiness, wealth, status and power, look good at all times, never give up and deny fear . . . or else I'll be meaningless, a failure, worthless, not good enough, humiliated, impotent, a useless, pointless scumbag . . . therefore I have to prove I'm none of these things by getting more, having more, being more* . . . and round and round it goes, in a variety of iterations, trapping us in an addictive cycle of *proving* we are *not* what we fear. And while we are in its grip, the only mind-talk we hear is, 'I really want to do THAT next.' Desire gets a lot done because it drives us into doing stuff, but it is a state of proving, not of creating and manifesting. Eventually it destroys and undermines our results. But until then it feels powerful, delivering fixes of temporary worth every time we get more, have more and be more.

Ultimately, this doesn't last. We soon crash back into our *scumbag-not-enough-ness*. We get lifeshocks that expose our proving motives. Deep disappointment sets in. Accordingly, we press on with proving ourselves again, pursuing the false promise of ultimate satisfaction, fulfil-ment and freedom that never comes. Next time disappointment becomes depression and, the time after that, depression becomes despair. I feel tired just writing this. It is an insidious and dangerous force, entirely self-centred and blinding us to our *true longings*. The bank of desire is forever in debt.

This is what I was doing in my early thirties, until I started to pay the price. Even when we become aware of what it is costing us, the full price may not be felt until much later. It is hard not to wonder what this period of my life did to my health and what part it may have played in the illness I live with now. I don't have evidence for that, of course, and object to anyone attempting to explain my cancer, especially with inferences that it may be my fault. At the same time, I aim to own my part in my experience and I am clear that my never-enough-fuelled workaholism took its toll.

The state of 'desire' is mostly invisible, even to the supposedly self-aware, and some schools of personal growth are feeding it like a beast. Indeed, the reactive mind will protect desire as something noble and even sacred. Just last night, I saw a promotional post on Facebook entitled, 'How to Build a Spiritual Empire'. For real. The cognitive dissonance was startling and the desire conspicuous – except to the person who posted it and the thousands of people who 'liked' it. What could be more alluring than 'a spiritual empire' to prove my value and importance on this earth?

Much of our 'success' is built on this state of self-deception. It produces 'haves' who never have enough, underpinning the immense discrepancy between the wealthiest few and poorest many. It is an invisible engine driving the increasingly extreme need for fame and physical perfection. It has made talent shows some of our most popular viewing in the past decade or more. It is a primary reason why so many successful and famous people experience depression. Some commit suicide because nothing they achieve seems to free them from their pain.

The state of desire is only *exposed* when something obstructs its path, when our lifeshocks force us to notice we are in its grip. When we fail; when we fall; when we are brought to our knees by Something Greater than anything we can achieve, pursue or control. Which is where the greatest successes of *being* are so often born.

The Only Battle That Counts

I wasn't always in this driven state during that lonely period in my thirties. There were times when I loosened my grip and let the river carry me, when I trusted my innate value and was able to serve with nothing to prove. But I was also blind to the 'desire' that crept in and the way my professional boundaries crumbled in its wake. I wanted what I wanted too much to set them where really needed and, with my 'pay the bill' mindtalk still running, I opened myself up like the January Sales, with all my best goods on offer.

One of the ways I did this was by forming a partnership with another consulting firm, but failing to create a clear contract about what we could and couldn't do with each other's material outside of and beyond that relationship. I raised the issue when we first started working together. It wasn't that I didn't think it was needed. It was that I buckled to their suggestion that my request demonstrated a lack of trust. Of course, it didn't. But we had won a big contract together and I *wanted* to work on it more than I wanted to risk an early conflict with my new partners. So, in my state of 'desire', I caved. We collaborated and co-created for seven productive years. There was sincere mutual respect and deep friendships formed. One of our leaders became godmother to the daughter of one of theirs. We cared for each other. We hung out.

I lay no blame for the ultimate breakdown of our relationship, and know my reactive behaviour played a real part in it. I asked too much of myself and everyone around me paid a price. Of course, they played a part on their side too. When we agreed to stop working together, it became important to navigate the separation as professionally as possible, ideally to our mutual benefit. We had done some truly wonderful things together. We had touched thousands of lives with material we all valued. We had built something together that mattered to us all. The dialogue was tough and everyone felt bruised. Looking back now, I am still filled with sadness about it all.

Eventually, the separation negotiation all but broke down during a discussion about the use of each other's material. We had become very skilled at delivering each other's consulting and training practices. In some cases, we had integrated these and similar iterations of certain aspects were also in the public domain. This was fertile ground for misunderstandings. At the same time, I felt clear about the difference between what we had developed and what they had developed, much of which had happened before we even met. I had assumed that the lineation was clear and that we would maintain these boundaries outside of and beyond our partnership. From their perspective, we had taught each other our approaches so that we could use them independently in our services to other clients (essentially helping each other excel with combined best practice) and they had no contract telling them otherwise. This was very exposing for me, reminding me of the agreement I had asked for at the beginning and the way I had caved when they seemed to take offence. My 'desire' had overshadowed my wisdom.

We never resolved it. We agreed on other matters like who would work with which clients going forwards, but hit the wall on this issue. I could not persuade them to omit our methodology from their portfolio and, knowing their business had far greater market penetration than ours, I feared it would all come back to bite us hard. A few months later it did when I ran a pilot project for a major blue-chip company and potential new client. I didn't know the other consultants were already working there until, at the end of the pilot, the client said, 'I acknowledge that you are very good at this, but cannot hire you because we are already working with a business that teaches these skills.' This was the first of several such instances.

It was an exposing lifeshock at several levels. First, it highlighted the cost of my desire-driven need to prove my somebody-ness instead of protecting my business interests from the beginning. Second, and more surprisingly, it exposed the part of me that hated working in corporate settings. I found the sudden shift from a collaborative partnership to a competitive relationship deeply disheartening. In fact, if I admitted it, I found the fiercely competitive business world I had chosen to work in disheartening too. As I engaged with the lifeshocks, I remembered that I hadn't gone into this line of work to help corporations make more money, but because I saw them as potential levers for social change – powerful enough to influence the world we live in and support

issues such as poverty, unemployment, inequality, home-
lessness. Somewhere along the line I had lost sight of this
purpose and hadn't noticed how painful I often found it
to end up increasing their bottom lines rather than
contributing to social change. The other consultants were
helping their clients become more profitable and were
happy doing it, but I had wanted my clients to serve
'nobler causes'. I had been running an agenda that wasn't
theirs.

At first, I wondered if there was a legal case to pursue.
But Brad, who saw his part in what had played out, was
far less concerned with what we had to lose as a business
than *what we had to gain as human beings*. He didn't want
to invest large amounts of money and energy in trying
to protect what we had already failed to protect and
controlling what would be hard to control. We had not
set up our business to 'win' in the market, but to be of
service and earn our livings while doing it. Indeed, the
essence of our 'business strategy' had always been this: *to
follow the lifeshocks and let them lead us home*. Home to
ourselves; home to each other; home to That Which Is.
In our view, this was where *lasting* success resided. Our
purpose was not to engage in a competitive battle, but to
wage a battle of the spirit against our own fear and self-
deception. Its rewards cannot be found in a model or
method, however brilliant. The talk needs to be walked.
The wonder needs to be lived.

I continued leading my business for a few years after
this happened and endeavoured to expand our client
portfolio to include more organisations from the public
and charitable sectors. I wasn't ready to walk away or
find a completely new source of income, but it never

really fed my soul after that. The final lifeshock came after I was hired by a woman who had been a client twenty years previously when employed by another company. She had also contracted the other consultancy to pilot a course with some senior leaders and recognised some of what they were teaching. When she asked if I was aware of what they were doing, the reactive part of me wanted to draw her into my side of the story and influence her decision to engage them as suppliers. But her apparent loyalty to the essence of what we had taught her all those years ago, which manifested in her gratitude for the way it had freed her spirit at a difficult time, reminded me how many purposes can be served with these kinds of tools. My once-collaborator, now-competitor was working to improve her business results, but I truly didn't want to do that anymore. In that sense, her business needed their services more than ours. My heart wasn't in it. I realised that I didn't need to lay claim to some methods. I needed to reclaim my true calling, to be true to what I had wanted to do from the beginning – play my part in creating a more inheritable world. I was suddenly willing for my earnings to fall dramatically (which they did) in order for my spirit to rise (which it also did).

This was the last project I delivered as a business consultant and I have never regretted letting it go.

Such is what exposing lifeshocks give us: the chance to be fully authentic, to find our true path in life and to accumulate an inner wealth that no amount of material wealth can match. Whoever we are and whatever we're up to, they will hammer on our pretences and call us back to love. Knowing this is the case is an epic relief.

It lifts us off the throne of judgement and restores us to our rightful place as perfectly imperfect human beings fumbling our way to the light.

The Success That Seeks Us

It isn't that we're supposed to 'get it' after one lifeshock; that if we don't change our false beliefs the first time we notice them, then we are more fucked up than we fear. There are no quick fixes and there is nothing, ultimately, to 'fix'. We are not broken. We have been deeply wounded and hurt along the way and sometimes parts of us 'break down'. But 'I'm broken' is a game-over belief that generates utter desolation and a profound sense of hopelessness. Life becomes the pursuit of fixing what's wrong with us instead of embracing what's right with us, what's whole. No, we are not broken. We are just learning what it is to be human. Our beliefs run deep and we cling to them like life rafts in an ocean. They can also solidify into 'identity'. Our part is to stay vigilant and let the lifeshocks chip away at these lies.

This is not a purely rational exercise, nor a simple affirmation replacing 'I'm not enough' with 'I am enough'. It's more a stripping away of mindtalk so that truth – which is not an idealistic, utopian end point, but something accessible to every human being at every moment – can make itself known. When 'desire' retreated as a strong motivating force in my life, my worth was left standing as something permanent, God-given and non-negotiable, like a mountain in a valley, and with as little to prove.

Since then the state of desire that drove me so hard in my thirties has never fully had me in its grip. Sometimes desire sneaks up on me and I am momentarily seduced, but it doesn't have the same power over me any more. I know this because I am living with cancer and I desire to stay alive more than any desire I've ever held, especially as the deeply loved wife and mother I am privileged to have become. But mortality is the one thing none of us can bypass. It is too real for me now to deny my humanity or spend my days desiring what can never be gained.

Brad died some years before I closed our business, then cancer sealed the decision, but I had lost my passion for it after the breakdown of that consulting partnership. Not because I couldn't recover from it, but because I saw the extent to which I had misdirected my passion. I realised I wasn't a 'business woman'. I had been in love with *literature* all my life, and grieved over ink stains on my primary school story, for heaven's sake.

Ironically, it was in this desire-free, nothing-to-prove space that I wrote *The Cancer Whisperer* as a parting gift to the world before I died. I had no ambition other than for it to reach some like-minds who needed another way to deal with the disease. It simply wasn't *for me*. Yet, in worldly terms, this book is one of my greatest successes.

I now find myself serving in a vast context of untold suffering, and doing all I can to shift prevailing cancer paradigms: the top-down doctor-patient relationship that hinders people taking charge of their own healing, to whatever extent they can; the treatment of patients with physical disease, but not of people with emotional dis-ease; and the entire way we treat cancer as an enemy instead of an intensely potent source of lifeshocks that may awaken our spirits and free us from all the unnecessary, additional suffering generated by our reactive minds.

I deliver regular talks and workshops to cancer patients these days. I provide support to thousands of people around the world. An international band of 'cancer whisperers' has formed and, with it, profound connections between strangers whose shared experience of living in the face of death forms instant bonds. Barriers are down. The kind of resistance I met when serving in organisations is low among cancer patients. I am meeting a ripe, raw readiness to wake up, learn from life, claim what is on offer in our most vulnerable moments, answer that unfathomable longing to be spiritually free as much as, perhaps even more than, to be physically well. I continue to serve as a trainer and leader in Brad's educational programme, teaching people to learn from their lifeshocks. Currently, I earn significantly less than I used to, but I am back in complete integrity with my vocation. My lifeshocks have exposed the true longings that crouched beneath my mind's desires. They delivered me to a 'success' that, Brad used to say, 'we are so busy seeking, we do not notice it seeking us.' And for this to happen, *the successes of the soul need to come first.*

The Second Practice: Truth-Telling

Because I think a thought doesn't make it true. Most thoughts are profoundly false.

K. Bradford Brown

The Truth Challenge

Some assert 'there is no truth', but the aim of challenging our mindtalk is to *ascertain the correctness* of what we are believing. Human perception is a very complex realm because it is so subjective, but correcting our false thinking is an essential first step towards aligning ourselves with Life As It Is. This involves a conscious examination of the veracity and viability of our perceptions.

The truth-telling I am describing in this book also relates to *feelings*, which have a physical reality. They physically exist. They can be *ascertained,* and this is why feelings are always *true,* even if the thoughts that cause them are false.

To ensure we don't replace one myth with another, I am including specific distinctions and accuracies to assist anyone who engages with this practice.

The Principle of Veracity

Once you have re-experienced the lifeshock and written down your mindtalk, the next step is to challenge each line as *true, false* or *I don't know*. Everything we think can be evaluated this way. Without exception. Brad used to say, 'There is only one belief I am asking you to take on: all mindtalk can be challenged.' Here are some important guidelines:

What's true?

1. The lifeshock is always true. It happened.
2. Feelings are true (even if what causes them isn't). And remember 'I feel *that. . .*' is followed by a belief – usually false.
3. Any data-based facts are true.

What's false?

1. All 'have tos', 'shoulds', 'musts' and 'oughts' are false. These are *demands*, not true wants or choices. I may *want* to do my best, but I don't *have* to. I may *want* to succeed, but I don't *have* to. I may *be willing* to work long hours, but I don't *have* to. *Shoulds, musts* and *oughts* are cousins of 'I have to'. The compulsion or obligation robs us of our personal authority and free will. It also sets up resentment.
2. All absolute statements and generalisations: *I am bad, I*

am unworthy, I am too much; they are better, they are untrustworthy, they are evil; life is cruel, unfair, unjust, etc.

What's 'don't know'?

1. *All* statements about the future (which none of us ever knows).
2. All thoughts about what other people think – unless you ask, and they confirm your thoughts as true. 'Yes, I do think you're a coward, now you ask!' But even this does not make what they think true! These may well be false judgements coming back at you. We can apply *true, false* and *don't know* to these too – as when I knew that the promotional email describing me as going from being 'nobody with nothing' was false.
   NB: When we think, 'They think I am. . .', we are the ones thinking it! This is called 'projection'.
3. Assumptions about others, the world, the future.

It is also worth emphasising the power of 'I don't know', to which we can assign a lot of our mindtalk. I learnt the full power of this when doctors started predicting my future, including when I was likely to die. The fact is, no one can know the future, and nothing is cast in stone (as has been borne out by the fact that I am still here). *Not knowing* is profoundly liberating. As I wrote in my previous book, 'I choose to live on the sacred frontier of *not knowing*, where what I imagine meets what is so. This is where I stand still, ready to break for freedom from whatever I believed was real but wasn't.' If all you get is 'I don't know', you are already free.

For example

Returning to Elizabeth's lifeshock of her husband saying of his lover, 'She feels wonderful in my arms', this is how she challenged her mindtalk.

Mindtalk:

I'm left behind.

False. 'He may leave me, and I may leave him, but that does not put me behind. Whatever happens, I am *here*.'

I'm abandoned.

False. 'I am not abandoned. I am here. He is here. I am able to take care of myself.'

I'm helpless and isolated.

False. 'I have many resources, including this process. There are many people in my life who will help me.'

I can't survive this.

False. 'I am still here. I am surviving it. I have had dark nights of the soul before and survived.'

I'll never stop crying.

False. 'I can't cry forever! And I am deeply hurt. There will be crying. Grief is appropriate.'

I'll never trust again.

False. 'Trust is mine to give or not give. And I haven't been honest with myself. I settled for the beautiful lies instead of seeing the ugly truth.'

No one loves me just as I am.

False. 'I have not loved myself just as I am.'

I will never be safe again.

False. 'There are no guarantees that vows and promises won't be broken. None of this makes me "unsafe". It shows that I cannot control him.'

I will never stop feeling lonely.

False. I won't always feel this way. I have children, friends, a community, And I have often felt lonely in this marriage.'

No one will ever find me sexy.

False. 'Being sexy isn't one of my life goals. Living vivaciously and juicily is.'

I am ugly.

False. 'I haven't take good care of my body, but I shine in several ways.'

I am being violated by my husband and his lover.

False. 'They have been deceiving me. Violation is an outrageous accusation.'

He is a spineless coward.

False. 'He has lied to me for quite some time. This is a sign of weakness, but I have seen his courage at times too.'

I am unsafe, at risk, in danger.

False. 'He is not threatening me. I can put boundaries in place to minimise what he says and does in my presence.'

The only choice is between acceptance and madness.

False. 'The clear choice is acceptance of what has happened and the sanity of handling my mindtalk.'

I have to protect myself.

False. 'How would I do that anyway? It is happening and now I know about it.'

Go to war.

False. 'I don't have to or want to. I would prefer to leave.'

Or else I will crumble, disappear and die.

False. 'I am intact. I am here. I am alive. As I clear these lies, I feel calm.'

I can't do it.

False. 'I am doing it.'

It's too much grief, too much pain.

False. 'It is as much grief and pain as it is. And I need to feel it for it to pass.'

My heart can't take it.

False. 'My heart took a direct hit and is still beating.'

I won't ever recover.

False. 'It may well take time, but my recovery has already begun.'

I am broken.

False. 'I am grief-stricken, but I am still whole.'

So, I have to stay small and keep quiet.

False. 'I am not small or quiet. I don't wish to be in this situation.'

I have to try and save our marriage.

False. 'Part of me wants to, but a lot of this is fear. More of me wants to let go.'

Et voilà!

Three Roads to Truth

Note how Elizabeth didn't just put *true*, *false* and *don't know* on each sentence. She qualified them with objectivity and reality-based statements. This is the *truth-telling* part.

Again, I am aware of some techniques being taught about truth-telling and changing our 'limiting beliefs' that I believe are not helpful. Among them are these:

1. *Affirmations. E.g: 'I am pain free'* (when I'm not) and *'I manifest material abundance'* (when I am in

debt). This is not truth-telling. It is wishful thinking.

2. *Turning beliefs around.* E.g. 'He is cruel and heartless' becomes 'I am cruel and heartless', as if everything we think about others is a projection of what's so about ourselves. No, no, no! This is not truth-telling. It is a reversal of false judgement, whether it had been projected or not.

3. *Replacing one absolute with another:* 'I am the best mother in the world' is no truer than 'I am the worst mother in the world.' This is not truth-telling. It is replacing a lie we don't like with a lie we do.

Nor is this a question of replacing 'I am not enough' with 'I am enough' or 'I am selfish' with 'I am selfless.' It is so close to truth, but not quite. *I am enough. . . for what? I am selfless (except when I'm not). At my best, I am loving and generous. I am okay with myself as I am. My essence is human, even innocent, and sometimes I screw up big-time. The truth for me right now is that I care about this and can see my part in what happened.* Now we are being accurate instead of absolute. This is the truth-telling we can practise with integrity.

There are three key ways to approach this:

1. *Replace the lie with the truth:* 'I am not good enough' might become 'I am okay with myself as I am.' You might also add, 'And I'm not perfect' to ground it. I often write something like, 'I am deeply loving (except when I'm not). At my best, I am brave and audacious.'

2. *Discern the truths within the lies*: 'It's false that I am a failure, but I failed to achieve this particular result. I am someone who takes risks and is willing to learn from my mistakes.' This way we are still taking responsibility for our results instead of using 'truth' as a form of false positivity or as disguised abdication.

3. *Let the truth make itself known*: the truth is *always* there, waiting to be seen and claimed. When the lies are cleared away, truth is what remains. You may find it just arises from within when you verify a belief as 'false'. It may come to you, as if from another realm. You may be surprised. This is called realisation.

For example, when I verified, 'Cancer is a killer disease' as *false* (because it doesn't always kill), I heard 'Physical disease is a manifestation of emotional *dis-ease*.' This stunned me and, of course, I could not prove it to be so. But it led me into a transformational inquiry and turned my relationship with cancer on its axis. I have since found considerable evidence to support it.

If you want to change what you feel, tell the truth...

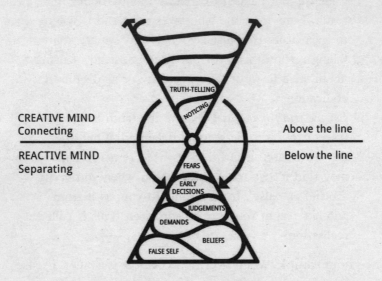

Copyright © K Bradford Brown 1984.

7

Power

A wave only has power because it is attached to the ocean.

David Templer

The Brink

I have lost my balance. Literally. I walk like a drunk, tipping from side to side, and fall over if I turn my head too quickly. My eyesight is off-beam, too, like headlights pointing at the kerb instead of the road. I get extremely dizzy turning over in bed at night and vomit when I sit up in the morning. At times, I mix up words when speaking. Most days I have headaches. Some are blinding. And I can't walk down the stairs without assistance. My husband is bringing me meals in bed and gives me his loving arm to lean on when I potter around the garden each day, just for fresh air. I am becoming increasingly dependent on him. I can't go to a shop without him driving me there. I can't tuck Gabriella into bed because bending over makes the room spin. I can't walk through the fields to see the herd of horses that always greet me as a friend. *I can't, I can't, I can't.* Every day I lose a bit more control over my body. Every day I seem to lose another piece of myself.

These symptoms started a couple of months ago. They came and went for a while and, at first, my medical team thought it was an ear infection called 'labyrinthitis', which causes vertigo. But, the fact is, my brain tumours are back.

I had a good run at 'normality' after the Gamma Knife radiation successfully removed the multiple lesions that appeared last time. For nine months, I strode out into the world as a healthy human being. Not that I was kidding myself. I knew this was a temporary reprieve, but felt vital and grateful and seized the day. *The Cancer Whisperer* had come out in paperback and I travelled around the UK giving talks to cancer patients, promoting it in the media and basking in this surprising new opportunity to be of service. I had also started writing *Lifeshocks* after the Gamma Knife procedure, but set it aside for a while to be out in the world as much as possible, instead of at the beautiful black-and-white, mother-of-pearl-encrusted desk my husband gave me for my fiftieth birthday. I have been getting on with my life.

I spent much of last winter on a temporary outdoor ice-rink in Tunbridge Wells with my daughter, now seven, who makes all the bitter in my life sweet. Tentative at first, she was soon speeding around in her pink and white skates with the same confidence she roller-skates round the kitchen table at home. She is, as I say, so much what I longed to be at her age: all muscle, agility and exploding into each moment. She beats up each day and leaves it knocked out in the corner before cart-wheeling her way to bed. She fulfils a longing I have only ever satisfied fleetingly: to be truly at ease in my own skin. I watch her in wonder sometimes, vicariously delighting in the tautness of her muscles and the way she swings from the highest bar at the back of our wooden staircase in the hall, which is open at the back like a ladder. I can't imagine skating with her now and wonder if I ever will again. My situation seems so bleak today, so immutable. The symptoms are worsening and there is not yet a viable solution on the table. I have been exploring all possibilities since the news of my brain tumours sunk in, but today it is hard to feel hope.

Lifeshocks often come in waves, one after another, lapping on the shore at our ankles and slowly building in size until we get soaked. This is how it went when learning about my brain. First, I received a phone message from my neuro-oncologist telling me my latest scan was 'fine' and to carry on as normal. That word alone was a clue. 'Fine' told me almost nothing. That's what we say when someone asks us what we're feeling and either we don't know the answer or don't want to be honest. It's a barren word. But, on this occasion, I took it at face value and didn't chase the details. This is unlike me. I usually hunt down details like a sleuth, but I was taken in by his cheerful tone of voice and deeply desired it to be true.

Two months later, he called me into his office and informed me that things weren't so 'fine' after all. He was sitting behind his desk when I walked in and he already had the images of my last two scans up on his computer screen. He shook my hand as I sat down and was soon explaining a few spots that looked like scarring. 'The problem,' he continued, quite matter-of-factly, pointing at a particular blurry zone near the brain surface, 'is this area, right here. *This lesion is new.*' Another wave splashed against my ankles. I leaned forwards to look closely at a small, white circle with a flat side where it butted up against the inside edge of the brain's lining. There was a narrow space between that edge and the skull, where fluid buffers the brain to protect it. 'It seems to be in the meninges,' he concluded, 'which means we can't target it with Gamma Knife again. *We need to do whole brain radiation instead.*' This time I got drenched.

I sank back in my chair as the lifeshocks penetrated my being. He kept talking, but his words floated over my head while streams of fear and fury flooded my body. I knew how dangerous this was. I knew about leptomeningeal disease, a rare complication whereby tumour cells spread to the membranes and gain access to the cerebrospinal fluid pathways. I was aware that it moves through the fluid pathways and spreads out like an octopus, depriving the brain of oxygen, neurological functioning and cognitive acumen until the patient finally slips into a coma before dying. Now I was blindsided – not just by this information, but by the way he had let me believe I was okay when I wasn't. I deeply objected to this deceit. First, he created an illusion of wellness (which I readily bought into), however well intended; now he was shattering it like glass.

This is what lifeshocks do: shatter illusions. Mostly, I am ready for the shattering. I have trained for it. But, even as the glass shards spread out at my feet, I tried to cling to this illusion by asking for another scan because the tumour appeared to be up *against* the brain lining rather than *in* it. Partly, I didn't trust what he was telling me. Partly, it was easier to blame him than admit I had ignored my intuitive suspicion of his original message.

Mostly, I needed to keep pretending I was fine. This is how the 'reactive mind' tries to protect us from reality: by pretending what's happening isn't really happening, even when it is staring us in the face.

But the lifeshocks keep coming until we get it, the next a little louder than the last, and each taking us that much deeper into ourselves (when we let them). Just ten days later, the neuro-oncologist scanned my brain again with a much finer-cut machine and, sure enough, it delivered a tidal wave of reality: multiple new lesions in the tissue and lining of my brain. I could see at least seven spots in different areas, but the lifeshock that struck deepest was seeing three streaks of cancer spreading out in the fluid pathways at the back of the left hemisphere. This time it was undeniable: leptomeningeal disease.

I have managed to avoid whole brain radiation since I was first diagnosed with 'terminal cancer' three years ago. At that point, too, my brain was riddled with tumours, but I was able to clear them with a powerful new drug called Afatinib (along with other complementary interventions) that has now passed its shelf life in terms of its effectiveness in blocking further progression. Whole brain radiation (WBR) is quite standard in these circumstances, but it can later lead to serious neurological damage, including dementia after as little as a couple of years (though not in all cases). Now, I was being offered it again.

Instead, I asked for a tumour near the surface to be removed and biopsied for possible mutations that might open other avenues. I found a neurosurgeon who was up for this, calling WBR 'a last resort'. He was refreshingly honest about it, explaining that in the 1980s and

1990s, WBR was given to patients like me because they were almost certain to die from their primary cancer before the dementia set in – which was invariably a kinder way to go than dying from secondary brain tumours. These days, because more effective, life-prolonging treatments are available, living with incurable cancer can be more like living with a chronic illness, at least for a few years. In my case, I have no active tumours from the neck down because the Afatinib has been holding everything in those areas steady. But the challenge is that the blood–brain barrier is a highly effective security system which few drugs can penetrate. This makes the brain especially vulnerable in a situation like mine.

It makes my entire being especially vulnerable, too. In recent weeks, I have been doing all I can to find a viable alternative to radiating my brain indiscriminately. Some possibilities are surfacing, but they are all long shots rather than certainties. The reactive mind wants certainties. It doesn't want to decide between one risk and another. It clings to control like moss to a damp wall. I am trying to be patient, to do the research that needs to be done and identify the best way forward, but it is taking time and my symptoms have become debilitating. The lifeshocks are relentless, as lifeshocks are when something essential to the spirit is at stake. And I can't see what that is yet.

For now, I'm walking a tightrope between 'the courage to change what I can' and 'the serenity to accept' what I can't; between the belief that it is 'impossible' to reverse this and my demand that I do just that; between what I have the power to affect and what I am powerless to alter. One minute I am researching the latest trials for my particular cancer mutation and the next minute I am planning my funeral. Both seem entirely appropriate. Once again, as was so in the gravely ill period following my initial diagnosis, I am living on the brink: that place where our sheer mortality drops before us like an escarpment and our ultimate powerlessness to be anything other than human is laid bare. And yet, while I can't quite grasp what life is trying to tell me, there is something paradoxically empowering about this powerlessness; something that smells of autumn and tastes of wine.

Time to Be Precise

Having participated and worked in the Human Development movement for over a quarter of a century, I have long been concerned by the concept of 'personal power'. On the one hand, I have been eager to find a version of it I could live with and nurture. On the other hand, I have become wary of how seductive promises of releasing one's 'personal power' can appear, and how ripe for the ego to claim dominion in pseudo-enlightened clothes. 'Personal power' seems to have become an end in itself, with little definition or nuance. The Human Development market is flooded with 'personal power' products, some of which have integrity and some of which don't. I have purchased and participated in at least a dozen over the years, during which I have been alarmed – and sometimes temporarily taken in – by false positive *beliefs*, which feed the illusion of limitless personal power, being taught as *truths*: 'you can do anything';

'anything is possible'; 'you create your own reality'. To name just a few.

It is certainly true that we create our own emotional experience through what we believe, and act in line with those beliefs (although it is important to note that there are also clinical and chemical exceptions to this). It is also true that we can harness our inner resources – vision, purpose, skill and sheer hard work – to create espoused results. There is plenty of evidence to support this, and some great tools to become effective at it. However, human beings *can't* 'do anything' and 'anything' is *not* possible. This is omnipotent thinking. We don't have wings. We are not immortal. If we are trapped in flames, we burn.

Equally, the belief that 'you create your own reality' contains some liberating truth. Indeed, I teach people that our results reflect our dominant intentions. What we actually do tells us what those are. We may make a commitment not to eat sugar and, within a day, devour a packet of chocolate biscuits. This is because we have not noticed our unconscious *conditions*. 'I will give up sugar *provided that* it is easy.' 'I will apply for the job I want *provided that* I have no self-doubts.' 'I will support my partner to fulfil his aspirations *provided that* he still makes me his priority.' And so on. Our 'provided thats' are the unconscious intentions that so often win. When it comes to manifesting our power through purpose, commitment and discipline, this is very important to understand.

At the same time, there is a shadow being cast in the personal growth world by the tenet that 'you create your own reality'. There is an absence of awareness about the sheer *privilege* of being able to engage in personal growth at all. There is a lack of consideration for people's particular contexts, including their education, cultures and formative lifeshocks. Try saying, 'you create your own reality' to a shivering refugee being pulled off a boat in the Mediterranean, a young black man being pulled over by the police for the colour of his skin, or the people of Sierra Leone who just lost hundreds of compatriots to a massive mud slide. No. This is irresponsible language that posits blame or deserved 'karma' where it is not due. 'You create your own reality' may be psychologically mature in some ways, but it is spiritually *young*, because there is an arrogant assumption that what we intend for our lives is more important than *what life intends for us*.

In my twenties, I worked for a management consultancy that put me through fifteen days of intense personal-growth training. We were taught that 'there is no truth', 'there is no reality' and 'you can change reality by changing your perception of it'. As someone who was already aware of how transformational a shift in perception can be, I was almost convinced by these generalities until the trainer said, 'The wall is only a wall because you see it as a wall. If you see it as pure energy, you will be able to walk through it.' At this point, I challenged her to do just that, to *be* what she was teaching, but she couldn't. The wall was adamant in its wall-ness. And I resigned from the company soon after.

The fact that there are so many 'personal power' offerings in the market testifies to a deep need in our culture, a need born of people's profound sense of powerlessness and inability to live the lives we dream of. It may also be born of the fear of our ultimate mortality in a world that distances and anaesthetises death as never before. Either way, we are reaching for something within that will bring us peace, joy, security and intrinsic worth – and better we reach for this within than chase it outside of ourselves. In itself, this is a huge leap forward. It is also what I have spent much of my adult life helping other adults to find. However, we need to be aware of how cunning and powerful the reactive mind can be. *The more we are on to it, the more ways it finds to trick, dupe and seduce us – just like cancer mutates in response to the treatments we throw at it.*

This means we need to be increasingly vigilant as we awaken and evolve. We need to notice when the ego basks in the glory of being a 'life coach' or 'spiritual teacher'. We need to beware the teacher who cannot see their own shadow and is not willing to have it pointed out. The belief that we have 'arrived' developmentally or spiritually is a clue that we have lost ourselves again. Equally, the Human Development movement needs to be aware of the shadows it casts, one of which is the emergence of 'personal power' teachings that fuel a false positivity and the myth of our omnipotence: the notion that we have power *over* reality, that we are ultimately in charge.

At the other end of the scale are 'spiritual' teachings that discourage the quest for personal power because we are all 'completely powerless' and everything that happens is 'God's will'. Again, there are some essential truths here to reiterate: we *are* all mortal and impermanent; we are *not* in control of what happens; none of us is exempt from loss, frailty, vulnerability and death. These are the truths that 'you can do anything' and 'anything is possible' seek to deny. At the same time, being taught that we are completely powerless can compound existing false beliefs that disable our ability to act, serve and shine as responsible, creative and compassionate human beings. It can become an enlightened excuse to turn away from the world instead of playing an active part in its evolution. More than this, it can fuel people's sense of impotence, self-loathing, hatred and violence – which is what an underlying conviction in our powerlessness can lead to.

This is where the principle of veracity comes in. First, we need to get over our perceived powerlessness, which manifests in a variety of core beliefs: *I'm helpless, I'm out of control, I'm weak, I'm ineffective, I'm a failure, I'm needy, I'm useless.* All these beliefs generate a state in which we become victimised by whatever is happening and unable to respond effectively. They suck up our inner power. As I have explained and want to reiterate, core beliefs like this are invariably false. The 'I am' makes them erroneous – as if 'weak' or 'helpless' marks someone's entire being, like the lettering through Brighton rock, permanently branding who 'I am'. We need to understand that *who we are* and *how we behave* are not the same thing. We are not our behaviour. That we fail at something does not make us 'failures'; that we have weaknesses does not make us 'weak'. The reactive mind does not get this. It turns one into the other at lightning speed, writing us off with sweeping judgements instead of discerning the difference between our *doing* and our *being*. When my daughter crosses a behavioural line, like when she threw skittle balls at the television in a rage at the age of three (smashing the screen irreparably), I do my utmost to say, 'What you *did* was not okay' – which she is then required to repeat back to me so I know she got it – 'but YOU are okay. You are always, always okay.' Then some appropriate consequence (versus punishment) for that *behaviour* ensues. Happily, she hasn't smashed anything since.

While working to overcome the *false limitations we impose on ourselves*, we also need to accept the *true limitations set by life.* The walls we run into. The events we cannot control. The deep-down vulnerability of our ultimate humanity. We need to challenge and release our delusions of grandeur and false entitlements, which are born of beliefs that over-inflate our powers: *I am superior, I am better than, I am above, I am super special, I am always right, I can do no wrong.* This is where we go when we cannot bear the pain of 'I'm powerless' (and its various cousins) a moment longer. We pretend we never even had that thought in the first place. We bury it deep in the unconscious and lash out at anyone who suggests we see ourselves that way. Instead, we steal our worth from others because 'at least I'm not like them'. We avoid pain by asserting power *over* others instead of reclaiming the power of knowing who we are and what we are legitimately worth. Somewhere between our perceived impotence and assumed omnipotence lies our true power. It is time to drop the generalities, abstractions and absolutes. It is time to be precise.

Reactive Power

I grew up around 'powerful' people, some of whom ran the country and many of whom walked with an air of assumed superiority. I also grew up with two highly assertive parents who match each other in professing their opinions on any given subject. Apparently, I was a placid baby until the 'terrible twos', when the will announces itself and tests parental boundaries to the limit. I tested my mother's hard, throwing tantrums and defying her at every turn (for many years). She once said to me, 'By the time you were two your will was stronger than mine.' This is saying something, because my mum is a force to be reckoned with. She is also a deeply private woman who keeps her heart in her inside pocket rather than wearing it on her sleeve as I do. As such, I will not write about her in much detail. It's not that she hasn't been a potent source of lifeshocks in my life. All mothers deliver formative lifeshocks to their children. It's just that I don't need to share this publicly to get my message across effectively. I don't need to transgress her boundaries as I did so often as a child.

However, I don't think she will mind me describing her as a unique, extrovert, dominating character with an independent spirit and a penchant for the dramatic in the way she speaks. When she is cold, she is 'simply arctic'; when she is hot, she is 'roasting alive'. And when she hears me talking about what I do, she says, 'Thank God I'm so shallow!' If you can imagine Lady Bracknell from Oscar Wilde's *The Importance of Being Ernest* booming, 'A *hand*bag?' on learning Ernest had been adopted after being discovered as a baby at Victoria Station, then you have an idea of how my mother gets her point across. It is very effective and, at times, very funny.

She sacrificed a lot for Dad's political career, having been a talented cellist and having once ridden for the

Junior British Equestrian Team. She was a model politician's wife in many ways, but was far from passive. In 1983, the then Secretary of State for Trade and Industry, Cecil Parkinson, was revealed in the press to be having an affair with his secretary. But when Cabinet ministers were instructed by Downing Street civil servants to hold hands with their wives in public to demonstrate their devotion, my mother retorted, 'Certainly not! If anyone who knows us saw Nick and me holding hands in public, they would think one of us is having an affair!' And when Margaret Thatcher allowed the United States to use British air bases to bomb Tripoli, without consulting her entire Cabinet, my mother wrote an outraged letter about it to *The Times*. Then, when Dad explained he would have to resign if she sent it, Mum redirected it to Margaret Thatcher instead. At the next Cabinet meeting in Downing Street, a civil servant grabbed Dad to say, 'Mr Edwards, we have had rather an unfortunate letter from your wife. What should we do with it?' To which my father hilariously replied, 'I stand between two omnipotent women and have no intention of interfering. Pass it to the PM.' In other words, I received very clear messages from both my parents that being a strong woman was a completely okay thing to be; perhaps the only way for a woman to be.

Learning what that really meant, however, and what true strength really looks like has been a life's work. Indeed, this is a developmental journey for all of us, one that passes through a number of different phases of ego development as we mature. In childhood terms, there is an early phase when there is no world but 'mine' and the world exists to serve 'me'. The child develops the notion of blame and desires things to be a very particular way, or else. In most cases, the child grows out of this into a phase when their sense of value and identity depends on belonging to a group (often at the expense of others).

At my primary school, there was a girl called Jenni, who bullied other children most days. I was afraid of her, but she liked me and picked me as one of her 'friends', which seemed far safer than being one of her victims. This meant doing her bidding or ending up at the receiving end of her spite, which happened on the few occasions I stood up to her. We were about nine years old at the time and there was a girl in our class we were mean to regularly. Her name was Alice. She was physically ungainly and often twiddled her hair anxiously. I colluded in the teasing and ostracising almost without question, but for the low-grade disquiet that gurgled in my chest and which I medicated with chocolate and denial. You see, I knew what it was like to be in her shoes. I knew how it felt to be targeted by pointing fingers and mocking jeers. I was the one whose breasts were already forming and who stood several inches taller than my friends. I was the ungainly one who felt humiliated when bouncing around the netball court in netball bibs designed for flat-chested girls. But this didn't stop me joining the persecutors, if only to spare myself the same treatment. Such is the shadow of a bully: cowardice, and the failure to admit one's own fear.

One day, when Alice brushed past Jenni in the corridor as we bustled from class to the playground for a break, Jenni wiped her arm where Alice had touched it. 'Yuck. Alice muck!', she said before wiping it on to someone else's arm, as if passing on a disease. That person copied her, passing it on to someone else with 'Yuck. Alice muck!' This went on for several minutes as 'Alice muck' was passed around the class amidst raucous laughter and the acute cruelty that nine-year-old girls are disturbingly capable of. As the 'muck' was passed to me, I saw Alice with her back pinned to the wall, immobilised, as if she was trying to make herself disappear. I felt sick. My fear of Jenni and desire to protect myself was matched by an intense wave of empathic loneliness such as I had never experienced. It seemed that it wasn't fear pinning her to the wall as much as deep resignation, a giving-up on herself that erased her existence along with her pain. For me, it was a moment of pure shame, a glaring lifeshock that offered an opportunity to break from the group and risk not belonging in favour of being Sophie. I failed. *It's only me against them,* I told myself. *If I don't join in I will be next. Exiled. I have to protect myself. I have to hurt her too.* The pull of my mind defeated the pull of my heart. Instead of putting my arm around Alice to assure her she was worthy of a loving touch, I wiped someone else's arm, muttered 'Alice muck' and ran away, as if to pretend I hadn't. I colluded with the group to oppress another human being. The shame still burns as I write.

In my view, this is what happened on a grand scale in Charlottesville in August 2017. Sometimes the name of a place becomes synonymous with a shocking event or tragedy: a global lifeshock that gets everyone's attention. Charlottesville was one such. I simply need to write the word to conjure an image of white supremacists marching with Tiki torches and Nazi flags in *2017* that sends shivers down the spine. Well, it certainly sends shivers down mine. A young black man was badly beaten. A white woman, protesting against the supremacists, was killed by someone driving a car headlong into the crowd of protestors. The marchers did not wear hoods to hide their identities. They marched openly, as if emboldened with permission and fearless of consequence. It was a blatant, unapologetic declaration of supremacy, resentment and hate.

These were adults, not children, but no more mature psychologically. Contrary to how it can look, assumed superiority is rooted in fear, not in any sense of innate worth. In the absence of that worth, a group of people will tap into strong negative emotions like anger and resentment to feel 'powerful'. They create belonging by getting into agreement about how they see the world, no matter what the truth or facts, and conspire to impose their reality on others. Then collusive oppression, akin to what happens in many school playgrounds, is unleashed. Indeed, psychologically, this kind of *reactive, controlling* power still belongs in the playground. It hasn't grown up yet.

In this instance, the resentment had been brewing for many years, restrained by cultural political correctness and a lack of approval from national leaders, festering throughout the first black president's eight years in office, and unleashed by his successor. Trump's election campaign tapped straight into the resentment of white supremacists and disillusioned white-collar workers: the people who believe they have lost their rights, powers and place in the world to black people and immigrants. He expressed what they believed. He voiced their frustration. A leader whose 'I, my, me and mine' centre of gravity has earned him the label 'man-child', and whose leadership style is the embodiment of *reactive power*, Trump harnessed ill will that may have run deep enough to win him the White House. Resentment is a corrupt, potent force rooted in a deep sense of impotence, and can only assert itself at others' expense.

Limiting Lifeshocks

In order to respond to lifeshocks consciously and creatively, someone needs to be home. This means returning to *the authentic self*, in which resides a natural inner authority that we often see in toddlers. It arises as they develop a stronger sense of self and begin to state what they think and want without hesitation or self-consciousness. When Gabriella was a baby I called her 'my chicken' for some reason, and various versions of it evolved over the next couple of years: 'chick-a-bee', 'chick-a-boo', even 'chicken soup' for a while. I know. A bit blech, perhaps, but I was drunk on mother love at the time. One day, when she was standing next to the fridge in our kitchen, I asked her, 'What do you want for lunch, chicken?' She was two years old and responded with complete authority, 'I am not chicken! I am Gabriella!' And that was that. It was Gabriella from then on.

This was her authentic 'I' speaking, her young but unequivocal sense of self. This innate authority – the part of us that consciously *authors* our lives instead of being buffeted around by reactions to unwanted lifeshocks, the nature of which we barely suspect – is the epicentre of our true 'personal power'. This is a far cry from the power asserted through the 'false self' which compensates for the 'feared self'. Often, this sounds like a child's demanding, whining 'I' that complains when things don't go its way and throws a tantrum to regain control. As our false selves claim increasing dominion, the authentic 'I' shrinks beneath belittling self-accusations and unachievable demands. We try to claw back power by presenting ourselves as *ever strong, ever right* and ever better than, lest people find out how *weak, worthless, useless* and *unlovable* we believe we really are.

This process is so insistent and insidious that some of us can completely camouflage the underlying accusations and walk through life convinced they aren't even there. Equally, some of us hear them loudly and relentlessly – a downpour of daily self-criticism, even when we get lifeshocks we might like. For example, when someone says, 'You look beautiful', the reactive mind will chime in, 'They're just saying that' or, 'What are they after?'

The former behaviour inflates our authority and the latter shrinks it. Either way, the authentic self, which acts from intrinsic and unwavering self-worth, is locked up in a concealed room constructed by false beliefs we put in place from a young age. Effectively, we leave the building to a squatter asserting convincing rights.

The more degraded our inner authority becomes, the more power our aggrandised 'self' will try to steal from others – by putting them down, taking a position of superiority, believing itself to be 'better than', blaming others when things go wrong and standing on their necks to grab a modicum of self-worth – sometimes literally. This is the psychological platform on which racism stands.

Equally, we can slowly erase our true authority by taking a 'less than' position. Our reactive minds demand that we *stay quiet, hang back, don't make a fuss, don't draw attention, put others first, be modest at all times*. While appearing more passive, these 'have tos' are also designed to maintain an illusion *of control. Exposing* lifeshocks often challenge the 'less than' attitudes, but *limiting* lifeshocks can confront the manipulating, controlling aspect too. False modesty is a manipulation, a way of protecting ourselves from perceived external threats or fitting in with the expectations of others in order to be accepted and belong. This too is a form of false, egotistical power.

Whether we diminish or inflate our sense of self, we are attempting to assert power over our perceived powerlessness, to keep it invisible, even to ourselves. Either version erodes our inner authority like clay.

When this happens, when we claim powers that do not belong to us, when we attempt to control the uncontrollable and deny the ultimately undeniable, *limiting lifeshocks* come our way. This is the second of three key manifestations of lifeshock, this kind confronting our omnipotence – our arrogant, dominating, bullying, superior behaviour. These lifeshocks remind us that we are not above others. Nor are we in charge of Life Central. Seeing Alice pinned against the wall was a limiting lifeshock that slapped my bullying behaviour in the face and invited me to stand up for her in my true authority, regardless of what anyone else did or said. But my self-protective conceit, and underling belief in my own powerlessness, won.

A case in point

As a consultant, I have seen limiting lifeshocks rain in on dominating leaders with controlling management styles. In one retail organisation, there was a regional director who I had heard about from many staff long before I met him. He was a legend in the business and the people in his department were almost universally terrified of him. During the initial research process, they warned me about his 'relentless criticism' and 'perfectionism'. Believing nothing was ever good enough for him, they dreaded his visits to their stores. They had formed collective strategies to hide their mistakes and cover their arses. On the days of his visits, they posted a sentry in the car park to look out for him and send a warning that he was coming, like a meerkat on the lookout for predators.

He was particularly critical if certain products were no longer available on the shelves, especially the ones he wanted to take home to his family. As such, the staff kept those products in the storage room – effectively denying them to customers – until he arrived at the store. Then, following a warning from the meerkat on lookout, a team was quickly deployed to put them all on display before he walked through the shop doors. It was an impressive and very well-organised deception in which all staff members colluded. They made me hoot with laughter. I was in the store when this happened, and witnessed the kind of operational excellence this leader was demanding of his people. The irony was delicious.

Yet, I also wondered what was driving this man to hold such seemingly impossible standards and bully his employees when they fell short. The time eventually came when I was asked to deliver a leadership training session for him and his direct reports. The dynamic was fascinating. They agreed with almost everything he said. Very few of his team questioned, let alone challenged him. Some stuck their necks out and he was quick to criticise, but there were occasions he listened too. He wasn't entirely closed to input. He just held a very high bar. I found myself warming to him and was aware I needed to stay as objective as possible. I bided my time while building rapport with him, to the irritation of some team members who wanted me to say what they were afraid to say.

Instead, I observed him closely. I noticed his dedication to the business and his commitment to its success. He frequently spoke about 'living the company values', which included 'trusting and respecting each other', 'serving our local communities' and 'going the extra mile for customers'. He was holding some important bars, however controlling his manner.

'Are you aware that most of your staff are scared of you?' I asked him, once I was confident I had won his respect.

It was a significant limiting lifeshock for him. He really didn't know.

'Why would they be frightened of me?' he asked, only slightly defensively.

I turned the question to his team to answer. They were hesitant, understandably, but I pointed out that this was their opportunity to change things. Slightly squirming, they started to give him feedback about being 'critical', 'not recognising what we do well' and 'getting angry when things weren't perfect.' That one hit his jugular.

'But they *should* be perfect,' he retorted. 'We should do our best at all times.'

And there was my moment to work with him. I had already introduced them all to mindtalk and I knew it was important that he didn't lose face. So I agreed with him what I was going to do before doing it and secured the commitment of his team to write down *their* mindtalk as they listened. He was up for it and this is what came out:

Things should be perfect because we need to be our brand.

We should be what we say on our tin.

We should be impeccable in our dealings with customers.

We should live up to our values at all time.

We should deliver excellence. Nothing less.

This is the right thing to do.

It is the responsible thing to do.

'And if you don't do all that?' I asked.

It will damage our integrity.

We will deliver poor results.

We will have failed in our duties.

I will let the business down.

I will let customers down.

We will become mediocre.

I will fail at my job.

We will lose our jobs.

'And what would that make you?' I pressed.

A bad manager. A failure. A fraud.

'So what do you have to do to stop all that happening?' I continued, writing it all on the flipchart.

I have to hold the highest standards.

I have to do whatever it takes to deliver.

I have to point out all our mistakes.

I have to safeguard the integrity of our business.

I have to do what's right.

This is who I am.

As I listened, I felt real compassion for him, and genuine admiration. This was a man with deeply held values and finely tuned ethics. His bullying behaviour was driven by a strong desire to do the right thing. His intentions were noble and he had a rare, if sometimes misguided, integrity that needed preserving. All he needed to do was dispense with all the false 'shoulds' that were running the show and making people blind to how much he cared. It wasn't easy, but again, line by line, I helped him challenge his mindtalk until he found new ground to stand on:

I care deeply about the business, my people and my customers.

No one is perfect and I don't need to demand that.

I will continue to hold a high bar.

I will recognise successes as well as pointing out mistakes.

I will enrol people into my vision instead of being angry when they don't get it.

I will listen to my team.

I will make fewer demands and more requests.

I will learn to inspire instead of intimidate.

I am not a failure or a fraud.

I don't have to prove my integrity because it is solid.

This man's influence in the business was huge and his new behaviour was a major turning point in changing a bullying culture into an empowering one. The rest of the workshop was imbued with dialogue and co-operation. But the impact of the changes other leaders saw in this man led to behavioural changes in the whole culture. And his staff stopped holding his favourite products back when he visited their store.

Relevant to all

None of us are exempt from limiting lifeshocks that invite us to redefine or redirect our power. Not even dictators and warmongers. The price may become very high indeed, but as Gandhi said, 'Remember that all through history, there have been tyrants and murderers and, for a time, they seem invincible. But in the end, they always fall. Always.'

As parents, we also receive a fairly continual flow of limiting lifeshocks from our children: every 'no' to a request; every answer that doesn't come to our questions; every way they insist on being themselves when we want them to be like *us*. All too often, we think we can control our kids, that we *should be able* to control our kids, that we are *bad parents* if we can't. I wanted Gabriella to love reading and have pressured her about it sometimes. She resolutely doesn't. At times, I wish she would *sit still* and demand she does so. Then I watch her body twitching with energy until she can't contain it any more and leaps up to swing on the back of the stairs again. These are frequent limiting lifeshocks to remind me that my job is not to control her, but to learn who she is and create a space for her authentic self to bloom. Sometimes, parents assert reactive, punitive power in order to maintain the illusion of control in the family home. Tragically, some parents take this to highly abusive and dangerous levels.

Most of the lifeshocks in that consultation with my neuro-oncologist were also *limiting lifeshocks* too: the initial dubious 'fine', which suited my need to keep my disease at arm's length; 'the new lesion here', which I met with anger that he had deceived me instead of accepting what he was saying; 'we need to do whole brain radiation', which threatened my mental powers more than I could bear to deal with; seeing the leptomeningeal disease on the scan, which confronted me with my mortality again. This was when I finally yielded to reality. I did not have the power to undo it or, at that moment, make it go away. These limiting lifeshocks are filling my days as I write: spinning out, falling over, vomiting when I wake up, being handed a walking stick before getting up, the headaches, John bringing me meals in bed, medical doors closing one after another, even as I continue to explore every alternative to whole brain radiation. Each one reminds me of my mortality and calls me back to my humanity until I literally have no place left to go. My last lines of defence are being crushed.

Thankfully, I am aware of these lifeshocks. I am also aware that my most persistent challenge in life has been my relationship with my physical body. To a large extent, Western culture has mistakenly located power in brains, brawn, beauty and genitals, as if intellectual acumen, physical strength or attractiveness, and sexual prowess can assuage the underlying powerlessness we cannot shake. In my teens and twenties, I was far too uncomfortable in my body to claim much physical or sexual power. I sought power *over* my body rather than *in* it. Instead, I relied on my brain. I used my intellect to inflate my 'I', compensate for my physical flaws and make me worthy of existence. When teenage boys retreated from my prematurely big breasts and older men saw them as justification to hit on me when I was under the age of consent, I learned to disarm them intellectually. In my self-loathing, bulimic years at university I could conceal my 'craziness' with brilliant essays. When relationships failed and loneliness intensified, I bolstered my self-regard with the high achievements of a quick-witted workaholic. And when I wrote myself off as unlovable, I settled for being 'admirable' instead. In other words, I asked my brain to do more than its day job. I asked it to house my power.

I have made big strides since then. I have learned to live in my heart as well as my brain, to listen to my intuition as much as my intellect, to be led by love. Slowly, with the help of many lifeshocks, I have become more self-accepting. At times, I have even walked tall and proud in my skin. But I have never fully tapped into my physical strength, the inner athlete I left on the school running track in the pre-sports-bra era. I have come to terms with the body I was given, but never really celebrated it as a gift, as the source of my pilgrimage into self-awareness or the sensual, empathic, feminine vehicle that has carried me through the world. I can't quite reach it, but I sense these limiting lifeshocks leading me into a new relationship with both my mind and body. I just can't see it yet.

Responsive Power

However powerless we are to undo what was done (as I wished I could with Alice), however much we want to send unwanted lifeshocks back from whence they came, we always have the power to *respond*. This is how Nelson Mandela brought an end to Apartheid from a prison cell on Robben Island. It is how Martine Wright, who lost both legs in the 7/7 tube bombing in London became a Paralympian. It is why so many volunteers arrived in Houston with private boats to rescue people who were stranded in the aftermath of Hurricane Harvey in late August 2017. It is why tens of thousands of peaceful protesters marched through Boston, just days after Charlottesville, to dwarf a small group of white supremacists holding a 'free speech rally'. It is what Viktor Frankl gleaned from his experience at Auschwitz when he wrote, 'Between stimulus and response there is a space. In that space is our power to choose our response. In our response lies our growth and freedom.' This power is not personal. It is *relational*. It is an interaction with someone or something outside of ourselves.

By constructing the *false self* to conceal the *feared self*, we are reacting *against* lifeshocks. We are saying 'NO!' to what is before us. We act it out in indirect ways. Some of us become cool, distant and reserved, closing our hearts, withholding our emotions and disconnecting from who we are with and whatever is happening. Some of us become angry and aggressive, blaming and criticising, dumping our emotions on others while lashing out against the situation. Either way, we reject what *is* happening, whether we like it or not.

This 'no' is the foundation on which we build the false self, brick by self-deceived brick. No to our situations. No to all the people we hold at a distance. No to our true feelings. No to the pain. No to the fear. No to the vulnerability. No to the lack of control. No to the lifeshocks. *No, no, no. It should not be this way.* This is what the reactive mind finds a thousand different ways to express in its wholesale denial of Life As It Is. It is the epitome of powerlessness. We also pay a heavy price by holding on to the pain, rage or numbness of our unexpressed 'no', sometimes for many years. As long as we withhold this 'no', our real 'I' is silenced and its innate power diminished. And as long as we exercise *reactive power* – not just power over others, but attempted power over empirical reality – we have no authorship, no real power to *respond*.

When I was first diagnosed with cancer, I was completely blindsided. The lifeshocks came thick and fast: *'The mass in your lung is a tumour'*; *'it has spread to your lymph nodes and bones'*; *'you have tumours on C3 and T5 vertebrae, which could paralyse you'*; *'your condition is incurable'*; *'it would be wise to put your affairs in order'*; *'you have multiple metastases in your brain'*. To name a few. As each lifeshock landed, the 'no' inside me got bigger. I recognised their limiting nature, their insistence that I yield to my mortality and lay all I thought I knew at the altar of humility. Even so, I wanted to push it away and pretend it wasn't happening. I wanted to walk away from the doctors and hospitals. I wanted to return it all to sender.

At that point, I was powerless to find my way forwards. But I knew I needed to come to terms with my diagnosis, to accept what seemed unacceptable, to exchange my need to control the situation with my ability to respond to it. This meant expressing my 'no'. Once all the data about my condition was in, which involved several scans over a six-week period, I went for a walk to some nearby fields where only sheep and horses could hear me. It was winter. It was very cold. The air cut my lungs like a knife. But I welcomed it. I could *feel* each breath and each breath reminded me I was *alive*.

The lifeshocks from my diagnosis had concertinaed in my diseased neck and tight shoulders, which limited my mobility on this occasion. Sometimes your whole body needs to say 'No!' The ground was hard and sprinkled with a thin layer of frost, like icing sugar. And there I stood, screaming 'No! I can't take this! I won't take this! It's too much for me! Fuck cancer! Fuck all of this! No! No! No! No! No!' At first, I needed to press it out, but after about a minute my throat opened up and poured grief-stained, despair-spattered rage into the icy winter air.

Twenty minutes later, I walked home slowly. I was the calm after a storm. 'I have cancer,' I whispered repeatedly until the words felt easy to say. 'This is real. I can do this. *I* can do this. I have trained for this my whole life. I trust lifeshocks. It is what it is. *I* have cancer and *I* can respond.' Just emphasising the word '*I*' helped bring me back to myself, to the part of me that could face *into* reality instead of away. I felt open in a way I hadn't for some time, as if a thick screen had been pulled back between the world and me. The blue sky was bluer. The crisp air was crisper. The naked trees were more naked. I was letting life back *in*.

This is something I have taught others to do many times, usually when they are overwhelmed with anger or despair. It's called a 'No Process'. It is a very physical and vocal release of our reaction to a lifeshock. It can be done in a field, at home (preferably with loud music), a car (I suggest not in a Sainsbury's car park); any private space. You simply close your eyes, go back to the lifeshock, feel the feelings and see what they want to say: *No! I won't! I can't! Fuck off! It's too much! How dare you!*

Go away! Then you belt it into the ether. Open your throat, punch the air and let the rage rip until you feel your energy shift. GET. IT. OUT. Then breathe, go back to the lifeshock and see if you can open up to it and meet it with 'YES'. If not, let the 'no' rip again.

In this way, 'no' delivers us to 'yes'. And, in this case, 'yes' delivered purpose and productivity – researching my disease, exploring my options, putting my affairs in order, asking my doctors every question I could think of, starting my blog. Saying 'yes' to all this did not, of course, mean I liked it. I didn't and still don't. It meant I *accepted* it and could therefore *respond to* instead of *reacting against* my diagnosis. I knew what outcome I wanted, but prepared for all possibilities. By accepting the variables over which I had no jurisdiction, I could see where I *did* have jurisdiction and where I could *act*. My 'yes' unleashed my 'creative mind'. Three years later, I still have cancer. I am very ill right now, but I am still here.

Noticing and channelling our inner 'no' to lifeshocks – in conscious, non-destructive ways – is the beginning of reclaiming our inner authority. My seven-year-old daughter is extremely good at it. When her 'no' arises in the form of anger, her whole body stiffens like a board as she vocalises her indignation. She embodies her 'no'. Just a few days ago, when she was furious that I wouldn't give her Maltesers just before bedtime, she lay on the bed as the muscles in her thighs clenched and said, 'Mummy, my legs are angry!' And they were. I encouraged her to kick them around a bit and voice her fury, which she did. Then she forgot about the Maltesers and was back to herself again.

Back to herself again. First, 'No!' Second, acceptance. Third, the *ability to respond*. There can be no response (vs. reaction) until we accept the lifeshock, until we say 'YES' to the fact that it happened. This does not mean liking it, condoning it, agreeing with it or being resigned to it. It means seeing it for what it is, a factual event that is out of our jurisdiction, but within our remit to respond to. 'Alice muck.' White supremacists marching in Charlottesville. Leptomeningeal disease. It means saying: 'Yes, I can take this. Even this I can take.'

In my early thirties, I introduced Brad at a public talk he was giving in London. As I stood at the front of the room and looked out at the audience, a lifeshock greeted me. Sitting a few rows from the back, slightly to my left, was Alice. I recognised her instantly. Part of me wanted to run from the room, not to avoid her, but to be sure not to put her off listening to what Brad had to say. 'I'm not who I was!' I wanted to shout. 'I see you. I give a shit. Stay!' She did stay and I waited to talk to her afterwards. She was understandably guarded as I approached her.

'I can't believe you're here,' I told her.

'I can't believe you're here either,' she answered. 'You're one of the reasons I came.'

This time I didn't defend or run away. I was able to apologise for how I had treated her. I was able to share some of what I had learned from Brad and encourage her to do the course so she could find real healing (which she did). I was able to make some small amends for my part in her suffering. I was finally given the opportunity, after all those years, to *respond* to the young girl I had abandoned in a school corridor; to honour her in the way my heart had wanted, but my mind had not allowed at the time. And in doing so I was back to myself again.

The Power of Surrender

As we mature psychologically, we become more capable of exercising *responsive power*. By encountering the limitations of *reactive power*, and experiencing its costs, we shift to new levels of awareness. We learn how to collaborate with others. We take increasing responsibility for the quality of our experiences and the results we create. We enter into mutually supportive, even mutually transformative relationships in which 'power over' is replaced by 'power with'. Of course, we still get trapped in self-deception too. We revert to the false self when fear takes hold. The *reactive mind* still tries to control the uncontrollable. We repeatedly succumb to the lies that are held as truths in our culture, a number of which show up in soap operas and pop songs (I know these are from bygone days): 'Love hurts'; 'I can't live if living is without you'; 'The sun ain't gonna shine anymore'; 'You're dangerous because you're honest'; 'Money makes the world go round'; 'Second chances don't ever matter, people never change'; 'Fame! I'm gonna live forever!'; 'Total eclipse of the heart'. Oh my. Mindtalk is *everywhere!*

But there comes a point on this journey when we recognise that the work of reclaiming ourselves, of *noticing* and *truth-telling* and *choosing* anew, becomes a daily commitment if we are to live as our authentic selves.

This is not everyone's cup of tea by any means. It takes work, inner work, which the reactive mind will talk us out of at every turn because it wants to remain in charge. But more and more people are engaging in this inner work. More and more people are now recognising the interpretative, meaning-making, story-telling nature of their thinking. There is a palpable shift in consciousness occurring at this time in our evolution. There is an equally palpable, systemic reaction against it, as suppressed prejudices resurface, opportunistic attitudes clamour against liberal ones and 'alternative facts' are presented as truths in the body politic. It can seem daunting indeed to break from consensus consciousness and dismantle our defences on an ongoing basis so that we can respond with clarity, creativity and inner authority to the challenges we face – personally and collectively.

But we are being assisted all the time. Whenever we are kidding ourselves, we get lifeshocks. Although some schools of human development see external events as random, impersonal and accidental,[5] we may also recognise lifeshocks as replete with purpose beyond our normal seeing. We may begin to observe persistent themes in the lifeshocks we receive, like relationships repeatedly ending in a similar way. And if we miss a lifeshock another will come. And another. And another. And another. Until one penetrates the *false self* to reveal the *feared self* underneath; until another penetrates the *feared self* so that the *authentic self* can be revealed, restored and reclaimed.

To this end, there is nothing random about the events of our lives. Lifeshocks take us deeper and deeper into

---

5 Even Brad used to teach an exercise in which we would take a lifeshock we didn't like and repeatedly say, 'This has no meaning other than the meaning I give it', until we could view it completely free of interpretation.

self-awareness and alignment with That Which Is. They are not all of the same magnitude, but they persist in peeling back the layers of fear and self-deception, carrying us from recognition to acceptance to integration to realisation of what is so – about ourselves, others and life itself. There is no arrival point. There is just more shedding and budding to be done.

Today, I am a winter tree again. Open to the elements and wounds of life. I wonder why I keep getting brain metastases when other metastatic patients get none. I wonder why I am among the 5 per cent who get leptomeningeal disease. I wonder why my deepest fears – of losing my cognitive abilities, being absent in the presence of my beloved family, not being Sophie any more – are being served up to me again. It is time for more than acceptance. It is time for *surrender*. Not resignation. Not giving up. Surrender. To that which I cannot control; to a reality I can trust, but not fathom; to the possibility of losing my mind and of dying sooner than I want to; to the ocean my wave is attached to.

Surrender is a sibling of acceptance, but it is more grown up. Acceptance says, 'Yes, I can take this reality, however much I don't like it'. This is what lifts us into a responsive, versus reactive, state. But surrender goes further. It says, 'Yes, I submit to this reality completely' with firm faith in a higher power, allowing it to have its way with us until we find that same source *within*.

I have been on steroids for several weeks now. I have gained a lot of weight again and some days my reactive mind is more concerned about this than the mortal peril I am in. Seriously. It is that insane! I am aware of it, sometimes even amused by it. Each day I surrender a little more to being bigger than I like and less capable than I imagined I could bear. In truth, both seem equally significant and are somehow connected, as if the tumours in my beautiful brain are coaxing me into the right relationship with my beautiful body – not merely by embracing how I look, but by rejoicing in the human form through which my spirit has shone its light into the world.

Just last night, I was overcome by tiredness. My headaches were hard to bear and I was retreating inside myself, looking for shelter from the agony and solace from my fear. My brain was throbbing and, as I lay my head on the pillow, I could feel something pulling me into what I can only describe as a deep black chasm at the back of my consciousness. I felt terrified. The pull was irresistible. I told myself that if I fell asleep I would never wake up again. For a few minutes, I fought to stay awake, to stay alive for my daughter, to write the chapters of my yet unlived existence. But I was powerless in the face of my exhaustion and the force that was pulling me down. So, I breathed deeply, challenged my fear of dying that night as 'I don't know' and surrendered to the possibility that it may indeed be so. 'Thy will be done,' I whispered out loud half a dozen times as I let go of my heartfelt desire to wake up again and all my illusions of control.

I did wake up. Here I still am to tell the tale. I descended somewhere so deep it took me nearly an hour to lift my heavy head off the pillow. But something shifted inside me as I slept. My physical limitations were the same when I woke, perhaps worse, but I felt a love for and gratitude to my body that I had never felt before. Instead of wanting to escape it and wishing it would function 'properly' again,

I moved into its soft folds and diseased cells with renewed tenderness. I also felt a surge of fresh energy, more mental than physical, and an increased willingness to utilise whatever powers I have left. Within the pain and loss and uncertainty, a dove was singing at my window and a power was present that offered a pathway out of the impasse.

Having explored a range of 'long shot' treatment options, I have now made a clear decision (supported by my oncologist) to try out a drug called Osimertinib that I don't qualify for under UK medical licences because I tested negative for the mutation you're supposed to have. As such, I can neither get it on the NHS nor on private insurance. It is very expensive, far more than we can afford. But, having shared this decision publicly, someone stepped forwards immediately to give me the money for long enough to see if it could help me. And two lung cancer patients sent me surplus pills they hadn't taken, which amounted to a month's supply. Furthermore, since starting this chapter, an oncological conference has been held in Spain, the result of which is that the licence may change in the coming year. This means that if the drug works, I will be able to access it without needing to pay for it. Once again, following a complete surrender to the Great Unknown, I am being sourced. And I am reminded that surrender does not replace action. It facilitates action. By yielding to a higher power, we access our true power. This is how it is possible to be vulnerable *and* authoritative, humble *and* assertive at the same time. This is also the 'exquisite paradox' that the American spiritual teacher Ram Dass speaks of. 'As long as you want power, you can't have it. The minute you don't want power, you'll have more than you ever dreamed possible.'

I remain on the brink. I do not yet know if this treatment will make a difference, but I do know this: if I am afforded another chance to stay here, to live longer than many doctors and statistics predict under my particular circumstances, then I am being invited to live in *all* of me. All of me. To be whole, as Portuguese poet Fernando Pessoa suggests, by being 'complete in each thing'. Mind, heart, body and spirit. Flawed and fabulous, powerless and powerful at once.

I also know this: that true power comes to us from the source of everything; that through my brain tumours and lost balance, through my need to reach for John's arm as I walk in the garden and through every lifeshock that knocks on my deluded doors, I am sourced. And now I can awake each day safe in the recollection that when I believed I was about to die, I still had the power to *choose* it, to say, 'Yes'.

The Third Practice: Choosing

Choosing Is the Antidote to Demanding

The demands we make of ourselves can be extremely limiting. They can close off other possibilities, insisting that we do it *this way* or *that way* or *my way.* This creates tunnel vision, the underlying fear driving us in one direction and increasing our stress in the process.

Choosing is the antithesis of demanding. It is the exercise of bona fide free will and the means 'to select from a number of possibilities'. As I said earlier, we may *choose* the very thing that the reactive mind demands, but there is no 'or else'. *I choose to work hard, but I don't have to. In fact, I choose this because I love what I do, because it feeds my soul and because when I am being creative I feel more ALIVE.* Similarly, *I choose to do unpleasant treatments, but I don't have to. I choose to let nurses put countless needles in my veins, to drink disgusting Chinese herbs and to spend money on all this when part of me thinks I 'should' be leaving it for Gabriella. I choose this because I want her to have more of me and because I want to have more of my life.*

Where demands *block*, choices *release.* Where demands are rooted in *false fears and beliefs* ('I have to. . .or else. . .'), choices are rooted in *insight and purpose* ('I will or am willing. . .because of what I value.') Once we have identified what's true, new possibilities present themselves. This is important because *truths change our feelings* and *choices change our behaviour*. We can choose *how to be* as well as *what to do*.

<u>*For example*</u>

After challenging all her mindtalk about her husband's affair, Elizabeth wrote these choices:

'Go home, my love, go home. I want you to be at home where you are loved and smiled upon. That place is not here.'

'I choose to defend nothing and hold on to nothing.'

'I choose to hand back the rings, the expectations and the vows.'

'I choose to put them down and release them.'

'I choose to feel my pain until it is done.'

'I choose to turn over the page and begin anew.'

'I choose to find new ways to love Elizabeth.'

'I choose love. I will not give up on it. I won't take my eyes off it.'

'I will keep walking.'

And her road opened once more.

Discerning Is Heightened Choosing

The practice of 'choosing' is about being focused and committed. It involves deploying the power of our *word*, which is arguably the most powerful force available to us as individuals. We don't just choose to behave a certain way. We commit, with our full authority.

We also need to be discerning. Discernment is an elevated form of this practice. It is highly intuitive. It sees self, others and the circumstances, taking them all into account. This is how we see surprising gifts and extraordinary possibilities. It unleashes our creativity in response to lifeshocks. *Choosing* is how we take back our power from reactive forces. Discerning is how we find light inside darkness and walk our true paths again.

One thing Elizabeth discerned is how lonely she had felt in her marriage over the years and how she needed to find new ways to love herself instead of expecting that all to come from her husband. She even recognised this as her part in his affair.

And thus the layers of the false self continue to peel away.

We Can Choose Our Beliefs

It is worth noting that when we are below the line – self-deceived, reactive and separated – *our beliefs have chosen us*. However, when we are above the line – clear, responsive and connected – we can *consciously choose* our beliefs: 'I choose to believe I am worthwhile, that I have innate value.' 'I choose to see other people as essentially trustworthy.' 'I choose to believe that life is not out to get me, but to help me get myself.' Again, this is more accurate than asserting positive absolutes: 'I am enough. People are trustworthy. Life is benevolent.'

Sophie Sabbage

If you want to change how you behave, make truth-based choices. . .

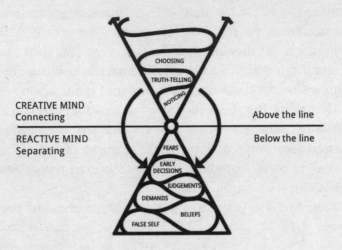

Copyright © K Bradford Brown 1984.

8

Love

Your task is not to seek for love, but merely to seek and find all the barriers within yourself that you have built against it.

Rumi

In my eyes, my husband is so of the divine and in the divine that he doesn't even know if he believes in the divine. Instead, he walks through woodlands noticing the colour of the air and wondering why herons so frequently lift their long necks from rivers as if to salute him when he walks by. Sometimes they just rise from behind the trees with their wide cloudy grey wings extended in full flight. I rarely see them when I walk alone, but when I'm with John they appear as if they have been waiting for him and belong to him. The first present I bought him was a picture of a heron to hang on his office wall.

He has tried to join them, to lift his legs off the earth and fly with the sacred. At sixteen, he left home and travelled overland, as a long-haired hippy, from the UK to India, passing through Afghanistan before Russia had invaded and devastated the stunning city of Kabul. He sought out Indian gurus to enlighten him, meditated daily, practised yoga, smoked a lot of weed and was eventually sent home by the British Embassy having contracted Hepatitis C, which nearly killed him. He wandered, but was forced to return, landing in the January snow at Heathrow wearing a kaftan and Jesus sandals. He then moved to a cottage in North Wales, which had no electricity or running water and no neighbours in sight. For two years he worked as a shepherd, relishing the solitude, the bleakly beautiful mountains of Snowdonia and the chilly walks to the well on winter mornings where he often had to crack the ice to get water. He frequently harks back to this time, as if he isn't quite himself without the something he left there.

Later, he spent ten years in an esoteric community that arose in the 1970s in the wake of the New Age and in which John continued his search for the purpose of human existence. Having had no interest in the conventional aspirations of Western life or its religious offerings since the age of fourteen, when he attended his first 'communion' and found it pointless, this organisation gave him the chance to study mystic traditions: the work of Gurdjieff, astrology, palmistry, religious ceremony, unseen worlds, clairvoyance, telepathy, higher intelligence, Fallen Angels and the esoteric laws of the universe. Once again, he removed himself from the normal world in pursuit of something other. He even changed his name during this time and lived in Israel for two years, helping to establish a branch there, and became fluent in Hebrew.

Eventually, having encountered the limits and shadows of this community, he and his partner, Christine, left it behind them to start a family. Two months after the birth of their son, Sean, Christine was diagnosed with bone cancer and John was slammed back into the prosaic grit of being human once again. He quit his job to raise their boy while she endured gruelling treatments for nearly three years and they got into debt that took over a decade to clear. This involved John working as a sales director for a telecommunications company, where he eventually became the managing director and hung a sign on his door saying, 'Le Grand Fromage'. He just couldn't take himself seriously in that context. The wandering hippy and secluded shepherd were still trying to take flight like herons rising above the trees.

By the time I met him, his twenty-year relationship with Christine was over and he was earning £8 an hour caring for autistic children whose families didn't want to put them in institutions. He had a gift with these kids, but will be annoyed with me for writing that because his humility is watertight. Before we got together, I remember listening to him wax lyrical about these children and why 'my job is not to help them learn our language, but to make sure I learn theirs.' His father had died from multiple sclerosis when he was six years old and he was raised by an angry, alcoholic stepfather who drank heavily every weekend, frightened John as a boy and regularly left him at home alone while going to the pub with John's mother. It was only when John discovered his untaught affinity with autism that he began to realise his stepfather had likely been on the spectrum, undiagnosed. The condition had coloured his entire childhood and sown some seeds of empathic wisdom that these children were now benefiting from. On our second date, he took me to the wedding of one of his clients. The bride had three sons on the autistic spectrum and the groom had a severely disabled daughter.

John was put in charge of them all during the wedding and, as I watched him interact with these children in ways that made their eyes sparkle, I fell irreversibly in love.

When we first met at that leadership course in Oxford, which was led by another mentor of mine, Professor William Torbert – author of and creator of *Action Inquiry* – John was on the brink of wandering away again. He was single, his son was grown up and nothing was tying him to the conventional world in which he had never felt at home. So, life sent him another force to earth him in the depths of his humanness again: me.

I was forty when this happened and had finally let go of the 'soul mate' notion, which tantalised me through my twenties and tormented me through my thirties. I had loved and been loved a few times, but nothing had matched that description. Nothing that fitted me like the last piece of a puzzle. No one who astonished me into being my unreserved self. Until John. I didn't know it, but I hadn't been ready to love someone so completely or for someone to love me that much.

I had hoped for it, longed for it, prayed for it and given up on it. I had nearly got married twice, but for the wrong reasons. I didn't see myself as desirable enough to attract what I ached for and didn't believe that what I ached for really existed. I didn't want my married friends judging and pitying me. And I didn't want to be alone. Sometimes, in my loneliest hours, I regretted these decisions and wondered if I should have said yes instead of no.

At the same time, I had enough self-awareness and sense of purpose not to sell myself short. Brad was at hand to pull me back from anything less than true love and anything that might distract me from whatever I might be destined for. He saw me as an agent of change in a suffering world, encouraging me to channel my gifts in a spirit of selfless service while seeking a partner who was not going to clip my wings. He was also teaching me how to love and be loved.

I had *felt* love before I met Brad, but I didn't suspect what love really was. I thought it was just a feeling, an emotion we reserve for those we trust, care about and feel safe with. But when I saw Brad working with people on his courses, I witnessed a way of loving that I had read about in scriptures but relegated to folklore.

Before I knew him, Brad once ran a course at a hotel in Houston, Texas. It was some time in the 1980s. When they broke for lunch and walked out into the lobby, there was a commotion. A small crowd had gathered around a man who was holding a gun to a woman's head and threatening to 'kill the fucking bitch'. Apparently, she was his ex-girlfriend. The gunman was raging at the top of his voice and an unarmed security guard was trying to talk him out of it, to no avail. Presumably, the police had been called. Instinctively, Brad stepped into the fray with, 'You're mad as hell, aren't you?' in a tone that matched the gunman's. This established instant rapport: *I see you and I see your anger.* The man said, 'Yeah, I'm mad as hell' and continued to rail about what he believed this woman had done to him and why she deserved to die. Brad played it back to him: 'So you're mad because. . .and she deserves to die because. . .and she hurt you by. . .' until the gunman started to calm down. Brad was *for* him and, at some level, the gunman felt it. Eventually, when Brad saw a small opening to respond, he said, 'I'm concerned for you. If you pull the trigger, you will spend the rest of your life in jail.' *I'm concerned for you.* Not for *her*, for *you.* In that instant, the man released the woman, dropped his gun and ran.

Brad called this way of being 'for-ness': the willingness to see beyond what another human being has done to their essence – the deep-down essential part, the part that is the same as us; the part that has worth, no matter what. He taught me that a person is not their behaviour, that we can hold people accountable for the most deplorable actions, while also holding space for a revival of their loving and lovable essence. This is what Sister Helen Prejean did with the death-row inmate, Matthew Poncelet, as depicted in the film, *Dead Man Walking*. It is also what Archbishop Tutu did at the Truth and Reconciliation Commission in South Africa, where he sat, day after day, listening to accounts of the horrors white people had inflicted on their black neighbours. He called it 'an incubation chamber for national healing.'

When we are *for* someone, we can listen without judgement, even if we are appalled by what they are doing. We can go after the false self without going after the person because we are ultimately on their side. We can speak truth to nonsense, truth to lies and truth to power. For-ness shames no one, but it will rip self-deception to shreds in order to free another human being from the unnecessary suffering it causes. Love softens us, but it is often far from soft. It can be as fierce as frost that splits rock.

Along with everyone he trained, Brad did this with racists in South Africa during the Apartheid era, bringing them to their knees with remorse and back to their feet with forgiveness. He did this with rapists and murderers in US prisons, reducing reoffending by helping them get the psychological chasm between 'I am a criminal' (which consigned them to a permanent fate) and 'I have committed crimes' (which liberated them to take responsibility and change). He did this with bullies, addicts, liars, manipulators, victims, survivors, pleasers, fixers and avoiders, sometimes taking a sledgehammer to their false selves while holding their essence in his palm like an egg about to hatch. Using more forceps than hammers, he also did this with me.

Once, I asked Brad why he never took a hammer to my self-deception and he responded, 'You have that covered Sophie. You hammer yourself quite enough.' He also told me that I was so open to his feedback there was no need to be confrontational. 'You are one of the least defensive people I know.' With him, this was true, because I trusted him completely, but my defencelessness did not extend to everyone else. Even in close relationships my guard was often up: with my parents, siblings, friends, lovers, even partners I loved and lived with. I had too many secrets and too much shame. I was also still riding one of the four horses of the psychological apocalypse: *I am unlovable*. Most 'core beliefs' are cousins of these four horses and, by the age of thirty, I had managed to dismount the other three: *I am invisible*; *I am unworthy*; *I am crazy*. I entered my fourth decade confident that I was *seen, valued* and *made sense*, even if I was still perceived as weird and intense by some of the people in my life. I also knew I was loving. But lovable? No. I was nowhere near convinced.

This began to shift for me when I discovered the power of my own for-ness in a surprising way in my early thirties. I was seeing a man called Daniel. We got on very well, laughed a lot, enjoyed each other's company and found each other attractive. But the sex was terrible. It was awkward and fumbly, as if we were both completely new to it. I was conscious of it, but couldn't figure it out. Then, a few months into the relationship, he had spent a weekend in Devon and came to my flat on Sunday evening looking sheepish.

'I've got something to tell you,' he said, anxiously.

Most of us have had *that* 'lifeshock' at some point in our lives! But I was intrigued more than alarmed and waited for him to spit out whatever it was. Eventually he did.

'I slept with a man last night.'

Far from feeling hurt or angry, I felt utter relief and laughed. He relaxed instantly. Suddenly it all made sense. The lifeshock dispelled some lurking something-wrong-with-me mindtalk, but more importantly I wasn't 'not enough of a woman for him' as I had imagined. I was entirely too much of one.

I could see his distress ran far deeper than telling me what he had done, and took both his hands in mine, feeling simultaneously *for* him and *for* myself.

'So how long have you been living in that closet?' I asked him, calmly. He was twenty-seven at the time.

'As long as I can remember,' he replied, as tears filled his eyes. 'I'm so sorry.'

For the next hour or so, I listened as he poured his heart out about his sexuality and how scared he was to tell his parents. I wrote down all his mindtalk: *They will hate me. They will reject me. I will disgust them. I will disappoint them. They won't be able to handle it. I have to protect them. I have to protect myself from their judgements, from the world's judgements. I have to hide who I am. I have to fake love. I have to pretend to be heterosexual. I have to bring girlfriends home. I have to settle for what I don't want. I can't be happy. I can only have secret sex. I will never ever find love.*

Together, we challenged it all. Every statement was 'false' or 'don't know'. Here was a man who had closed his heart to what he truly wanted *and* to who he authentically was. Just as he had given me what is called an *evoking* lifeshock, I had given him one in return when I laughed with sheer relief. This is how *evoking* lifeshocks work. They are often pleasant, easy to like, but anything that opens the heart qualifies – including my boyfriend telling me he had slept with a man. My instant acceptance of his sexuality opened his heart in turn. It reflected what he was hoping for from his parents. It encouraged him to tell the full truth to *someone* and, in so doing, unburden his spirit.

That very evening, I drove him to his mum's house before his reactive mind could convince him to back out of telling them, which is what he had now chosen to do. It was not what he feared at all. It took some adjustment, but they had suspected it for quite some time – a suspicion his mum had put aside after he brought me home to meet her. Acceptance of his sexuality followed and, more importantly, his own acceptance of himself. This primed him for love. Three months later he moved into a flat in my street with his new boyfriend and we hung out as the friends we were far better suited to being.

Life does not just evoke us to love others. It bears divine witness to how lovable we really are and evokes us to *let love in.* That conversation was as much a turning point for me as it was for him. It helped me rejoice in my femininity and stop apologising for it. It gave me complete clarity that I wanted a man who wanted *all* of my womanliness, from its curves to its compassion, from its passion to its power. This was the self-acceptance I had been seeking for most of my life.

Distinct from *limiting* and *exposing* lifeshocks, *evoking* lifeshocks speak to our relationships, eliciting our tenderness and clemency, our empathy and lovability – not just in relation to people we know, but to complete strangers, perceived enemies, the planet we live on and humanity itself. These lifeshocks call us back to love.

Processing lifeshocks we don't like is the sleeves-rolled-up, snot-filled work of freeing ourselves from lies that curtail us. This is the work I have been doing for more than half my life. John did not suddenly drop out of the ether in a flurry of good fortune after Brad died. I worked my psychological butt off through all the years that came before him, dismantling my defences and planting hedgerows of self-acceptance through which love could enter. I listened to my evoking lifeshocks. I let them melt the hardened crusts around my heart and teach me how to love.

But engaging with lifeshocks we *do* like can bypass the lies altogether, opening the heart to connection and wonder. They are on offer in abundance, yet we often close to them instead of opening up. Sometimes we resist them directly; other times we simply pass them by. A sunset. A kiss. A warm greeting. A bird singing. A compliment. A thank you. The falling of rain after a drought. One summer, I was working in my Battersea flat when I heard the rattle of hailstones on the large panes of glass in my living room and the skylight above me. I had a deadline. The storm was distracting. I wanted it to stop. But the sound intensified as the hail hit harder and faster, sending a chill through my body. I noticed the muggy air that had hung over London all morning dissipate. Evoking lifeshocks were tapping on my windows in their hundreds. So, I closed my computer, walked barefoot up the staircase in a T-shirt and leggings, and stepped out through the skylight on to the roof. The sky was silver. My hair was drenched in seconds. And I stood, face up to the hail, breathing, opening my pores, feeling the stones melt like tears on my cheeks. It was exhilarating. I felt awake and completely alive.

And then there are the evoking lifeshocks we let in without any effort: a child saying, 'I love you Daddy'; a newborn baby being placed on your chest; a girlfriend laughing instead of crying when her boyfriend admits to being gay.

These moments are as unexpected as the ones we don't like. They confront our mindtalk head on, yelling, 'Wake up! It is not what it seems! You are not what you fear! It is *this*. You are *this*. You are loved. You *are* love! Take heed!' This is how life speaks and this is what I did for my boyfriend that day. He brought me his shame and I took him into my for-ness. He said it was the most complete acceptance he had ever experienced.

It wasn't that I was always alone before John. It was that I was alone in a longing that none of my lovers could meet. Within weeks of our first date, John took part in a More to Life course that I was leading. In some ways, this seemed like a bad idea, akin to having therapy with a family member, even though my training partner would be the one to interact with him. It also positioned me as the 'teacher' and him as the 'student', which made me very uncomfortable, but didn't seem to bother him at all. Others were surprised by this too and, during the course, someone asked John why he had chosen to do a weekend I was leading.

'Because Sophie needs to know that I can be with her awesomeness and still feel completely okay about myself.'

That chest-cracking lifeshock was when my heart knew there was no turning back. In one sentence, he had epitomised the collapse of all my relationships with men: the way they had invariably attempted to lower my sun and dwindle my light. Sometimes it was blatant, like exploding flares of criticism, competitiveness, aggression and envy. Other times it was subtle and passive-aggressive. But the message was the same: *know your place, do not outshine me, serve my needs.* For a while this suited me perfectly, matching my self-imposed unworthiness to the letter. What would love give me to show me the parts of myself I have failed to love? Lovers who failed to love them too. Sometimes the *absence* of love is what evokes us back to love.

In my mid-thirties, I let myself love a woman to see if it would end the loneliness and answer my longing. It wasn't just experimentation. I loved her. I gave it my very best shot and was open about it. She remains a close friend. But, in the end, I couldn't sustain this shift in my sexuality. People thought I had come out of a closet after many years, but I hadn't. My attraction to mcn was too real and lasting for me to relinquish permanently. But this relationship gave me a taste of what it was like to be loved by someone who didn't need to put me down. And I must admit that, to some unconscious degree, it had also been a way of giving 'men' the finger, which I didn't want to sustain either. It was bitter and unbecoming. It was as big a wall against what I really wanted as I could build. I had come a long way since my twenties when I either erected walls, which denied anyone access, or took them down, which granted too much. One had locked me in loneliness; the other laid me open to looting. I didn't want to go back to that, even if my heart was breaking a little more each day.

John seemed to sense all this from the beginning. A few weeks into our relationship he said he knew I was not to be messed with. He realised he needed to be fully in from the off or not get started at all. It was as if he saw the wounds that don't bleed and the way my gated soul unlocked in his presence. I became as defenceless as I had been with Brad, but with a greater intimacy and vulnerability. This wasn't an act of will as much as the sudden crumbling of a cliff after years of erosion. A total collapse.

During the course in Oxford, there was a steady stream of evoking lifeshocks beginning with John intending to say, 'That was amazing facilitation' after I led the first session, but blurting, 'You're beautiful' instead. This was how it went with us. Something was at work before and beyond us, as if our souls were throwing their arms around each other while we shook hands and said, 'Hi, I'm John', 'Hi, I'm Sophie.' One evening, I sat on the floor, with John sitting on a chair behind me, as a group member told a story called 'The Robe of Love'. The words floated over my head while John stroked my arm so gently I could hardly tell if it was his fingers or the breeze blowing through the window. On the second evening, he brought out his guitar and played Blue Grass music to us all, something he would continue to do while courting me, introducing me to singers like Maura O'Connell whose Irish folk songs found their way to the top of my playlist.

He also talked about his recent heartbreak, the death of his first relationship since Christine and the pull of the wilderness, that place where he could wander across the world's edges, touching that invisible, sacred something he had only really found when he was alone. 'Don't go!' my heart screamed, silently. 'It is *here*. I am *here*. Stay here.' I felt desolate at the very prospect of him being anywhere but at my side.

He did come to my side on the last day as I was walking in the garden of the abbey where the course was being held. We strolled slowly as he smoked a roll-up and asked each other about our lives as if there was no attraction between us. But again, our souls were stronger than our reserve and, as we returned to join the group for the final session, he took my hand and said, 'Sophie, you take my breath away.'

Of course, grief – which opens the heart – created a channel for all these moments to flow into me without resistance. Only an open heart can love and be loved. Mine was gaping that week. I had recently returned from California where I had attended Brad's memorial service. We had known his death was coming for a while. He had been living with Parkinson's disease and Lewy body dementia for several years. It had been so painful to witness the steady degradation of his rare and refined mind, I often prayed for him to be taken and felt relief for his soul when he died. But this loss was acute. My go-to person for fear, upset and outrage had gone. And the person who saw me more clearly than I could see myself had gone too. Ours had been a different kind of love story, a love of the spirit between a teacher and his student that left my branches heavy with fragrance and fruit.

Was it a coincidence that John appeared so soon after Brad died? Or had there been a man in my life who wasn't 'the man in my life'? I didn't see it at the time, but one of my girlfriends had. She had once said to me, 'I don't think you will meet your person until Brad has left this earth.' I told her not to be so silly and carried on loving Brad as I had loved no other. It sustained me in invisible ways. It had been enough.

But it seemed she was right. A vast space had now opened up for John to move into and grief had made me translucent enough for him to really *see*.

Neither of us mentioned meeting again after the course. This wasn't a holding back so much as a catching up with something that was several steps ahead of our awareness.

Our love was like a tugboat, pulling us along behind it. But I had enough awareness to send him a five-word text as soon as I got home: 'Got your breath back yet?'

And the relationship was on.

At the time, I lived in a flat on the top floor of a converted Victorian school with a spiral staircase leading up from the living room to a roof terrace. This looked across Battersea Park at the landmark chimneys of the power station standing like sentinels over the River Thames. When John first came to see me there, he gasped at the view before exploring my home and noticing how empty the fridge was. A litre of semi-skimmed milk. A tub of hummus. A Diet Coke. A ready meal from M&S. I resisted his suggestion that we go to the local supermarket, explaining how much I hated walking down aisle upon aisle of food. I didn't mind admitting such things to him. Our connection was too fine for false impressions. I wanted him to know what he was getting into, warts, weaknesses and all. In response, he transformed a trip to the supermarket into a romantic date. He held my hand as we walked down the aisles. He nuzzled my neck when we paused to choose products. He asked what meal I wanted him to cook me and selected all the ingredients for a cauliflower curry. We picked out a fine red wine and I laughed all the way to the checkout. It was better than the most expensive dinner date I had ever been on and set the tone for all that would follow.

Three months after our first meeting, I flew to Florence with a man who embraced my frailties and 'awesomeness' in equal measure. We wanted to spend a few days in a city as beautiful as what we were experiencing: a love with nothing to prove or hide. We stayed in a small hotel just a five-minute walk from the Ponte Vecchio, the famous medieval bridge that spans the River Arno at its narrowest point and hosts merchants displaying their goods on either side. Our room had ugly, vertical, black-and-white stripy wallpaper, but it didn't bother us. Nothing bothered us. We spent hours every day wandering around the city, talking, discovering, disclosing, deepening. I barely remember what we talked about. I remember sharing a chocolate-orange dessert by putting the spoons in each other's mouths and savouring the flavours like prolonging an orgasm. I remember how we laughed at a tourist T-shirt that said: 'Heaven is where the cooks are French, the lovers are Italian, the police are British and everything is organised by the Germans. Hell is where the cooks are German, the lovers are British, the police are French and everything is organised by the Italians.' And I remember him teasing me about the number of shoes I brought with me for such a short visit. In turn, I teased him about his obliviousness to what he was wearing. I had never met anyone less vain. One morning we walked past a shoe shop with a large window and one bright blue, high-heeled, crystal-encrusted pair of shoes on a display mount in the middle. It stopped John in his tracks and he looked at it intensely for a few moments as if trying to solve a puzzle.

'This is why you have a shoe fetish, isn't it?' he asked eventually. It has nothing to do with walking or getting somewhere. It's a religion!'

'Yes!' I replied, laughing and astounded by his determination to understand me right down to my toes.

He dived into my details and I dived into his. He told me about his life: India; Wales; Christine and her cancer; his love for their son; his years in the esoteric community and all he had learned there; his first home on a farm in Kent before his father died and how he was suddenly wrenched from this life to a small flat in London where his mother worked as a cleaner to make ends meet; the funeral he didn't go to and the goodbye he didn't get to say to his dad; his love for his mother who had died some years previously following a stroke. There was a deep loneliness that ran like an undercurrent through all his stories, the pain of not being *seen* and prioritised and appreciated, though he never actually said it that way. It was as if any expectation of such things had long since turned to ashes. And I began to see that the longing I met in him ran as deep as the longing he met in me. He showed me all the empty places I could cram with love.

He read my palm one evening and I can't remember anything about it except the sensation of his finger tracing the lines. He taught me about what Gurdjieff called the Law of Four, which can be expressed as the four seasons, the four Archangels and the four beasts: the bull (earth), the bird (air), the lion (fire) and the snake (water). These archetypes can be seen in human behaviour and everyone has a dominant trait. The lion character pads about, often wild-haired, holding themselves upright and feeling easy in the limelight. The bird character rarely stands still, pecking at everything, flitting from this to that, ever watchful, moving in nervous rushes, treading lightly. The bull moves solidly, head down, with heavy footfall, determined but unable to change direction easily. The serpent slides gracefully through the world, preferring the edges of the room rather than the centre, quick to notice the movement of others and effortlessly merging with the background. He said one of the things he fell in love with was my walk; that I pad like a lion towards the places he is loath to go. In turn, I fell in love with the light he shone in the shadows, his serpentine elegance and ability to discern the tiny nuances of his surroundings. We complemented each other. We each rose where the other fell.

Above all, I remember how we flowed into each other like a confluence of rivers. It was the few days between Christmas and New Year. Florence was cold, but sunny and teeming with tourists. I taught him how to 'Zen walk', which involves finding a space to move into instead of trying not to bump into anyone. You simply place your attention on the space instead of the people and step into it. Even in dense crowds there is always a space, however small. With breath and attention, you can weave your way through crowded streets like weft through warp. And thus, we navigated the city of Florence: finding the space, finding the opening, finding each other. Neither of us had experienced anything like it before.

Not long before I met John, I had more or less accepted Elizabeth Gilbert's definition of a soul mate as someone who will 'tear down your walls and smack you awake', but 'not as someone you can live with forever'. This helped me come to terms with my unmarried status and reassured me that a sprinkling of soul mates had crossed my path – not least among them, Brad. But here was someone who did just that for me, and I for him. Someone I wanted to live with forever. It seemed there was nothing we couldn't say to each other and there was nothing painful about any of it. On New Year's Eve, we went for dinner at a restaurant right next to the Ponte Vecchio. John was enthusing about the past few days when, as was his wont, these words fell out of his mouth as if someone else was saying them:

'I guess I'm asking you to marry me.'

'Guess?!' I retorted, instantly, as if that was the only word I had heard. 'Guess is a buffer word. It cushions you against commitment. What's behind it?'

I was expecting this question to reveal his reservations. After all, we had only known each other for three months. I was also worried he would think I was saying no. Instead, without defence, he unpacked it over the main course, ripping off some internal layers as if diving for pearls. I loved this. He was so utterly willing to *look*. And it was far from what I imagined, as so many lifeshocks are. Eventually, he explained that, while he hadn't married Christine, he had been married once before, in his early twenties.

'It was so easy to get a divorce when it didn't work out,' he reflected. 'That's what's behind "I guess", Sophie. Marriage just doesn't seem permanent enough for you.'

His eyes were wet with tears and his voice so round with sincerity that my reactive mind had no room to manoeuvre. He wanted to commit to me more fully than a marriage could accommodate. He was in that deep.

'Ask me again without the buffer,' I replied, reaching across the table to take his hand as the New Year's fireworks began to explode outside.

We married seven months after our first meeting. Initially we married legally, with a registrar and only immediate family present. Then we married publicly in a carefully designed multi-faith ceremony led by a priest called Roy Whitten, who co-founded More To Life with Brad and who honoured all faiths as beads on a single string. The 'hymns' came from Christianity, Sufism and The Beatles. The poetry came from Hafiz, Rainer Maria Rilke and Pablo Neruda. The vows came from us. At the party afterwards, monsoon rains breached the marquee, flooded the dance floor and made the poppadums soggy. It was as if the heavens had opened and poured blessings upon scorched earth.

That was ten years ago as I write. What a long, steep, metamorphic road we have trodden since. At this moment, he is at home with seven-and-a-half-year-old Gabriella, having picked her up from school, as he does most days, while I am on a writing and healing retreat. This morning he sent me a picture of the very first plait he has put in our daughter's hair (normally Mummy's job) and told me her teacher gave him a house point for his efforts. Parents don't get house points, but John does. John breaks new ground wherever he goes, just by being himself. He doesn't plan it. He doesn't suspect the power that pulses through him or the holy breath that permeates his corporeal being. He doesn't discuss what is sacred because he *lives* what is sacred.

John sees it as his role to help me be of service to the world as long as possible and, while he still works part-time for Professor Torbert, he is the home-maker. He does the washing and cooking. He puts the bins out, burns excess rubbish, mows the lawn and tends the garden. He goes to the supermarket to do our weekly shop and ensures everything Gabriella needs for school is ready for her in the morning. He says he wants to create a space for God to enter every day.

And he does.

And He does.

If John really had his way, he would have travelled the world with me these ten years on the spiritual quest he started when he dropped out of school and set off for India. He doesn't realise that he is a hand in its glove, that it is invisible to him because it encompasses him. The challenge for John is fully inhabiting his own humanity. Part of him is still trying to escape it, to skim across his humanness like a stone across water, never fully dropping into it and landing on the sea floor. This is why he often mentions his ageing, the slowing down of his physical capacities, his inability to run any more having damaged his cartilage as a marathon runner in his thirties – little indications to me that he is willingly inching his way back to where he came from and won't stay a day longer than he needs to, thank you very much.

But life keeps holding him here, in his body, anchoring him to the earth with a wife who has cancer and a high-voltage daughter who insists he plays football, carries her to bed when she's tired and catches her when she hurls herself into his arms. He is by no means perfect. Some days he runs headlong into Gabriella when she is detonating into another moment and blows a gasket. Then he shouts 'enough!' and storms outside into our apple orchard where the tree bark mimics his scars. His own bark snaps because he does not nourish it. You see, he was meant to fly off into the spiritual planes when he hit sixty, not be driving a daughter to school and a wife to the cancer clinic. Instead, we keep rooting him in what he tries to spiritually bypass – the sacred *on this plane*. We are the living lifeshocks that call him back to his humanity, his flesh-and-blood beauty and the Love that loves him through us.

I know this life is not what John envisioned when we met in an Oxford abbey and resurrected each other's hearts. Just two months ago, we needed to decide at which point in my decline from brain tumours would he need to remove me from our home: when I'm wheelchair bound (no); when I go blind (no); when I can't control my emotions (probably); when I don't recognise my daughter any more (yes). I want to die at home in my own bed and be carried out of the door feet first. I want John at my side when I take my last breath. I want to be as present to my dying as I have been to my living. But Life may not design it that way. And what I want for myself fades into mist compared to what I want for the two human beings I love most. This made our conversation necessary and easy. Because, in all the creases of our experience with cancer, there is so much 'collateral beauty' and so much love to be claimed.

Brutal as it has often been, cancer has delivered a torrent of evoking lifeshocks into our marriage, from when we first heard the word 'terminal', to seeing my daughter blow out candles on her seventh birthday, to my longed-for husband, whose surname made me more Sophie than I had been before, lending me his arm this summer so I could potter around the garden without losing my balance. A love that began at the deepest part of its ocean continually finds new tributaries to flow into. This is no bed of roses. It is poignant and acutely painful because being broken open *hurts*. This is different from the heartbreak that *losing* love can bring. Hearts never break from loving. It is the shield we put around them that shatters. This isn't always pretty. It is snotty and messy. The heart melts like a candle and changes shape.

Each chapter of this book seems harder to write than the last one, as if I am getting closer to That Which Cannot Be Named. At times, I don't know how to do it justice, how to give testimony to the miraculous ministry of lifeshocks or the love that seeps down like dawn the instant we find our 'yes' to them.

This 'yes' is pivotal and is, necessarily, preceded by 'no' in many instances. This is the difference between false positivity and true acceptance of what is happening to us. Lifeshocks can be ferocious. By definition they are *shocking*. Sometimes we need to rail against them, as I needed to do with my brain tumours. We need to permit our deep-down humanness to see nothing but darkness and cry out from our pain, 'My God, my God! Why hast thou forsaken me?' Only when we pass through the eye of this needle can we begin to fathom the *for-ness* that awaits us when we say, 'Yes. I accept what is happening. Even this, I accept.'

BC (Before Cancer), I would not have dared to write this book. Brad's widow, Anne, asked me to write it several years ago, but I wasn't ready. I didn't have the authority or certainty that being gravely ill has given me. I hadn't learned to walk the high wire. I didn't have a head for such spiritual heights. And I hadn't met John.

When, on occasion, someone suggests that it is possible for me to actually get well, to join the rare ones who cured the 'incurable', something inside me resists. It always surprises me. At first, I thought it was simply fear of getting my hopes up only to have them dashed. Tied to this is my reluctance to presume any kind of 'special' status in the eyes of Something Greater. *Don't get cocky. Stay humble. Keep your spiritual powder dry.* But there is something else at play. There is something at the razor's edge that I miss during periods of relative wellness and normalcy. I can't rest in certainties when I am brushing with death. Instead, my pores open like the jaws of a whale swimming through plankton. The tiny nuances of life get in. There are no filters, no searching. There is nowhere to go, but *now*, *here*. The crowds disperse and silence roars in my ears. Light sweeps the cobwebs from my corneas. Love enters everywhere. And, for a time, I feel utterly, ironically, alive.

This is a problem because I want to walk this earth as long as possible and there is a counter-intention at work. Sometimes, cancer seems to be a manifestation of life's insatiable appetite for awakening. It's as if I need the vehicle of suffering to encounter the divine, just as John seeks the divine on uninhabited hillsides and in hidden worlds. But it isn't suffering that pulls back the veils. It is the surrender that suffering can necessitate. The dropping of guards. The opening of gates. The yielding of my will to Thy will. I don't want my life to be in peril in order to bathe in the essentially loving nature of the universe, but when it is in peril all doubt about that truth is erased. Perhaps this is why I become unexpectedly grumpy when my body stabilises, as it has very recently. The filters return. The reactive mind gets its claws out. The fall of leaves on grass outside my window is less symphonic.

Since completing the 'Power' chapter, I have received more scan results and learnt that the new treatment is working – at least for now. I have regained my balance. My brain tumours are in retreat and I have been graced with another astounding reprieve. When my oncologist put my last two brain scans up on his computer to show the difference between them, I was stunned. On the first scan, some tumours needed expert eyes to identify, but there was one large white circle deep in the back of my brain that explained the severity of my symptoms this summer. Right next to it was the most recent scan and that large white circle had disappeared, at least to the naked eye. The radiologist called it 'a striking improvement' and it struck me like my first sight of the Grand Canyon had when I drove right up to it, quite unwittingly, when on holiday with a girlfriend in my twenties. Two hundred and seventy miles long, up to eighteen miles wide and a mile deep, two billion years of geological history rolled out in the blazing Arizona sunlight like a terracotta ocean with titanic waves rising and falling as far as the eye could see. On both occasions, I stood in sheer wonder of what I was seeing and stopped breathing in momentary disbelief.

These are lifeshocks to behold rather than notice. We can do this by relaxing the muscles in and around our eyes to soften our seeing. Instead of looking out from the ends of our eyeballs, we start looking out from behind the windows of our corneas. By taking three conscious breaths, in through the nose and out through the mouth as if blowing out a candle, we can achieve a meditative state with our eyes wide open. We can see the display of life, the nuances of its colours, the tones of light. We can walk through fields and forests in this state, letting what's out there pour into our senses like morning sunlight. We can see beyond the world's surface into the holiness of things.

This is a powerful way to open the heart and see things as they really are. Perhaps surprisingly, we can do this with the scan showing a large tumour as much as the one showing it has gone. In a way, that scan is *more* evoking because it displays the love I might *lose* and the joy I might be wrenched from on the screen. It also points to the increasing love I feel towards myself. My heart feels *safer* with the image of the tumour gone, but *bigger* with the image of it sitting at the back of my brain. Love doesn't lurk in comfort and safety. It seeks out the vulnerable and kisses all our wounds. This is what evoking lifeshocks do. Like them or not, they invade our isolation and call us back into connection. They hammer on our resentment until we find our forgiveness. They appear again and again, bent on melting the coldest hearts.

T. S. Eliot wrote, 'Humankind cannot bear very much reality.' For a period in my late twenties I refused to read or watch the news. I didn't want to engage with all that 'negativity' and wasn't willing to wrap my arms around brutal truths about the world I live in. Nor did I want to become so accustomed to all the horror that it didn't affect me any more. Instead, I focused on serving my clients and the students who attended my courses while closing my heart to the suffering in the world. Brad called me on it when I almost bragged about not reading or watching the news. I was on a seven-day course with him at the time and each day started with a reading from a recent newspaper article – to give us all lifeshocks about what was going on around the globe. Would we open up to them or close, respond or react, connect or separate? That's when I realised what I was doing or, more accurately, avoiding: the world's pain and every call to love it transmitted in my direction.

You see, we are being called to love every time news of conflict and violence lifts our head from our cosy lives. Just recently, an eight-year-old mixed-race boy was lynched in New Hampshire, USA, and nearly died. Reports of the modern slave trade abound, including countless children being sold and used for sex. Last summer, a friend of mine was pulling desperate refugees out of packed boats on the Greek island of Lesvos and, but for cancer, I would have joined her. The Rohingya people are fleeing almost unspeakable atrocities, including being beheaded in public places and gang-raped by soldiers. Hundreds of thousands have died in Syria while millions have been displaced. Racial and religious hate crimes in the UK spiked by 41 per cent after the Brexit vote. And hate continues to beget hate. We can turn off the television and throw away the newsprint, fatigued by more suffering than we can compute. We can let helplessness close our hearts, or we can keep watching. We can tune in and face in and let these realities crack open our sternums like surgeons with sharp knives. We can collude in the hate by pretending not to care or we can let life teach us love. In this sense lifeshocks are love-shocks. Every one of them is calling us home.

On 1 October 2017, as I was working on this chapter, news of the Las Vegas shooting came in: 58 dead and 489 wounded. One man stood at a hotel window with semi-automatic rifles and unloaded them on concert-goers. It was being called 'the deadliest mass shooting in US history' (which won't actually stand up in the face of its documented violence against African Americans and Native Americans). Former Fox News star, Bill O'Reilly, bizarrely called it 'the price of freedom'. The resistance to gun control actually takes my breath away. It is as blind and stubborn a denial of reality as humankind is capable of. And yet, thousands of Give-A-Shits lined up to give blood within hours of the shooting and heart-searing stories of heroism emerged: the man who acted as a human shield for a nurse who was trying to reach the injured; people who died helping others to safety instead of running to safety; the couple who got away, but returned with their pick-up truck to help more escape the carnage; first responders charging into the line of fire, and surgeons working twenty-four hours straight to save lives. This is how humanity meets the inhumane and how love responds to the loveless. This is love *evoked*.

These horrors are happening every day. When the heart stops, doctors re-establish a rhythm with electric defibrillation. They shock it back to life. *Similarly, we are shocked back into connection when we emotionally and spiritually flatline. When we withdraw from love, love comes after us.*

It is so easy to numb out and despair, to ignore the

noise that thunders in our chests, to join the shuttered hearts that give up on 'God' in forsaken bewilderment. Beyond fury. Beyond feeling. It is also easy to superficially turn to 'God' in order to turn our backs on suffering, to offer spineless prayers instead of actual help, or adopt a self-righteous, fundamentalist position that abdicates guilt, compassion and responsibility in one fell swoop. Either way, we go deaf to the lifeshocks, even when they are shooting at us point-blank. We add to the heartlessness. We fail to love.

But the hits just keep on coming and they will not stop. Love will not stop. It will rip off the decorations. It will sand down our rough surfaces. It will mess up our tidy corners. It will toss our expectations in dustbins. It will blowtorch our hard shells until we melt in its furnace. Because, as Brad so simply put it, 'The teachers of love are everywhere: griping, killing, demanding, bitching, resenting, dying, caring, asking, yearning for our loving response.'

In the wake of my deep relief and gratitude about the brain scan, I returned to this book expecting love to pour from my fingers like an avalanche. Instead, my sentences stuttered. My words yelled at me like angry parents. Doubt elbowed my fingers off the keyboard. The first three versions were aborted and fingers of tension reached down my neck to my shoulder-blades, even as I lay in the Tenerife sun on our late October family holiday. I wanted to write about my great loves and great teachers of love, but each became a bud that never opened, over-pruned and damaged by sudden frost.

I wanted to write about my dearest, darling, dazzling Gabriella, because of whom my love is bottomless. And

I wanted to write about the Lover, the Giver of Lifeshocks, the For-ness that reaches out to us through these moments and prompts us to remember how love-able we really are.

I realise now that I have been afraid to finish the book, that it might mean the fulfilment of my mission on earth and, consequently, the conclusion of my time on earth. *When it is done, I am done, so don't do it!* Oh my. The baffling, cunning trickster strikes again.

Love-ability is both the willingness to love and be loved. I sought the genuine article in both directions and it took me forty years to find it in a single relationship that would teach me the limits of happiness. Happiness is transient and turbulent. It is acquired, held on to and then lost. We pursue it in our ignorance, anticipating an omnipresence and mistaking it for wonder. But there is a difference. Happiness depends on stimulus. Wonder just is. It isn't ours. It is LIFE. We can step into it and express it, but we can never own it. Happiness is the bubbles on the swell of the ocean. Wonder *is* the ocean. Few of us are ready for that much beauty in that much fullness. We prefer the comfort of being up to our necks in angst and worry because it's familiar, cosy, and seemingly easier to contain. So, we protect ourselves from the lifeshocks we like as well as the ones we don't. We defend ourselves from wonder because once we are *in* it there is no more wondering what love is for.

I know how blessed I am in this. I know how many people never find this in a single relationship. And I know what it is to be lonely, to long for what does not come. The two people in my life who live closest to God, whose relationship with 'Him' is direct and intimate in ways I have rarely experienced, are also the two loneliest. Their paths have been so arduous and so hard for other people to relate to that they often find themselves isolated. As I write, they are both single. They both dig deep into themselves to root out anything that contributes to their suffering. They both love big. In the absence of human love, we can still lean into the Great Love that is available to us all, as they do. This does not necessarily bring comfort when the heart aches to be held in someone's tenderness, but it does help us put one foot in front of the other and take the next breath. Love evokes us in a million different ways: some soft, some tough, some seemingly merciless. In our self-centredness, lifeshocks will call us to love others. In our self-neglect, they will call us to love ourselves. And in our self-pity, they will call us to acknowledge the suffering of others, to put our pain in perspective and be of service to the world. We each have our barriers to break down. We each have our road to Love.

There are no cheap Easters. Cancer casts a shadow over the love I have been given, but it is cast by *light*. A couple of times John and I have talked about separating. Not because of a distance between us, but because I fear burdening his spirit. I don't want him to lose himself in me: my purpose or my needs. He has done too much of that in his life. I want him to stay because this marriage nourishes and uplifts him, but I love him enough to tell him he can go. We have difficult times. We raise our voices. We argue. We name the turds on the carpet. But, thus far, we don't let the sun go down on our anger. We just can't hold it for that long. We *work* at love and love *works* on us.

This chapter belongs to John. In many ways, the years I have been with him have been my most challenging, but they have also been the most wonder-full. Even on the parched days fresh rain has eventually fallen. The evoking lifeshocks persist like beacons in stormy weather: the breakfast he brings me on the mornings I feel too unwell to get out of bed; the supplements he lines up for me each day so I don't have to think about it; the kisses we exchange as we brush past each other in the corridor; his proud smile when we are out together in public; the tears that flow when cancer brings me to the brink again; the chevron of wild geese that flies over our garden on summer afternoons; the house full of toys I didn't believe I would ever inhabit; the dazzling daughter we were given a 10 per cent chance of having and the sorrow that accompanies the prospect of leaving her too soon.

John would change places with me in an instant and skip off back to the sacred in the knowledge that I could fulfil my destiny and raise my longed-for daughter with all the love we had forged to create her. But the shoes are on the right feet. His soul has chosen to serve, but he is not being allowed to live his purpose through me or withdraw from the world when I'm gone. He is being asked to look beyond me, beyond us. He is being asked to stay, to parent, to grow old gladly, to read the palms of trees, to witness Love in his own mirror, to see the clean space he has created for God in his own body, to walk the dog he thinks I only bought for Gabriella, to watch the herons rise.

Clearing Your Mind

The following process is the bread and butter tool for living above the line, in the 'creative mind'. It incorporates the first three practices: *noticing*, *truth-telling* and *choosing*. I have already given examples of these and outlined each step of the following process in the previous 'how to' pages. This is the process in full and, when mastered, it is an effective and reliable way to disarm the reactive mind.

Again, simple does not mean easy. The reactive mind will resist doing this and may well talk you out of it before you finish reading this paragraph. *Just skip this. Get to the next chapter. This is interesting but not really for me.*

Like all the skills in this book, this is best learned experientially and takes practice, but once you have it, you have it. I do about three a week. It is the most used workout equipment in my mental gym.

The Clearing Process

1. Re-experience a lifeshock (by going back to it in your mind's eye *as if it is happening now*) and feel your feelings.

2. Write down your mindtalk, unedited, line by line.
   Tips:
   To access more mindtalk, use 'if. . .then. . .' to
   hear the next line. *If I make a mistake, then I'm a
   failure. If I'm a failure, then I'm not good enough. If
   I'm not good enough, life will be miserable. If life is
   miserable, I may as well stop living it.*

   Then add, 'therefore, I have to. . .' or 'I
   should. . .': *If I'm a failure, I have to work harder
   all the time; I have to get everything right; I have
   to be perfect'.* Or else: '*I'm a loser. . .an idiot. . .a worthless waster of space. . .'* You may be amazed at how
   cruel your mindtalk can be and how deep it runs.
3. Challenge each line of mindtalk as *true, false* or *I
   don't know.*
4. Tell the truth about the lifeshock (e.g. *it really did*
   happen) and replace the lies with truths (see below).
5. In light of these truths, choose how to be and what
   to do now.
6. Visualise yourself doing it and being it.

For example

A man I have known for many years (I will call him
Richard) has been using this process since his twenties.
As I write, Richard is now forty-one. When he first took
one of our courses he had been taking drugs for many
years and it was consuming his life: marijuana, ampheta-

mines, LSD and ecstasy every weekend at clubs. He was using the euphoric high to avoid the pain he had been tucking away since childhood. At one point he took some very strong LSD and completely lost touch with reality. He ended up swimming in a duck pond at three a.m., convinced he was in the ocean. As a result he was taken to hospital, handcuffed, in the back of a police car and sectioned under the Mental Health Act. Some weeks later he did this process:

Lifeshock: Feeling the handcuffs being locked on to my wrists.

Feelings: Despair. Sinking feeling in my stomach. Fear. Terror. Sadness.

Mindtalk: (write it all down first, then come back to challenge it line by line)

> I am mentally ill – DK (i.e. 'don't know)
> I should be locked up – F (i.e. 'false')
> I am a danger – F
> I am a freak – F
> I am dangerous – F
> I am a laughing stock – F
> I will never get over this – F
> I am a fraud – F
> I am a failure – F
> I am the lowest of the low – F
> Everyone will find out – DK
> I will be laughed at – DK
> I will be talked about – DK
> Everyone will make fun of me – F

No one will respect me – F
No one will ever trust me – F
No one will ever love me – F
I will be alone – F
I will be unhappy – F/DK
I will have to run away and hide – F
I have to protect myself – F
I have to disappear – F
I have to change my identity – F
I will never be successful – F
I am a fuck-up – F
I am a bad, useless person – F
I am unworthy of love – F
Life is unfair and out to get me and take me down – F
Life is out to humiliate me and hurt me – F
I should be dead – F

Truth:

'I stripped off my clothes when I was under the influence of powerful and psychoactive hallucinogenic drugs.
I am a human being.
I have made some mistakes and done some embarrassing things.
I have fucked up but I am not a fuck-up.
These things do not mean that I am evil, that I should be dead or that I am unworthy of love.
Drugs can be dangerous, and taking them is not serving me.
Being sectioned shocked me into wanting to change.
I have a lot of courage and I can use this to stop.'

Choices:

'I choose to not take drugs any more i.e., I will not take Ecstasy, LSD, Speed, Mushrooms, Cannabis, 2CB or Cocaine.

I commit to being completely clean of the above drugs from this day forward.

I choose to forgive myself for all my past mistakes and find out more about why I made them.

I choose to trust what has happened.

I choose life and love.'

Visualisation:

'I see myself at a party, people offering me drugs and I am saying no thank you.

I feel strong and confident and solid in my choice.

I sense excitement about what might open up in my life.

I see myself being happy exactly as I am.

I see myself married with children.'

This lifeshock *exposed* his reliance on drugs and the fuck-up he had believed himself to be, but it also evoked him back to love – especially love for himself.

After this process, Richard kept his word and quit drugs. He continued clearing his mindtalk to keep himself on track and sought ongoing support.[6] He is now a

---

6 Brad had the greatest respect for the Twelve-Step Programme and we often send addicts who come to us to do it. Indeed, we generally don't let addicts engage in this work until they have reached the fourth step: 'Made a fearless and searching inventory of ourselves.' Of course, they need to declare their addiction for us to provide this guidance.

director of a charity. He is responsible for over eighty staff, over 200 volunteers and oversees a £3 million annual budget. He is happily married and his wife is expecting their second child. He is also becoming a trainer in the work that helped him turn his life around. He did not qualify to do this with a degree or psychotherapy training. He qualified by living it for nineteen years and using it to transform his own life.

9

Loss

And here am I, budding among the ruins, with only sorrow to bite on, as if weeping were a seed and I the earth's only furrow.

Pablo Neruda

Two Pink Lines

I haven't yet lost what I least want to lose by leaving her behind, but the actual losses in my life pale in the face of this prospect. Of course, it is Gabriella who will feel the pain of my absence, not the other way around. She will be the one left standing in a motherless space, without my chest to lay her head on or my voice to throw a blanket over her grief. Before I was ill, I used to say I would die for her. Now I say I would *live* for her. I would go to the ends of the earth to spare her this lack.

In a sense, I had already grieved the absence of her in my life before she came. I grieved her never arriving. As the years ticked by and my relationships tripped over, I slowly let go of being a mother, something I had once anticipated like green leaves in spring: too inevitable to wish for. At thirty-six, I considered going to a sperm bank and parenting alone. I even asked a gay friend of mine if he might like to co-parent with me so that the child not only knew who its father was, but had a relationship with him. We explored this quite seriously for about a year before deciding against it and giving it back to the gods. This may have been when I first realised that we can lose what we have never had. By the time John appeared, I had released my child to the graveyard of dreams, along with the illusion of finding a 'soul mate'.

Even when we first started dating, I didn't think about having children. I was forty, John's son was seventeen and Brad had entrusted me to take our business forward after he died. Besides, I didn't want to push my luck by attempting to resurrect two dead dreams at once. But this one resurrected itself without my noticing. It popped its head around the corner as John and I walked, hand in hand, around Battersea Park and little munchkins with chubby legs tottered by. The touch of his palm against mine seemed to send signals to my dormant ovaries. 'I want one,' I started saying, in jest at first, but then in earnest. 'I want one.' To my surprise, John didn't resist. He expressed some understandable reservations, but flowed into the possibility as if we were still Zen-walking through Florence. Our life together might be a little more crowded, but there was space.

We knew it was a long shot. I was forty when we decided to go for it and, following a fertility test, was told there was less than a 10 per cent chance of my getting pregnant. That 'lifeshock' was limiting enough for us to demolish any castles we had built in the air and to reconsider. We deliberated very carefully, aware of the responsibility having a child would bring – especially as older parents – and of the crashing disappointment we were likely to experience instead. In the end, we trusted life to bring us what would serve our highest good. We would be intentional, but unexpectant and unattached.

This was easier said than done, especially for me. I knew conceiving was virtually inconceivable, but the disappointments hit hard nonetheless. My business was thriving at the time and we were able to afford three rounds of IVF, privately. The first two failed. My heart sank each time I saw the single pink line on the pregnancy test, lifeshocks that both reminded us of our *limited* power in this situation and *exposed* my buried chests of sadness about the family I hadn't had. For a while, I wondered if this was the purpose of it all – for life to reveal the parched corners of my psyche and soak them in the sorrow they deserved. Perhaps there was a peace I still needed to find with my childlessness that being with John was offering me, and perhaps I needed to find it to fully be with John. However painful it got, I was willing for that to be the case.

IVF was not easy and the process became all-consuming when we were engaged in it. It was also weird to have sex taken out of the equation. On our honeymoon, John and I had spent four days driving to Andalusia in Spain, stopping to stay wherever we happened to be when evening fell. We had felt so free. He brought his Martin guitar and another he had given me for my birthday after I told him I liked to play as a teenager. We spent three weeks in a small villa nestled in the hills scattered with Moorish *pueblos blancos* – white villages – and every morning we sat on the front deck talking over coffee for at least two hours before deciding what to do that day. We swam, walked, explored the local area, made love *a lot* and he taught me to play 'Summertime' on my guitar. En route back to England, we drove across to Portugal to see my sister, Olivia, who was staying there with her partner, also called John, and their nine-month-old baby, Lilly. Like me, she had waited a long time to meet the 'right' man and it was wonderful to share in each other's happiness. I felt no envy of her being a mother. At that point, I was glad it was just John and me and had no idea how much would change when it wasn't.

Nor did the honeymoon stop when we got home. We were smitten and replete with joy. Whatever else we were doing folded into our bliss and became part of it. But when we started IVF, things changed. We were no less happy, but we were focused on something that was *missing* rather than present, which took us out of *this* and *now* and *enough*. An anxiety entered, a thirst. Following the first two disappointments, we agreed the third attempt would be the last. This was partly a financial constraint, but more a recognition of the real limitations we were facing. We didn't want to get pushy or greedy, but we did want to keep the door open a little longer. This time, we planned it very differently, stopping our busy lives and travelling to the Languedoc-Roussillon region of France for two weeks before the procedure. We slowed down and rested. We declared our intentions to the universe while consciously releasing our lurking expectations. We gave it back to life.

I remember feeling very peaceful when they planted two fertilised embryos in my uterus. John stood next to me, holding my hand, until we heard the doctor lift his head from between my legs and say one hope-saturated word: 'Perfect!'

Sometimes lifeshocks are that simple and potent. The moment I heard it, I was sure it was going to work. I didn't dare say so out loud, but felt the presence of Spirit in the room, a holy ghost. I talked myself out of this in the weeks that followed, my reactive mind dismissing it as silly nonsense and telling me to get ready for a child-less life. By the time I went to the bathroom to pee on another stick, I had accepted this outcome and was grateful to have found the soul mate I had given up finding. It was enough.

Slowly, a pink line appeared on the test, as it had with the last two attempts. But no. A second line appeared. John and I stared at it together, incredulous.

'Are you seeing what I'm seeing?' I asked him, my eyes glued to the little stick in my left hand.

'Yes,' he responded, wrapping his arms around me. 'Two pink lines.'

My pregnancy was challenging. I had a big bleed after ten weeks and thought it was over. It turned out I had miscarried one of the embryos, but the other remained. Still I continued bleeding and no one could work out why. In the second trimester, I was told to stay at home and stay still for the remainder of my pregnancy, which I did. I had regular ultrasound scans to see how the baby was doing and found out the gender as soon as I could. I would have been happy either way, but was ecstatic to be told it was a girl. The bleeding persisted. It wasn't heavy, but it was frequent and scary. Yet the ultrasounds kept showing a normal, healthy baby growing in my womb and the obstetrician said, 'There seems to be something wrong with you, Mrs Sabbage, but she is just fine!' And indeed she was. In every scan, her little legs were running. They were never still. The nurses laughed and told me I had an athlete in my womb. I could hardly wait to meet her.

We planned a natural birth, but that was ruled out when an ultrasound – conducted by a very determined obstetric nurse – eventually detected a haematoma in my womb. There was nothing they could do to stop it and were concerned I would bleed out if I gave birth naturally, so I agreed to a Caesarean section. Each step of the process required a surrender, a willingness to adapt to the lifeshocks graciously, a leap of faith. I was being granted the improbable without being allowed to take any of it for granted. My prayer was being answered, but not without some sacrifice and pain. This kept me humble and grateful. It poised me for inestimable love.

I was numbed from the chest down when the surgeon cut through my abdominal muscles, fascia, peritoneum and, finally, lower uterus. Twenty-four hours later, my legs would buckle beneath me when the nurse got me out of bed to walk.

The road to recovery from IVF and the Caesarean section was longer than I had imagined, but sometimes precious gains require significant losses. Great love does not come easy or free. It demands courage, humility and selflessness. And when the nurse lifted that little bundle of new life over the blue screen and placed her on my chest, I understood why Love, the pearl of great price, is a pearl of great *price*.

We named her Gabriella (derived from the Hebrew, '*gavhri'ēl*', meaning 'God is my strength'), with the middle name Grace (derived from the Latin, '*gratia*', meaning 'God's favour').

And then we were three.

After she was born, I stopped work and took nearly two years off. My new business partner held the fort and, while I was available for business meetings and strategic decisions, I didn't go out into the field to deliver any programmes. I didn't want to. All those years on the road, staying in hotels and training centres, coming home to an empty flat and empty fridge, were behind me. Gabriella changed everything. She moved into all the icy places and kissed them like spring.

John fell in love with her the moment I passed her up to him in the operating room, where he stood by my side in a blue surgical hat and gown. Having cut the umbilical cord, he looked down at her surprised little face and the first thing he said to her was, 'Hi. I don't normally wear this hat!' She had just been plucked from my warm womb with no warning or rite of passage and, while she didn't cry much when she emerged, she was clearly startled. But the tone of John's voice calmed her more than I was able to in my anaesthetised state on the operating table. The surgeon laughed when he saw them together. She was John's spitting image. 'Well, I can see she belongs to you!'

But Gabriella's arrival came as more of a shock to John than either of us had anticipated. Having raised a son already, he had some sense of what lay ahead and what might need to be relinquished to love Gabriella into being. He was looking down a long trajectory of sleepless nights, school runs, the trying-to-fit-in traumas of childhood, adolescent angst, all the mundane tasks of parenting and all the sacrifices therein. He had put so much of himself on hold already to care for Christine when she had cancer, to raise their son, to keep a roof over their heads through years of financial debt. He never said it that way. He had loved them truly and dearly. But something had happened to him when we met. The parts of him that lay dormant came out of hibernation and stretched their limbs in the sunlight. In particular, our honeymoon was now over – the nobody-but-us, dive-into-each-other's-oceans time, the quality of which neither of us had known before.

As we grew accustomed to the new member of our family, I observed John's mood change. He was still loving and very helpful. He played with Gabriella in ways that brought tears to my eyes. He sang to her. He delighted in my relationship with her. But a cloud formed in his chest and he became irritable in ways I hadn't seen before. None of this bothered me. Part of me had seen it coming. Having another child in his fifties was a big deal and we had long discussions about the challenges this might pose before choosing to proceed.

Of course, we had not entered into it lightly. I also knew he had found something with me that he had been looking for his whole life and that the clouds which had formed in his chest during the decades before we met had never been acknowledged or cleared away. I knew his 'no' to this situation, which consisted of fear rather than resentment, needed permission before his 'yes' could fully throw its arms around his new daughter. He hadn't given his 'no' any consent until now and it was a deeply liberating revelation for him to be with someone who didn't just accept it, but encouraged it to have its say. To this extent, the 'no' that arose in Gabriella's first months had tendrils reaching back decades into struggles that had nothing to do with her. She just delivered the lifeshocks that flushed it all out. He was way overdue for a dark night of the soul.

We left my Battersea flat to live in a bigger house in Twickenham, where I had spent some of my childhood and remembered being happy. Somewhat foolishly, we bought it in 2010, the year the sub-glacial volcano Eyjafjallajökull (meaning island-mountains glacier) erupted in Iceland, spewing ash cloud into the atmosphere for many miles and causing travel chaos across Europe. In the period that we viewed the house and exchanged contracts, there were no planes in the sky. Once we moved in we realised we were living on a busy Heathrow flight path and, when the winds blew eastwards, planes roared over our house several times a day and made the walls shake. This often happened when Gabriella was sleeping, which was a significant achievement in itself. She didn't sleep through the night until she was three-and-a-half years old. But it distressed John more than anyone. He became so anxious about it, he used to track the directions of the winds every morning so he knew when the flight path would change. To this day, he still shudders when a plane passes overhead.

My lifeshocks about John's state intensified until we went on holiday to France in 2011, when Gabriella was one. She was walking by then, which propelled her into who she was determined to be even in my womb. Those running legs were so frustrated before she could use them. Within three weeks of her birth, she was straining to sit up, then, once sitting, she was straining to *move*. We bought her one of those harnesses you can hang from doorways so she could bounce in it for hours on end. In France, she could run about in the garden, tirelessly falling and getting up again, strengthening her muscles all the while.

One afternoon, John went for a walk and came back several hours later. He hadn't taken his phone and I was getting worried. It was nearly dark when he returned, covered in mud and splattered in blood, beaming from ear to ear with joy. For me, this was a pure evoking lifeshock. I hadn't seen him so happy since the day Gabriella was born. He told me he had got lost in the woods and had to struggle through mud and brambles to find his way back to the village where we were staying. That's when I realised that green fields, thick forests, muddy paths and open skies were as essential to John's soul as clearing my mindtalk was to mine. Consequently we moved to Kent where he was born and his parents are buried. We have been living there ever since.

John didn't think it would mean anything to him to return to his birth-place, but followed my lead on it. It meant far more than he imagined, as if part of him recognised the place from which he had been so suddenly wrenched when his father died; as if he had left a big piece of his happiness here. His spirits lifted within weeks of moving to the countryside and Gabriella continued to burst into her delicious being. She was the first kid at 'baby gym' to do a forward roll. She dribbled a football across our garden at the age of two as if she had been Pelé in a former life. From autumn onwards, she spent hours jumping in the big puddles that formed under the huge horse-chestnut tree that stands like a guard at our gate. A true Aries ram, she continued to head-butt her days.

In between her bursts of self-expression, she wrapped her little body around mine to seek safety and reassurance, which made my cells sing. Just like her birth, there was no rite of passage. She was full on, then full off. There was no drifting off slowly to a story at bedtime. There was trampolining on the mattress until she collapsed into sleep, usually with her head on my chest. Once she said, 'Mummy, why do I have to close my eyes to sleep?' She didn't want to miss a minute. And nor did I. My heart had never been so full.

She was exactly four-and-a-half on the day I got the scan results that showed a tumour in my right lung. When my oncologist said my disease was 'incurable' and I read that I had 'one of the deadliest cancers in existence', all the colour drained out of my world.

Loss Lifeshocks

I have explained that lifeshocks are deeply personal, that what is limiting for me may be evoking for someone else. But loss lifeshocks tend to limit, expose and evoke most of us simultaneously. They confront our need to control things and keep things the same. They expose fears and judgements we have been denying. And they evoke our hearts by confirming what matters to us most.

I didn't lose Gabriella the day of those results and she is yet to lose me, but I have lived with that likelihood ever since. Sometimes it looms large, like an erupting Mount Vesuvius, as it did this summer. Other times, it lurks in the background like a black lake I can see out of the corner of my eye. Nothing confirms my mortality, exposes my fears or evokes my love more than this prospect.

I had known real losses before this happened. I felt the death of my maternal grandmother acutely, the one who made us giggle in the police car when they found a bomb in our house. I loved going to stay with her. She moved into a cosy bungalow in Worcestershire after my grandfather died when I was ten. I remember him vividly – his white hair, white moustache and kind eyes, but there wasn't enough time to really know him. He had been passionate about salmon fishing and, at the age of seventy, was fishing in Scotland with a friend when he hooked one. He was struggling to reel it in and called for help, but his friend had just caught one too. And thus my grandfather, having reeled in the biggest salmon he had ever caught, dropped down dead. They were found lying on the riverbank, side by side, and Granny served the salmon at his funeral. I thought this was all very cool. I thought she was very cool. She looked after us when my parents were embroiled in politics and I felt safe with her. She also made the best green peas.

At thirty-four I lost two friends to suicide in the same year, both of whom were in their thirties as well. One of them was a spiritual brother whose death shook me to the core. Nick (whose name I have changed) was a tall, wiry, elegant man with a not-quite-of-this-world ethereal quality. As long as I had known him, he had found the world a distressing place to be, although he did his best to participate in it through his work, marriage and friendships. But he was always participating in something 'other', like a nomad in search of an oasis whose waters had comforted him a long time ago. It wasn't that he ran from hardship. His yearning was to *merge* not separate, to escape a world too certain of itself to accommodate faith as fierce as his.

Nick once told me he felt happy at his sister's funeral the way people do at weddings because she had achieved the union he longed for. He often talked about 'missing home.' The clues were there and, when he died, my sorrow was cauterised by deep lashes of regret. *I should have read the signs. I should have trusted my instincts. I should have listened closer and challenged harder. I should have saved him. I should have locked him in life's wonder. I should have stapled him to love.*

But whatever losses came before, it was Brad's death which seemed to smash the sun into tiny pieces. I lost him slowly and watched him lose himself slowly. This was true for everyone who loved him, especially his closest family members. I write this with great awareness of their pain, which likely outran mine by miles, and in the hope that they understand how deeply I loved him too. As I mentioned earlier, Brad had lived with Parkinson's for at least five years before it was diagnosed and, later, it was accompanied by Lewy body dementia. These diseases joined forces. Piece by piece, he lost his physical capacities to one and his mental capacities to the other. It was like watching an eagle repeatedly snatch fish from the water and carry different parts of him off: his voice, his memories, his mobility and, at times, his sanity.

I continued travelling to San Francisco three times a year for our board meetings, right to the end. It didn't matter what we got done. It mattered that I treated him as still capable of doing things at all. In the few days that

I would spend with him at his home, I witnessed his struggle up close. When his disease was diagnosed, his doctor told him, 'Parkinson's dooms you to live consciously.' In other words, every movement took conscious effort. In order to write something, Brad needed to tell his arm to tell his hand to tell his fingers to tell the pen to move on the page like this. His handwriting got smaller and smaller until he couldn't read what he had written and, eventually, couldn't write at all. His hands didn't shake uncontrollably, as happens with many Parkinson's sufferers. Instead, they froze, and the freeze would spread to other parts of his body like ice across a river. Life was still teeming beneath the surface, but it was invisible and out of reach.

At times, speech eluded him too. When this happened, I tried to reach inside his silence for words he couldn't utter and lend him my voice for a while. This took all the empathy I could muster, but I became quite good at it. Sometimes, when I sat close to him, my muscles cramped and my own voice sagged, as if Parkinson's had broken in like a hooded thief to steal some pieces of me too. It tried to get between us, but didn't. Instead, it helped me fill the neglected cracks that form when we take someone's presence in our lives for granted. Some people expressed concern that I was still asking him to work and 'expecting' him to engage in board meetings when he was so very ill. But it wasn't about getting something *from* him. It was about giving something *to* him. For Brad, not being able to create and contribute was a living death. Our mettings gave him a chance to continue, if only in short bursts. And sometimes they brought him back from wherever the eagle carried him, restoring his lucidity for hours, even days at a time.

On one visit, Parkinson's laid him out on the floor for over two hours. We were in the open-plan living room that connected to his kitchen. It was just the two of us at the time. He was sitting in a large brown armchair when his muscles started to freeze. Normally, this eased off after some medication, but not that day. His lips were sticking together but he managed to tell me that these freezes happened sometimes and not to panic. He asked me not to call an ambulance, but to ensure he took the right pills at the right time if he wasn't able to manage this himself. Then, bit by bit, his muscles and senses atrophied like rotting apples falling from a tree. His eyes motioned towards the floor and I helped him lie down without any bangs or bruises before slipping a cushion under his head. And there he lay for what seemed like forever, unable to move or gesture or speak. At first, I was so scared I sat next to him like a lemon, frozen and dumbfounded too. I wasn't ready to lose him or grow up without him. I had no idea what to do.

But I could see the light in his eyes. *So. Much. Light.* I sat very close, cross-legged, clasping both my hands round one of his. My mind was screaming, 'This should not be happening! Not this! Not to him!' It seemed so cruel of life to bring him to this, so utterly unfair. Tears streamed down my face as I sat with my teacher, whispering, 'I am here, Brad. I am with you. I love you and I am here.' There was nothing more to say. There was just being and loving and letting that be enough. I knew he was in there, aware of what was happening, riding it out. At one point, I suggested it was time to call 911, but he squeezed my hands as if to say, 'No. Stay. This too will pass.'

Time seemed to freeze with him in sympathy. Occasionally, I reminded him to breathe and deepened my breathing too. I became calmer. I dropped my demand that this should not be happening and accepted that it *was* happening. I began to trust the lifeshocks again, to remember all he had taught me, to feel the presence of something that enters the stillness, that *is* the stillness. My sadness didn't subside, but my fear did. My heart opened like the mouth of a river and poured itself into his. Then gratitude flew over like a flock of starlings congregating at dusk to keep warm.

After a while, to my amazement, Brad's belly started to move. It rippled with laughter that could not escape his lips and the light in his eyes blazed brighter, like a cluster of camp fires on a moonless night. I didn't know why he was laughing, but it was infectious. It was emphatic. It was *yes*.

First, the movement in his fingers returned, then his voice. It reached up to me in an almost inaudible whisper that forced me to lean in close. 'Thank you,' he said. 'Thank you for finding me. . .for loving me. . .for choosing me as your teacher. . .for being my teacher today.' His belly was still now. Tiny tears escaped their ducts and slipped down his jawline. I wiped them away with a tissue.

'Why were you laughing, Brad?' I asked.

'Because Parkinson's has doomed me to live consciously! What else would Life give someone who has dedicated his *entire* life to living consciously? What else would "God" doom me to?!'

And there it was. The teaching, embodied. By now, I was massaging Brad's legs to get some blood circulating. And I knew there was a place this disease could not find him, where truths cannot be stolen and the human spirit cannot be bowed. I sensed a road back to reality rise before his faithful eyes and leave fear behind, in the far-off distance, wondering where he had gone.

'Be very careful what you ask for, Sophie,' he continued as I helped him sit up. 'You might get it.'

It's not unusual for a lifeshock to be *limiting*, *exposing* and *evoking* at the same time. This is very personal because lifeshocks have our names on them. They press on *our* perceptions, *our* pretences, *our* fears. Seeing two pink lines on a pregnancy test after three rounds of IVF was one of the most evoking lifeshocks of my life. But those two pink lines could be a *limiting* lifeshock for a teenager who has no desire to get pregnant. We open and close to different things, depending on what we value and the beliefs we live by.

Yet, lifeshocks relating to loss seem to bring the whole enchilada, whoever we are and however we are living. As I say, they limit, expose and evoke us all at once. We may not notice them all. We may not let them touch us. But loss is as inescapable as winter and its landscape is so much bigger than death. We lose jobs, relationships, youth, health, marriages, hope, memories, homes, control, appetites, dreams, direction, meaning, faith. We are designed for loss, just as trees are designed to shed leaves and flowers to shed petals. This is the nature of change and change is what answers our innate longing to grow.

But how we resist it. How we insist certain changes *shouldn't* happen. How we hold on to what we are losing as tight as we can. Of course we do. We want familiarity and security, comfort and control. And we hardly know how to let go. No one teaches us this as children. Despite the inevitability of loss in our lives, we are taught to acquire, achieve and gain, not how to relinquish, release and surrender. We are not pre-pared, which is also a letting go, a paring away of whatever might get in the way: fear, attachment, reluctance to be mortal. These are obstacles to releasing what we lose, including that which we deeply love. Deep love is not the problem. It will release a loved one in pain rather than hold on. It will mourn rather than moan. It is the part of us that knows how to surrender.

Love is what we surrender *to*.

Surplus Suffering

It is entirely natural to *want* things to be different, to resist loss. I did not want Brad to suffer. I did not want to see him struggle like that. I did not want to lose him. Equally, I want to be well more than anything. I want to be here for Gabriella, to see her grow up, to love her into life and teach her how to learn from her lifeshocks. I want a cure to be found for a disease that is devastating the lives of millions. I want these things truly, sanely and deeply. Wants are *true*. Not the 'have to have' wants I explained in the chapter about 'Success', which are just disguised 'shoulds', but our deepest longings.

The problem is not that we *want* things to be different, but that we *demand* things be different. In reality, life is a continual flow of victories and losses, joys and sorrows, peaks and troughs.

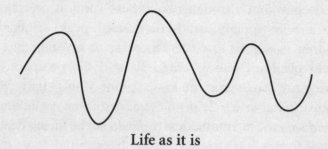

Life as it is

However, according to our reactive and expectant minds, life *should* look *up* most (if not all) of the time.

Life as I think it should be

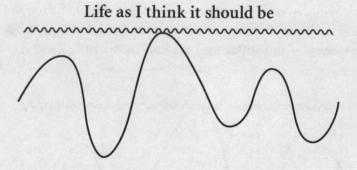

And this is *the* problem. Believing we know how things *should be* is playing God. It's an aspiration to omnipotence that refuses to accept *what is so*, however much we don't like it, and strangles our ability to *respond* – in all our loving, creative, discerning humanity – to what we object to so deeply.

In my mind, Brad *should not* have been immobilised like that and he *should not* have had to deal with Parkinson's or the dementia that followed. I would put seeing him freeze that day at the bottom of one of life's troughs – not the deepest, but a trough nonetheless (until it morphed into a belly-rippling, gratitude-infused peak). Equally, children *should not* lose their mothers at a young age. I would place my cancer diagnosis and the prospect of leaving my daughter at the lowest point of this chart. My reactive mind cried, 'It *should not* be this way! Children *should not* grow up motherless. I *should not* be facing death in my forties. This *should not* be happening! It wasn't supposed to be this way.' In other words, my life *should* look like the line at the top of the diagram. This is how I add denial, fear, anger, depression, defiance and resentment to the situation. This is how I add *unnecessary, surplus suffering* to the loss, pain and grief that is a natural part of living. And the distance between the straight line at the top and the bottom of my lowest trough is an exact measure of the suffering I add to my sorrow.

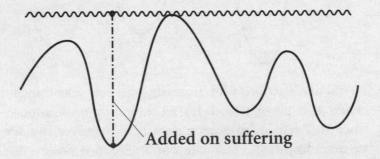

Added on suffering

© *K. Bradford Brown PhD. 1983.*

Perhaps this can seem deceptively simple. Much of the time, we are rational enough to recognise that life is not always going to unfold on our terms. And yet. When we suffer *loss*, when the lifeshocks seem unbearable, this is precisely how we add injury to apparent insult and utter misery to natural pain. It is no coincidence that 'life as it is' looks like the movement on a hospital cardio monitor, and 'life as it should be' is almost the flatline, the death-like perfection demanded by the 'reactive mind'.

Only from my 'yes, *this is so*' could I be with Brad in a way that brought him some comfort in the midst of distress, and even some power in the face of powerlessness. And with his 'yes' came realisation, gratitude and joy. Only from my 'yes, *this is so*' could I begin to simultaneously prepare my little girl and her daddy for a life without me while unleashing my creativity on the situation in such a way that I am still with them and still able to contribute something to the world. And only by embracing the 'downs' as willingly as we embrace the 'ups' can sorrow find its rightful place alongside wonder. This is what it means to be fully alive.

Loss slams our would-be omnipotence more effectively than anything else. It is the frequent and final reminder that we are not in charge of Life Central, we are not immortal and reality will not unfold on our terms. I now operate in a context where loss lifeshocks rain on my world. Just a few weeks ago as I write, my dear friend Annie died. I received a text from her husband saying she had 'passed away peacefully with Carmen (her daughter) and me at her side'. For a moment, I wondered why we say 'passed away' instead of 'died'. It seems to have become the new normal. Is it another way to soften reality's harsh edges and anaesthetise ourselves from mortality? Perhaps 'laid to rest' has replaced 'buried' for the same reasons. It cushions the blow.

Annie had lived with breast cancer for eight years. I had only known her for two years, but kindred spirits with cancer don't waste time or buffer love. In cancer communities, guards are down and friendships easily formed. I need to maintain some boundaries because I hear from so many patients these days, but some just find their way from the confines of my Facebook group or email list to the contact list in my iPhone and the vacant rooms in my heart. Several have died: Lorena, just after her thirtieth birthday, from lung cancer; Andrea, mother of three, the youngest of whom was four, from breast cancer; Katie, who married Daniel shortly after her diagnosis and died two years later, aged 34, also from lung cancer; Catherine, whose daughter was Gabriella's age when she died from breast cancer; Jenni, a script writer in her sixties who had the same type of cancer as my father is now dealing with, 'mesothelioma'; and Annie, who has left the biggest hole of all. There are many more who have died in this time – patients I had some contact with, but didn't know well. It is a world of profuse loss.

Cancer patients live on the brink, where there is no ducking the mortality we spend so much of our lives ingeniously devising ways to deny. This is where we learn we are neither indispensable nor inviolable. It is where we are too tired to pretend to be anything other than who we are. And, as I will show, it is where love bursts its banks, flooding all the stranded spaces in our souls.

It is a strangely enlivening thing to live with dying –

the likelihood of my own as well as the actuality of other people's. When you love someone with cancer – or Parkinson's coupled with Lewy body dementia – you need to be ready to lose them. It never seems to get easier, but it isn't meant to be easy. It is meant to herald a new season. This is the natural order. Loss is the spouse of change.

The Purpose of Grief

As far as I can see, grief begins where the widely acclaimed Kübler-Ross Grief Cycle ends. I have looked at it every which way I can and keep drawing the same conclusion. She breaks it down into five stages (the first four of which she later said can occur in any order): *denial, anger, depression, bargaining* and *acceptance.*

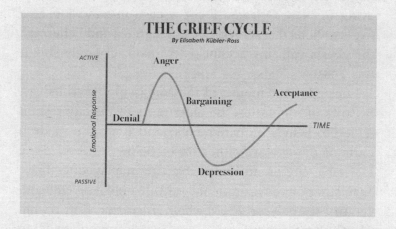

THE GRIEF CYCLE
By Elisabeth Kübler-Ross

ACTIVE

Anger

Bargaining

Acceptance

Emotional Response

Denial

TIME

Depression

PASSIVE

I am not refuting that this is how many people react to loss (or the thought of loss), but it seems to trap grief in a cycle that does not honour its essence. Indeed, the grief I have come to know and trust through my own experience hardly seems to feature at all.

I first bought into The Grief Cycle intellectually when I studied it on a Masters programme as a way to help organisations through major change – as well as a way to facilitate someone through deep personal loss. But not any more. I feel indignant for grief these days, the way I do when Gabriella's teachers don't understand her or recognise her gifts. It appears to me that, as a society, we have not done it justice. To a great extent, we have reduced it to a necessary and 'negative' emotion that has to be endured for a temporary period in order to find 'closure'. We have shrouded grief in black and borne it as a burden that weighs the spirit down. We have mistaken it for what it is not.

After school, I took a gap year before starting university, as privileged teenagers often do. I spent most of it living in New Orleans. I got a cash-in-hand job at a five-star hotel that served English high tea and I charmed the guests with my accent. I was excruciatingly shy. It was 1985.

Located at the mouth of the Mississippi, with its vast network of tributaries, the older parts of the city rest on its levees (sandy embankments) and the more modern parts of the city are either on or below sea level. 'The inevitable city on an impossible site' managed to thrive against serious environmental odds from the seventeenth century to the year 2005, when Hurricane Katrina hit. Multicultural, multifaceted and utterly unique, it is an artery for trade in the Deep South; an island *in* but not quite *of* America, peopled by political pioneers and lawless musicians that mainstream society isn't ready for.

When I was there, it had one of the largest LGBTQ populations in America, second only to San Francisco, in an era when AIDS was new, misunderstood and rife. It seemed to be one of the few places LGBTQ people could go without being treated like lepers. Known as 'The Big Uneasy', New Orleans has long been home to those that convention couldn't house and custom couldn't conquer. I fell in love with it.

I returned twenty years later, six months after Katrina ripped through the city. I had watched the BBC journalist, Matt Frei, return to the same dead bodies day after day, asking why no one was coming for them, calling for action with increasing intensity until personal indignation replaced professional objectivity in his reports. When a consultant who worked for the US government asked me to come and meet some of the city's leaders, I wanted to see if I could help. By the time I arrived, the whereabouts of tens of thousands remained unknown and the once thriving French Quarter was a shadow of itself. Bodies were still being found in the Ninth Ward and St Bernard's Parish, two of the poorest and worst-hit regions. I visited both. The houses were piles of rotting tinder. Cars were buried beneath rubble or rusting in driveways. People were still picking through the rubble for remnants of their homes and lives. I had to pinch myself to remember I was in North America, land of wealth and power and opportunity. The citizens of New Orleans were still counting the days and mounting loss, waiting, standing on tiptoes to see what their leaders would do to help them.

My visit was brief, but intense. In one week, I met politicians, community leaders, residents who had lost their homes and others still looking for their families. But the person who taught me about what gives birth to grief was Ricki, the bellman at my hotel. He was a tall, slightly overweight African American in his forties who gave me a Southern welcome as warm as a steaming bowl of gumbo on a chilly winter's day. The hotel was high and my room was on one of the top floors. As we stepped into the elevator, I noticed his elbow was bleeding and asked if he was okay. This simple kindness seemed to open his heart like a peony and, in the time it took to reach my floor, he had eloquently related a series of lifeshocks about Katrina. They seemed to stream from his latest wound.

'I didn't cry when I gashed my elbow, even though it hurt like hell,' he told me. 'I didn't cry when my home blew away and all my possessions were swallowed by the flood. I didn't cry when the streets became rivers and the bodies of my neighbours floated past me like cheap timber. I didn't cry when I saw a man clean his teeth in the black toxic water. I didn't even cry when folks ignored the young 'un about to be raped just feet from the concierge in a hotel lobby. And I didn't cry when friends were trapped for days at the Convention Centre, waiting for food, water and kindness.'

By now, *I* was crying. He didn't know these were lifeshocks. He didn't know how these details put the scale of this city's loss under a magnifying glass. He didn't know how much I wanted him to cry. Perhaps I was crying for him. It was as if numbing out was the only way he had been able to cope with what was happening. He had been denying his pain. He had been angry, but not yet sad.

'What did you do with all those tears?' I asked as he unlocked the door to my room and put my bags in the narrow hall.

'I couldn't feel any of it,' he said. 'I just got more 'n' more depressed.'

He seemed to have been overwhelmed by the losses – his own and his neighbours'. It was too much to come to terms with, too fast.

There was no 'bellman and guest' divide between us by now. I asked him to sit on the edge of the bed and tell me the rest of the story. I made him a cup of black tea. No one in his family had died, but many in his community had. His wife and children were now living in Baton Rouge, a nearby town, while he worked in New Orleans and continued to bear witness to the effects of one of the deadliest natural disasters in US history – made immeasurably worse by the failure of leadership, and the lack of information and accountability. The lifeshocks continued pounding him like waves pounding levees.

Until he cried.

'I didn't cry until my daughter begged me not to bring them back to this city of unspeakable loss,' he told me. 'Then I cried. I cried with her and for them. I cried for everyone who lives here. Just like I am crying with you now.'

'Because the bleeding was so great,' I responded, putting my hand on one of his broad shoulders.

'Yeah,' he said quietly, as fully fledged grief broke. 'And it really did hurt like hell.'

Outside, the sounds of Mardi Gras 2006 reached up from the streets below. This is a two-week Shrovetide celebration when revellers pack the streets and floats move past, carrying people in flamboyant costumes and masks. It is a hurricane of feathers, jazz, Cajun food, alcohol, dancing, coconut painting and unrelenting festivities – notoriously the wildest festival in the country. People throw beads off the floats and those on the streets try to catch them: purple to symbolise justice, gold to represent power and green to signify faith. That year it was more memorial than celebration, a mighty funeral procession in true New Orleans style. 'Homeland Insecurity' banners and images of people being herded into melting pots floated down Canal Street. Those who had returned home reached up as if grasping for beads of hope – not waving, as the media reported, but still drowning and calling for help. It became an outlet for grief, outrage and the irrepressible Southern Spirit.

That day I simply sat with Ricki and his grief, which *began* with his acceptance of what had happened. This was evoked by his daughter's request not to return and, in part, by a stranger in a lift who noticed his bleeding elbow. It was a beginning, not an end, a big step on the long road towards healing. It was also a glimpse of the grief that would later walk with me, lovingly, through my days. By the time Ricki left to help another hotel guest, there was a bounce in his step that hadn't been there before.

I didn't engage in denial when Brad died. I was very ready for it and relieved for him when it came. I was grateful he had been released from his suffering, his inability to recognise his wife some days, the paranoia that invaded his last days because of the dementia. In the end, he had to be strapped down on a gurney and hospitalised because he became violent and was no longer in his right mind. I later learned that his doctors said there was no physical reason for him to die that night, but his last lucid words to a lifelong friend who visited him a few hours before his passing were, 'I want to go home.' She thought he meant home to his wife, but he meant *Home*, to That Which Is. I like to think he chose to die with as much intention and consciousness as he had chosen to live.

I don't recall feeling 'depressed' in the months after he died. I remember crying a lot, mostly in private because I didn't want to seem greedy with my grief. For a while, I felt like a ship adrift at sea without a compass. He had been my compass in so many ways. I do remember feeling angry after his memorial service – not because he had gone, but because divisions surfaced among the tribe he left behind that had been cloaked by his unifying presence. Apparently, this often happens after a great leader or teacher dies. He didn't name an 'heir' and, consequently, a few self-anointed heirs began vying for leadership. Conflicts and resentments surfaced that begged our attention. And, for me, grief was seconds beneath the surface for some years to follow.

In all the time I knew him, I had never seen Brad in a state of deep grief. In fact, until my last visits with him, I hardly saw his grief at all. His life was scarred with losses, including the death of his eldest son, Kenny, from a heroin overdose some years before I met him. I often wondered how he alchemised that experience, but he rarely spoke of it. He rarely spoke of grief. Nor did he teach me very much about it. He assigned it to the 'creative mind' (above the line), where it belongs, and created a 'lamentation' process for his advanced students, which took them into the belly of their unspoken pain.

But I never saw *his* pain in that way. His death delivered me into grief's arms in ways it would take me years to fathom, but even then I missed the true gifts that it had to offer. For all he taught me about human emotions, grief remained the one I was least prepared for when he left and cancer came.

As I discovered in the first months after my diagnosis, according to Chinese medicine grief is held in the lungs, a revelation that led me to unlock decades of grief that I had never acknowledged. This discovery, combined with my sorrow at the thought of not raising Gabriella, took me deep into grief's hidden vaults.

For twelve nights in a row I did not sleep. At all. I lay in my devastation, eyes wide open, trying to accept the unacceptable. During this period, we sent our medical records to a pioneering oncologist in Mexico who was reversing stage four cancer in some instances and 'didn't turn patients down.' For the two eternal weeks that we waited to hear from him, he became the lighthouse in our stormy seas. John took the call when it finally came. I was putting Gabriella to bed at the time. This involved lying next to her while she snuggled into my armpit and kneed me in the ribs a dozen times before her perpetually moving legs finally gave up the ghost. She looked up at me and said, 'Mummy, my legs won't let me sleep,' as if they had a life of their own. I wondered where they would carry her in the future and if I would be there to see it. I wondered. I yearned. I prayed.

John said walking up the stairs that evening was the steepest climb of his life. He had to tell me that the oncologist who doesn't turn patients down had turned me down; I was that far gone.

Grief didn't burst its banks when he told me. There was no wailing or gnashing of teeth. John was desolate, but his pain distracted me from mine. I could attend to it instead of cratering inside. I could kiss the top of Gabriella's head, now asleep on my left arm, and pull him on to the bed to curl up with us for a while and take what this moment had to offer: the great love we had found, which could only be matched by the sorrow we felt at the prospect of leaving each other; and our dynamic daughter, who wears her father's smile as she explodes towards tomorrow.

Four words. 'He won't take you.' This was the lifeshock that melted the freeze. It was also when I realised that grief, which I define as *the courageous expression of sorrow* (at least at its outset), does not feature in the widely-accepted 'Grief Cycle' at all. Denial is not grief. It is denial, a temporary shock absorber that refuses to believe what seems unbearable and keeps reality at bay. Anger is not grief. It is anger. It is another reaction against reality, a deep-seated insistence that this SHOULD NOT BE HAPPENING as it clings to some semblance of control. Bargaining (such as 'I would give anything to stay with my family') is not grief. It is bargaining. It is a would-be omnipotence that tries to talk That Which Is into giving back what's been lost. Depression is not grief. It is depression. Instead of expressing sorrow, we de-press it. We push it down so deep the soul itself feel heavy. Denial, anger, bargaining and depression are all below-the-line *reactions to loss*, ways to *resist* grief not experience it. They are all versions of 'Life as I think it should or should not be'. *They delay grief.* They do not belong to it.

Grief begins where this cycle ends, with acceptance, with *yes, this is really happening.* This acceptance releases our de-pressed sorrow, which in turn may bring us to our knees. Let it. Drop to your knees and let grief, which has too long been mistaken for that which blocks it, do the job it is meant for. Let it open your closed heart, just as love does, and drench you in sorrow's healing waters. This is grief's nature and purpose – to release us from the surplus suffering of 'No' to the loss; to heal the heart and restore the spirit through surrender to what is really so; to keep love alive and hold our lost loves close; and slowly, over time, to propel us forwards again. I have nothing romantic to say about it. It can be agonising. But sorrow is a cousin of love. Neither can be fully themselves without the other. Nor can we be fully ourselves without them both.

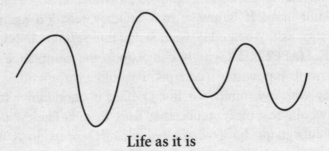

Life as it is

Bones and Love

In a few months, Gabriella will be eight and it is looking likely that I will be here to see it. I have been away from home for nearly two weeks, on retreat, to write these pages and keep my promise to my very patient editor who has extended the deadline for this book several times. One of the reasons I came away was because my stress levels were too high and my relationship with Gabriella was becoming strained. She was being age-appropriately defiant. I was needing to say things five times to get a response and often ended up raising my voice to make her listen. My reactive mind kicks in when I am tired and take on too much, a habit which seems to die hard. Cancer takes its toll on all of us. My fear surfaces in impatient parenting. I forget where my limits lie and what my priorities are.

At bedtime one evening before I came on this break, I asked, somewhat patronisingly, 'Where has my helpful girl gone?' – to which she replied, 'Where has my happy mummy gone? You are so grumpy *every* day.' For all my faults as a mother, I have raised a truth-teller, a deliverer of exposing and evoking lifeshocks like this one, which dissolved my irritation and melted my hardening heart. Sorrow scolded and forgave me all at once, reminding me what matters most, restoring me to my rightful mind and bathing me in love again. When I left, Gabriella knew it was not because of anything she had done, but because Mummy needed to go and find her happiness.

I miss home today. I miss John. I miss Gabriella, who has won the raffle at the school Christmas fair while I've been away. John sent me her beaming photo and I could feel him beaming for her. One of the dads at her school is a football coach and he started Saturday morning sessions for his daughter and other girls of a similar age who want to play. John always takes Gabriella. There are 'dad' things and 'mum' things. This is a definite 'dad' thing. She hasn't quite got the context of the game yet and some of the girls are a year older than her, but at the session before I left she dribbled the ball from one end of the pitch to the other and blasted a goal on the fly. The parents were cheering her on from the sidelines. None of the other kids could catch her. And John is still talking about it three weeks later. His 'yes' to being a dad again wrapped its arms around her when we moved to Kent, and has necessarily deepened with each day that he faces a future which may just hold the two of them. These periods when I am away are good practice. They find their way together. She settles into his love for her. And he settles into an unforeseen destiny, which he now acknowledges as his own sacred path.

Having seen a Santa a few days ago, who didn't look like the one she met last year, Gabriella asked John if he was real. Before he could answer, she figured it out for herself. 'It's his elves! They are all his elves! Because he can't be everywhere at once!'

This made me burst with pride. She finds school quite hard at the moment: the reading, writing and maths; the homework; the needing to sit and concentrate when her whole body wants to launch into the universe like a rocket; the fact that some of the other kids find these things easier than she does; the fact that she is the only one in her year who wears glasses; Dad taking her to school because Mum works and has cancer; not having siblings like most of her friends. But I see her fighting for her childhood, setting aside her suspicion that Santa may not be real and rolling with her imagination instead.

She may struggle to spell 'friend', but she doesn't struggle to be one. She has a kindness and empathy way beyond her years. Perhaps her context has shaped that in her. Perhaps I have shaped that in her. I am *far* from a perfect mother, but I teach her to feel, express and tell the truth. We have a deal about that. If she tells the truth – whatever she has done – I don't get angry. I have broken this promise twice in her lifetime and she called me on it big-time. But she finds it very hard to fib or keep a secret. She always dobs in her dad when he says, 'Fuck'. She knows the difference between who she is and how she behaves. She is beginning to know she has a mind that tricks her. She knows how to cry deeply when she needs to. And she knows how to love.

But she is so much more than anything we have shaped. She arrived with a wisdom that watches *Star Wars* and says, 'Mummy, when Darth Vader died his soul left and his body stayed, but when Ben died, his body left and his soul stayed.' – which is pretty much what happened. When she was four years old, she even knew she might have been a twin. We weren't going to tell her about it, but she asked. 'Where is my sister, Daddy? Her name is Emily. Why didn't she get here too?' This is a very real loss to Gabriella. She talks about Emily often and how much she wishes she had been born. When I see her deep joy as she plays with other children, I wish Emily had been born too.

Once, when Gabriella had made one too many requests for me to buy her something on Amazon Prime, with which she is all too familiar, I snapped at her impatiently and even threw the 'I'm not made of money' platitude at her. She laughed from her belly and assured me, 'Of course you're not made of money, Mummy! You're made of bones and love.'

Bones and love. For all my failings, this is how my daughter sees me. This the grace that meets my grief. And this is why grief has become a welcome companion, rising and falling like a tide, but always delivering me to the shores of what I cherish most. You see, love is less without it. Not quite itself. Grief reminds me to sow love more deeply in my family every day and, even as it brings me to my knees, it turns me back towards the light.

Brad is close again now because grief brings what we have lost back to us in mysterious ways. Sometimes I wish I could see him in person and teach him what grief has taught me. I wish I could unplug whatever sorrow he never got to name. We all have our blind spots, the places where our vision can't quite reach and the light doesn't quite touch. Perhaps, in my empathic way, I carried some of his grief for him and continued it beyond him when he had gone: his surplus sadness, his leftover love. I still miss him greatly, but I also feel his presence, as if his essence is sitting on the armchair in my bedroom, wearing a short-sleeved red shirt, a little Buddha smile and beige leisure shoes.

I need to trust that grief will also heal Gabriella if I go; that her losses will awaken her to her inner glory and be far outrun by these gains. You see, the light is not pain free. And grief is how we encounter the Joy that burns.

The Fourth Practice: Creating

The human mind is capable of remarkable imagination, both destructive and creative. This practice harnesses the creative imagination, the part of us that is connected to higher realms and willing to surrender to the will of Life instead of asserting our will *over* life.

Creating as an above-the-line practice is not about being artistic, although it certainly unleashes those abilities. Indeed, it is not about creating *things* as much as it is about *being* creative by aligning with the creation that is going on all the time. Nor is it a tool or process (although I am including one here that moved me more fully into this creative state). It is the action that arises from truth-based choices in response to our lifeshocks. It is the energy we release when we accept Life As It Is and become part of Creation, which comes through us in unforeseen ways.

This kind of creativity flows when we are utterly un-self-conscious. We become agents of Life, allowing ourselves to be directed beyond our personal ambitions into places we may never have imagined we would show up or serve. We become the artists of *living*; makers, innovators, ambassadors of truth and servants of Spirit. We source growth from suffering and turn our most painful experiences into canvases others can learn from. We live, breathe and act out of 'YES!'

For example

Richard's recovery from addiction is an example of pure creativity after he cleared out the lies. He started implementing his choices and living into his vision. He felt called to serve and built a career in serving the homeless. He listened to his lifeshocks all the while, uprooting core beliefs, discerning truths and realigning himself with Life As It Is. His is not just a life transformed. This was not simply a 'self-help' exercise. He has found his true path by responding to social issues he cares about deeply. This is what 'mastery of self in service to others and in response to personal and social lifeshocks' looks like.

The Grief Process

As I came to a new understanding of grief and found new ways to bring it to the surface, my 'creating' gates opened in a very surprising way.

In the first weeks of my cancer diagnosis, I remember sitting cross-legged on the floor by the fire at home, paralysed with regret about my life being cut short. It was deep winter. A dark, moonless night. I was alone. I had just come back from getting my final scan results and had needed to leave my car at the hospital because it was no longer safe for me to drive.

I kept hearing the words of my favourite poet, the Sufi mystic, Hafiz; words I had quoted a hundred times at the end of my courses: 'One regret, dear world, that I am determined not to have when I am lying on my deathbed is that I did not kiss you enough.' It filled me with sorrow. And as I closed my eyes to re-experience the lifeshock moment when my oncologist said, 'You may never drive again, Sophie', I felt my body tip forwards and my head started shaking, gently and evenly, from side to side.

'I wish this wasn't happening,' I uttered out loud. 'I wish I could drive and stay independent. I wish I had more years with my family, especially my girl. I wish I had taken better care of myself. I wish I had met John earlier. I wish I had become a mum sooner. I wish Gabriella's twin had made it into the world so she won't be so alone. I wish Brad was here to help me. I wish I had done more with my life, made a bigger difference, written books, used my voice, shouted what I have learned from rooftops, created more of a legacy, let myself be seen and known. I wish I had learned to *run*, to swim across lakes, to dance the Tango, to stand at the edge of high escarpments without being afraid. I wish I had loved the skin I live in instead of simply accepting it, at best. I wish I could see Gabriella grow up, teach her how to ride horses, how to listen to her heart and learn from lifeshocks, how to be herself and not what the world demands of her – or what she demands of herself. I wish I could be here for her. I wish I could live for her. I wish I hadn't set her life up to be so fucking hard. I wish I could spare John this pain and all the responsibilities that will follow. I wish I could have made this part of his life gentle and glorious. I wish Life would take this back. I wish God would take this back. I wish with all my soul that I could reverse this, call it a horrible cosmic mistake, wake up tomorrow morning to find the world has righted itself again. I

wish for more love, more life, more service, more fulfilment, more discovery, more wonder. I wish. . .I wish. . .I
wish. . .I wish I had kissed the world enough.'

I don't know how long this went on. I can feel the grief
crash through the walls of my chest again as I write –
enough to take my fingers off the keyboard and yield to
its waves.

Because this is what expressing 'I wish' does. Wishes
are *true*, free of demand, keepers of all the hopes and
dreams and longings we hold most dear. Wishes are the
warm rays that melt our frozen seas. By claiming them
and naming them, by voicing them out loud to the
universe, we can set grief free.

Then, as the waters begin to level, we can breathe
more easily again. We can give the wishes back to life
or give life back to the wishes.

Some were beyond my control, but others were ripe
for the picking. They showed me what I may still do for
as long as I am still here, for as long as there is breath
in my body and creativity in my being. In an utterly
unexpected twist of fortune, they marked the road I have
been walking ever since. They resurrected parts of me
I had buried. They enabled me to create anew. And,
above all, they gave me back my sorrow.

If you want your grief back too and any wishes it may
resurrect, here is the above as a six-step process:

Steps of The Grief Process

1. Close your eyes and re-experience a lifeshock that
   touched your regrets. Feel your feelings.

2. Connect with your regret, remorse, sadness.
   Breathe into it and let it expand.

3. Say out loud, 'I wish. . .I wish. . .I wish. . .' until all
   your wishes are out. Feel your grief fully. (Shaking
   your head gently from side to side may release this
   more.)

4. Breathe deeply into the release until your emotions calm.

5. Say out loud, 'I release my regrets and wishes. It is
   done.'

6. Choose what to do now with all that you have
   been wishing.

Earlier this year, I taught this process to a group of
people in Leeds. There was a woman there who had
been coping with something for some time. Having split
up with her partner, who was not the father of her
children, her teenage son told her that this man had
raped him several times. This lifeshock shook her to the
core. Firstly, it stirred up old memories of being sexually abused by her uncle on several occasions. This had
a profound effect on her sense of safety in the world
and she grew up desperately trying to protect herself,
living her life in fear, believing it had been her fault and
that if people knew her secret they would not want to
know her. It was also her worst nightmare, the one thing
she had wanted to spare her son and daughter above
all others, but that she hadn't been able to protect her

son from. Nor had she suspected what was going on, which led her to question her own perceptions and instincts.

By the time she disclosed this information on the course, she had cleared a lot of her self-recrimination and blame. She had challenged deeply accusatory mind-talk. She had recognised how she had invested more of her self-esteem in being a devoted and empowering mother than in anything else, and acknowledged that this lifeshock had shot her 'good mother' drama to pieces. This 'good mother' had become a false self because her worth depended on it living up to being exactly that at all times. This painful experience was already moving her into a more intimate relationship with her son and into a more humble, forgiving relationship with herself.

But she hadn't grieved what had happened.

That day, when she started expressing 'I wish. . .I wish...', she lay on the floor of the room and wailed with her entire body for forty long, redeeming minutes. Her sobs rose and fell like ocean waves in a storm. She went to the depths of it, giving permission to everyone else to empty their sorrow into the room. It was one of the most moving things I have ever witnessed.

I stood in the middle of this outpouring of grief and let it wash through my body like a holy river. This was the unpredictable and remarkable healing that cancer had taught me, the gift I could now give others, the peace I could now pass on. I felt as if I had become the eye of the storm, perfectly still, perfectly calm, being used by The Mystery. Its wonders to perform.

Creating is how we align with the Creation that shapes us all. . .

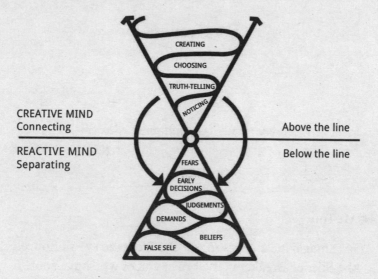

Copyright © K Bradford Brown 1984.

Forgiveness

Forgiveness is the final form of love.

Reinhold Niebuhr

#MeToo

Time magazine's 'Person of the Year 2017' honoured 'The Silence Breakers', the brave voices who have spoken up about a pandemic of sexual assault that has been boiling below the surface for aeons. Some of these voices are male. Most are female. The five people on the cover are all women, but the people who have declared 'me too' seem to span all classes, races, nationalities and occupations. The hashtag *#MeToo*, first used by a social activist called Tarana Burke and popularised by the actor Alyssa Milano ten years later, was used on Facebook by nearly five million people within twenty-four hours of Alyssa's original tweet. As I write, it has trended in at least eighty-five countries as an onslaught of exposing lifeshocks are flooding social media on a global scale. As *Time* reports, 'These silence breakers have started a revolution of refusal, gathering strength by the day, and in the past two months alone, their collective anger has spurred immediate and shocking results: nearly every day CEOs have been fired, moguls toppled, icons disgraced. In some cases, criminal charges have been brought.'

My own Facebook wall was deluged with stories: touching, harrowing, inspiring, bold, resilient, authentic, bitter, defiant, tender, raw, graphic, humbling, bruised and enraged. I wanted to add my voice immediately, to join a movement that matters to me and so many. I wrote several posts, but discarded all of them. Doubt kicked in. Depreciation. Comparison. An erosion of my own experiences. A fear of belittling the really brutal cases by chiming in with the lesser infringements on my person. I kept thinking of Nadia Murad, the Yazidi woman represented by the human rights lawyer, Amal Clooney, at the United Nations, who was trafficked as a sex slave by Islamic State at the age of nineteen and subjected to repeated beatings, gang rapes and cigarette burnings before she managed to escape. I kept thinking of the thousands of Yazidi women like her whose families were murdered before they too were trafficked as sex slaves. I recall the brutal gang rape of a twenty-three-year-old woman on a bus in India just a few years ago, where gang rape is rife. She died of her injuries two weeks later and, perhaps, as the BBC's Geeta Pandey suggests, triggered India's #MeToo movement, which has been gaining momentum ever since.

And then there are the approximated two million children who are victims of sex trafficking each year. That we have to approximate such a thing is a mind-boggling tragedy that few of us want to contemplate. Of course, this doesn't include the tens of thousands of children needing protection from abuse in their own homes in the

UK alone. Sometimes, the sheer scale of it makes my blood boil, but more disturbing are the days when my blood runs cold.

This is how I know that my anger has morphed into resentment. It slides underground and turns to ice. I appear to be calm, detached, indifferent. I allow resentment to banish the heartbroken helplessness that seems too much to feel and bear.

Brad defined resentment as *'ill will held over time towards someone or something for seemingly good reasons.'*

Well, what better reasons could I have for resenting than the violation of women and children by *sick, selfish, depraved, evil* adults – make that *men* – who have *no business walking this earth*?

See how absolute my condemnation, how righteous and unforgiving? That's the ice in my veins, a total intolerance for what I often see as inexcusable and unforgiveable. This is where what I like to think of my enlightened compassion for the human race seems to draw its line.

I'm not sure when my resentment towards 'men' began. I remember resenting my brother for being handsome and cool when I was frumpy and nerdy (like that was his fault). I remember resenting his mean friends for taunting me instead of dancing with me. And I remember resenting the lecherous adults who saw my prematurely ripe teenage body as a green light to have a good grope. By the time I went to university I was primed to join an embittered band of furious feminists who all too often masked man-hating as a human rights movement. This is radically different from the fierce, but forgiving feminism that advocates for equality of the sexes, the value of women's culture and the sacredness of Mother Earth, all of which I continue to espouse.

I wasn't really aware of my vitriol in my student days. I felt intellectually vindicated in my position, convinced of its reasonable and progressive purpose. When I wrote my feminist dissertation, I decried the phallocentric norms that strangled female expression (which they did) and compelled the likes of Mary Anne Evans to write under the male pseudonym, George Eliot. Mostly, my thesis was about how women had been silenced into insanity for centuries with practices like 'the rest cure', so eloquently described by Charlotte Perkins Gilman in *The Yellow Wallpaper*, which confined women with so-called 'nervous dispositions' to doing nothing except stare at the wallpaper in their rooms. There was a decent amount of truth in my well-received thesis, but the subtext was stained with bitterness.

That's the trouble with resentment. It is a cunning and largely invisible force that passes through our systems like the indiscernible pesticides on our food and toxins in our environment. We think we are eating vegetables, not chemicals, and breathing air, not poison. Resentment is so deliciously righteous and holier-than-thou. On the face of it, I loved men. I desired men. I slept with men. I sought their approval. I didn't think I was enough without one at my side. But my 'good reasons' stacked up over time while an underground reservoir of ill will twisted and turned through my being like a sewage system.

My ill will was easier to spot when dealing with blatant acts of aggression, like being rubbed up at a wedding by a friend's married uncle when I was seventeen and feeling my boyfriend's hands around my throat after a blistering argument. On these occasions, my own anger was hot, blaring, out in the open where I could see it. I could work on it. I could clear my mindtalk. I could release my rage with awareness and intent, then let it go. The lifeshocks were blatant enough for me to ask what I might learn and gain from them, even in retrospect. I was twenty-five when I first discovered how lifeshocks limited, exposed and evoked me into being myself. This didn't mean those experiences weren't painful. It meant I didn't hold on to them and they didn't hold on to me.

It was the more subtle, run-of-the-mill, seemingly acceptable but passive-aggressive encounters that slipped past my awareness into the reservoir beneath. Aggression is served straight up. It may be scary or brutal, but you know what it is when it comes at you. Wherever the actual punches land, its energy strikes directly between the eyes. Passive-aggression is hostility dressed up as 'sure, I'd be happy to'. It will smile and polish its halo while sticking the knife in. Then it will say, 'No, I'm not angry. I'm fine. Why are you getting so upset? Don't be so sensitive.' These days, I recognise it very easily. It goes right up my rectum and my rectum never lies. Passive-aggression is also the epitome of resentment: undiluted ill will pretending that it isn't.

I brewed my cauldron slowly. Bit by bit, I filled it with slights and snubs from the 'opposite sex' (note the adversarial and discounting nature of that term), being patronised and mansplained, having promising 'dates' turn into disappointing one-night stands. My first boss at the BBC was called Mario and I was one of four other women – three of us blonde (including me at the time), all in our twenties – who worked for him. We were known throughout the department as 'the marionettes'. Part of me found it amusing (the part that liked being included in the 'babe' brigade), but it pissed me off too. It implied we had all been hired for our looks rather than our abilities and my reactive mind popped it in the pot with all the other seemingly paltry discounts that came my way.

On the face of it, I signed up to the one-night stands, at least for a while. These were relatively few and far between, but there were just enough to make me wonder what made me unsustainable – a pit-stop rather than a destination. I smiled through them, usually with the help of some wine or marijuana, and took what pleasure I could get in my own passive-aggressive way, but I frequently left with a little bit of bitterness in my craw. Once, someone called me 'quite weird, but a damn fine fuck' before he fell asleep. So, I snuck away quietly after leaving an acerbic note that said, '*You wanted me for gratification. I wanted you for revelation. That's what I call a very bad lay.*' Which pretty much nailed why sex for its own sake invariably left me feeling blue. It would be many years before I indulged in a one-night stand again, but by then I was able to do so freely and gladly without expectation of more.

But there were some directly aggressive encounters that ended up in my cauldron along with the passive-aggressive ones: the time in St Mark's Square, Venice, during Carnival, when I was encircled by a group of young men who locked arms to entrap me until a friend came to my rescue; the time I was getting cash out of a machine in the Earl's Court Road when a complete stranger shoved his hand up my mini-skirt and violently

grabbed my genitals; the time a boyfriend offered me to
his waiting friends as if he was my pimp; the more-than-
I-can-count times I was hit on or groped by adult men
when I was a teenager; and the time I was raped on a
Greek island under the influence of too much tequila.
All this happened in my late teens and early twenties,
slipping past my awareness before I had garnered enough
self-regard to see these incidents for what they were and
protest.

Two years ago, I supported a woman participating in
a course I was leading. She was describing sustained
sexual and ritualistic abuse from the age of four at the
hands of her father, who had created a paedophile ring.
She had often been blindfolded and terrified. And this
went on for many years. It was one of the worst cases I
had heard about on these courses.

The details were horrifying and her willingness to share
them admirable. Yet, my heart closed more than it opened.
Her words didn't touch me. It was like she was speaking
behind glass. I checked I was *for* her rather than judging
her or recoiling from the horror. I also trusted what I
was experiencing and noticed that the energy in the group
was heavy. No one was leaning in to listen to her and a
lot of eyes were cast down. I interrupted her.

'Is anyone else in the room bored?' I asked. 'And not
wanting to admit it?'

Almost everyone raised their hand. At which point, I
told them to keep their hands up. I wanted her to get
the lifeshock. By now my heart was wide open to this
woman.

'What do you make of that?' I asked her.

She was stunned, but not defensive.

'They're not connecting with what I'm saying,' she observed accurately.

'Are *you*?' I pressed. 'Where are you? You are reporting these horrors like you're reading a menu! There is no *feeling* in your words. WHO is saying them?'

'I am!' she responded, with some strength in her voice. '*I* am.'

This time some tears came and she went on to explain that she had changed her name as an adult, partly so that her parents wouldn't track her down and partly to leave the 'victim' she had been behind.

By now my voice was soft and I was standing very close to her. The group was leaning in. 'Well, that makes sense,' I said. 'But I think you left part of yourself behind with your name. That's why you report what happened as if you weren't even there.'

This is what the reactive mind docs with sustained sexual trauma. The victims often leave their bodies or put thick glass between the present and the past. This woman was doing all she could *not* to revisit the terror. Part of her had given up on truly recovering, even decades later. She believed she was 'damaged beyond repair'.

At this point, she was so out on a limb, I asked the rest of the group who among them had been raped or sexually assaulted. *Over half* of the room raised their hands. Over half the room often do.

These are the experiences I have found hardest to forgive, but work hard to nevertheless. As I will explain, I have felt the cost of holding on to ill will. I have learnt that I am the only one who suffers for it. I have seen the way it forms like barnacles on a ship's hull, often just below the water line, and the damage this does to the human spirit. I have also seen forgiveness scrape the barnacles away so that I can move through life's waters with power and purpose, however rough the waves. I have felt forgiveness thaw the ice in my veins. I have let it put me back into the right relationship with my fellow man and restore my pride, dignity and integrity as a woman. My relationship with John would not have been possible if I had remained bitter, and my love for the world would be bridled instead of galloping free. So, in a spirit of deep kinship with all casualties of sexual assault, with a commitment not to see all men as perpetrators, a firm stand for this behaviour to be arrested in its tracks, a hope for *appropriate* consequences to be meted out, an equal hope that natural sexual expression is not curtailed and a refusal to resent any of it, I say: #MeToo.

A Living Hell

Nothing slams the heart more tightly shut than resentment. Nothing rejects evoking lifeshocks more fiercely than resentment. Nothing refuses to be exposed more stubbornly than resentment. And nothing asserts or defends its power more obdurately than resentment.

And oh, how we love and glorify it. We collude in it. We applaud it. We base entire friendships on it. We jump on its bandwagon. We create long-running soap operas with resentment at the heart of the narrative. We seek revenge for wrongs. We cry 'foul'. We build walls. We go to war. Nothing makes us 'feel' more right, more omnipotent, more superior, more vindicated, more elevated to the moral high ground or more martyred to a cause than resentment. It permits us to wallow in self-pity and indulge in revenge. It drenches our victimisation in the sweet honey of sympathy and even sweeter abdication of all responsibility for our suffering. It anaesthetises our pain (which anyone or anything but us is to blame for). It is as addictive to the psyche as heroin is to the body, and as poisonous to the soul. It is also as invisible and as inflammable as methane. We say, 'I don't resent my ex, I just feel sorry for him'; 'I'm not angry about how I was treated, just disappointed'; 'I have forgiven her. I just don't want to see her any more.' Many of us don't notice it and, if we happen to glimpse it out of the corner of our eyes, we don't want to admit it – especially if we are decent, kind, rational, positive, considerate and spiritual people. Especially if we are 'spiritual'. That's when it goes deep, deep, deep underground.

You see, resentment is insidious and elusive, the snake in the grass. This is largely because it is loaded with the payoffs I have started to name here. By resenting 'men', I got to be better than them, emotionally superior, more 'self-aware' (oh, the irony). I got to position myself against them in a pseudo-feminist display of righteous indignation and social victimisation. I got to bitch about them to girlfriends and collude in judging their defects. I got to jack up on quick fixes of artificial self-esteem by holding them in quiet disdain without being outwardly hostile. I got to impersonalise my perpetrators instead of facing the individuals who hurt me or even admitting what they had done. But mostly, I got to distance myself from the hurt, disgust and sheer embarrassment. I got to duck the lacerating self-criticism that lurked behind resentment's bolted doors. And I got to protect myself from believing I was at fault (which I wasn't in most cases, but feared

I was). *Superiority. Self-righteousness. Self-protection.*
Deeeeelicious.

But it isn't just the people we believe have done us
wrong whom we resent. We resent our nearest and dearest,
the people we've known the longest and the people we
love best: parents, siblings, friends, spouses, even our
children. It is important to grasp this. It is important to
recognise how ill will creeps into our lives like tangle-
weed, a dark green plant that grows flat on the ground
beneath other vegetation. We are completely oblivious to
it until we are lying in the dirt with its tendrils wrapped
around our ankles. Resentment just gets in without us
noticing. It binds itself to the petty as well as the significant: to the loo seat left up, the lid not put back on the
toothpaste, the kids interrupting when the adults are
having a conversation, my husband's back-seat driving,
Gabriella ignoring me *a hundred times* when I am asking
her to do something.

Resentment towards our children is probably the
hardest to admit, but there are usually 'good reasons':
the depth of their needs, the relentlessness of caring for
them, the sacrifices we make to raise them, the way they
take us for granted, the money they cost, the trouble they
supposedly 'cause'. This is normal, daily, family stuff for
many people, and much of the time our love for our kids
overrides it all. But little darts of ill will still strike and
they can accumulate into serious estrangement if we are
not attentive, vigilant and, above all, forgiving – which is
the epitome of 'easier said than done'. For this reason, I
am careful to tell Gabriella I have forgiven her after telling
her off for something and to ask for her forgiveness when
I have been unfairly reactive. And part of me still wonders

what she may resent me for in the future – being ill; not being like the other mums who take their kids to school every day; not living up to what I espouse in these pages on a minute-to-minute basis. That possibility is not something I can control, but I can teach my daughter to exercise forgiveness instead of expecting or pursuing perfection – including how to forgive herself.

Even when resentment is hot, vicious and vitriolic, we deny it. We are so utterly justified, so vehemently right, we don't see it as ill will, but as 'truth'. This is the torch that white supremacists proudly held up high in Charlottesville (in August 2017) and it is the wind beneath the terrorist wings that flew into the Twin Towers on 9/11. This is how online trolls unleash their acrimony so shamelessly and, in many cases, without even concealing their identities. This is how we commit rape, murder, child abuse and genocide without *seeing* what we have become or *feeling* appalled by what we do. Sometimes we resent individuals, as I resented the man who raped me when I was unconscious, and project that resentment on to anyone who reminds us of that person – like *all men*. And sometimes we resent entire races, nationalities or religions to the extent that we can't see any individuals among them at all. Suddenly *all* Muslims are terrorists, all Brits are anti-Europe, all Catholic priests are paedophiles and all women are whores. Resentment is how we dehumanise each other and still sleep like babies at night.

Are you feeling tired and a little heavy right about now? Are you wanting to put this book down or skip to the next chapter? Perhaps you are noticing a bad taste in your mouth, or are even beginning to resent reading these words, just a bit? *Lighten up, Sophie. Give me a frickin' break.* If so, fair enough. Why do you think I left it so late to mention this subject? We need to be *awake* to look at it. We need to be willing to scale the walls of our niceness and peer into the darkness we work so hard to deny. There are no exceptions. If you are human, to some degree or another, you will resent someone or something for a seemingly good reason several times over. 'Resent' comes from the Old French *'resentir'*: to feel again. And again and again and again. We churn it over. We recycle it. We chew on it for years. As I see it, resentment is the most cunning, baffling, duplicitous and dangerous force on the planet. It creates a living hell. This is what I am asking you to engage with. It is natural to feel resistant and appropriate to feel heavy. If you have come this far in these pages, if you tentatively sense or deeply trust the awakening power of lifeshocks, then this is where we pass through the eye of the needle – the point of pure, noncritical, ultimately forgiving *shame*. Or we can continue to use resentment as an illusory protection from reality and stay small, bitter and asleep.

I have a favourite T-shirt that says, 'I am mostly peace, love and light, and a little go fuck yourself.' I love it because it is both an accurate description of how I show up in the world and the pissy part of me I need to keep an eye on. The moment we acknowledge our resentment is the moment we unlock the cage we have been living in while believing we are free. Ill will is so very juicy. It is the power of the (perceived) powerless. It is the false fuel with which we launch our rockets, then wonder why we never make it home. In the absence of *true* power, *true* love and *true* self-regard, this is what we settle for in minute and massive ways.

Stepping out of the cage begins with *The First Practice*: *Noticing*. While it slips through our mental and emotional awareness, resentment shows up in our *behaviour*. Here are some types of behaviour that may give you a clue that you are nurturing resentments which you are unaware of:

Gossiping.

Bitching.

Complaining.

Feeling smug.

Plotting revenge.

Numbing out.

Shutting down emotionally.

Pitying *them*.

Withholding love.

Withholding sex.

Belittling others.

Self-justifying.

Lying.

Being cruel.

Feeling depressed.

Scheming for your own ends.

Displaying prejudice and discrimination.

Withdrawing from connection.

Being cold.

Being self-pitying.

Being abusive.

Ranting about *that person* in the privacy of your bedroom (often as if they are there).

Feeling hatred.
Lashing out.
Displaying false positivity.
Showing passive-aggression.
Succumbing to addiction.
Despairing.

I am aware this list is somewhat simplistic. Addiction and depression have complex causes. Withholding sex could be a conscious choice based on personal values. Numbing out and withdrawing from connection are often a reaction to deep, sustained trauma. I am not bypassing these complexities or putting it all down to one thing. *I am pointing out emotional and behavioural clues to the one thing we often miss among the complex causes*: resentment. We resent others. We resent ourselves. We resent politicians. We resent institutions like the police force and 'greedy' corporations. We resent entire nations, races or creeds. We resent drivers who cut us up on roads or tailgate us. We resent every lifeshock we say 'no' to (for as long as the 'no' keeps running). We resent the world. We resent God. And, if we don't believe in God (which is often because we resent him), we resent life itself – which is a 'bitch' right? 'And then you die.'

The price is so very high. Even so, until we can not just see the cost, but *feel* it and let it wrack our precious beings with the beautiful, burning, revelatory shame that breaks us wide open, we will resist letting resentment go. Its payoffs are just too potent. How to do this will follow and, with it, *how to forgive*. We are so often encouraged to forgive and assured of its benefits, but we are rarely told how. Forgiveness is not a concept or even a decision.

And, in my experience, it is bigger than any prayer. Brad defines forgiveness as *'the absolute refusal to hold ill will against someone (or something) for what they did or didn't do.'* Indeed. I have also come to believe it is yet more than that, but all this will follow too.

Betrayal

Fortunately, I learned the cost of resentment and power of forgiveness at my quarter-century mark. I prioritised forgiving the people closest to me and the ones I wanted to be close to. I was able to flush my unmet expectations down the river and drop the ill will, instead of allowing it to fester. I believe this was what opened the long road to John.

I also needed to forgive the men who had intimidated, hurt and mocked me. This became simple when I recognised two things. Firstly, *to forgive is not to condone.* I repeat: *to forgive is not to condone.* They are not the same thing. They are antithetical. Yet, all too often one is mistaken for the other and then it is no wonder that we refuse to forgive. Forgiveness does not say, 'This is okay. This is acceptable. Your behaviour is excusable. It doesn't matter. Please go ahead and walk all over me again.' No. Forgiveness says, 'I know my worth. I even know your worth. What you did was not okay. It had painful consequences and there are appropriate consequences for your actions. But I refuse to hold ill will against you for *my own sake.'*

Secondly, the costs outrun the payoffs by a million miles. Resentment costs us energy, health, vitality and emotional freedom. It costs us connection, love, intimacy, empathy, mutuality and compassion. It stifles our creativity and stunts our productivity. It denies us access to our full potential and bars the gates to our destiny. It prevents us from feeling, being and becoming. It shuts us down sexually or turns us into sex addicts, in a desperate hankering for the connection we have lost. It strangles self-expression, muffling our ability to say what we want, care about and need. It spits on grief, which can bring resentment to its knees.

Resentment makes us ugly on the inside, which often manifests on the outside through our drooping shoulders, tight jawlines, hardened faces and lacklustre eyes. It sacrifices our self-esteem to self-justification and self-righteousness. It turns our values into empty shells washed up on abandoned beaches. It bows our spirits and banishes peace. The object of our resentment does not suffer for it. Not. One. Jot. Only the person walking around with it pays the price. As the Buddha said, 'Holding on to anger is like drinking poison and expecting the other person to die.'

Resentment was one of the forces that seemed to be protecting the woman who had been repeatedly raped as a child *by her father* (and also by others). What greater betrayal can there be than that? Resentment distanced her from the pain. It enabled her to seem 'in control' and 'normal'. But it had also shut part of her spirit down. She hadn't just changed her name to protect her identity. She had changed it to *leave that person behind* and with it, part of her essential self.

'What was your name as a child?' I asked her.

And as she said the word, 'Lynne', with startling authority, the glass wall came down. Tears followed. An energy rose in her body that had been dammed up for decades. Her cheeks flushed pink and a half-smile appeared on her glowing face. The group leaned in. And she came back to life.

This was the price she had paid, not just for what had happened, but for the ill will she understandably carried and her conviction that she was 'damaged beyond repair'.

I worked with her a while longer, helping her face the fear again and reclaim her essence. It took time. It required her to feel the price she had been paying for the suffering she had meted out to herself by resenting and numbing and shielding. It took astonishing courage. Afterwards, she wrote these words to me:

'What stands out for me about our interaction is your clear confidence that I could re-experience the terror again and come out the other side of that. I had done this at times before, but had lost the reality of my experience again. When I did come out the other side, the clear message I got was how normal I was and not in fact damaged beyond repair. It was, and still is, a huge relief. Thank you for your support and for being brave enough to say you were bored.'

Except it didn't feel brave. It wasn't a question of 'how could I?' but 'how could I not?' It felt loving and easy because, in that moment, I wanted more for her than she had thus-far found for herself. I was *for* the woman, but not her ice-capped words.

Perhaps, most tragically and ironically, resentment also binds us indefinitely to whomever we resent, giving them power they have not earned and condemning us to remain at their mercy long after what they did or didn't do, even when they are dead. Just this morning, I watched a clip of a mother called Scarlett Lewis who lost her five-year-old son, Jesse, at the Sandy Hook massacre by Adam Lanza in 2012. He was one of twenty children, as well as six teachers, who were gunned down that day. She said,

'I felt like I was attached, almost like an umbilical cord, to the shooter right afterwards. All of my personal power drained out of me in the form of anger and through this cord into the shooter. I was dragging him around with me everywhere. For me, forgiveness was like a big set of scissors. And I took those scissors and I cut this cord that attached me to the thing that was hurting me.'

When I think of such a thing happening to Gabriella, my chest caves in like a sinkhole. I admire this mother so much. She has such excellent reasons to resent Adam Lanza, but she has chosen healing over hatred and compassion over poison. She even said of her son's killer, 'I think it is vitally important to remember that he was a human being too. And he was in a tremendous amount of pain'.

We need to find forgiveness for the seemingly small things as well as the big things. It is easy to discount them when comparing them to a loss like Scarlett's. But these resentments become toxic too if left to fester.

I have forgiven other perceived 'betrayals' in my life, including perceived betrayals of trust. When five trainers left Brad's programme to establish an alternative, seven years after his death, I saw this as a deep betrayal of Brad, his legacy and those of us who remained. I saw their departure as arrogant and potentially damaging. I resented their decision and many of the reasons they gave for it. All this made me right, noble (because I was staying to serve *even with cancer*), more loyal and ethically elevated. Mostly, it diluted the deep grief I felt at the loss of my friends and the loss of their talent in our midst. But I didn't hold on to this for long. I know better. I release my resentments as they arise, though they can still elude me until the lifeshocks expose them again and evoke me back to love. With forgiveness came the gifts that flowed from their choices and the responses of those who remained: the cessation of internal divisions since Brad had died; a recognition that there is no right path toward truth; an alignment of purpose among those who remained; a space for fresh creativity and truly collaborative leadership to enter; a reclamation of my own place among us; the return of prodigal students and a deep gratitude for it all. This is what forgiveness does: it *gives*.

Forgiving Others

When we open our eyes and hearts to the cost of holding resentment, forgiveness becomes the hand reaching down to pull us out of the quicksand. We will grab it without a second thought. But first, the costs need to tip the scales in relation to the payoffs. If that is the case, take another very close look at them: *moral superiority; self-righteousness; victimisation; emotional distance; the illusion of self-protection; self-pity; winning sympathy (versus empathy); abdicating responsibility; martyrdom; self-justification* and *vengeance*. Are these really benefits to who we are and how we want to be? Is this the kind of power we want

to wield and the values we want to embody? I hope not.
I suggest these are just *more costs*. And, if we take them
off one end of a balance-beam scale and put them on
the other, where they belong, we will not only offer
forgiveness to the person we have been resenting, we
may even be willing to ask for forgiveness too – for
holding on to ill will, for behaving in these ways and,
most ironically, for *becoming what we resent*. This is the
great tragedy of resentment: we react to someone else's
superiority, aggression, abdication and emotional distance
by behaving in the *same ways*. And thus the very literal
vicious cycle turns.

I am not suggesting we ask for and offer forgiveness
face to face. We need to be discerning about this.
Sometimes this may be very appropriate, as when addicts
make amends to the people they have harmed. This is
the ninth step of the 'Twelve-Step Alcoholics Anonymous'
programme. Even then, this is more about atonement
and restitution than forgiveness. As I said earlier, forgiveness is not condoning. It is '*the absolute refusal to hold ill
will towards someone (or something) for what they did or
didn't do.*' Ultimately, this is between me and me, you
and you. Its very purpose is to set *us* free.

A powerful six-step process which shows *how* to forgive
is summarised after this chapter. This needs to be done
with eyes closed and as an out-loud internal conversation
with the person we have been resenting. Expressing it all
in this way makes it a more *felt* experience, just as speaking
about a painful experience surfaces and releases the
emotions we had at the time. It also allows the cost of
holding resentment to flood the heart and body when
that moment in the process comes.

The following example is a process I did many years ago, but I just did it again for the purpose of sharing it and recorded it to transcribe here. This made it fresh, even cleared away some lingering remnants, and it can never hurt to repeat this process. Sometimes we need to do the process several times to deal with big resentments. This one is on the man who raped me in Greece. For the sake of this process, I will call him Janis (which was not his real name). I will also include some points of clarification at intervals:

Close your eyes and bring to mind the person you have been resenting. Say their name. Then own the full extent of your resentments.

Tip: This is not a blaming fest. If you say, 'You did this, that and the other to me' you are blaming, not owning. This begins with, 'I have resented you for. . .' Start each one this way. Go for the big stuff and the small stuff. No holds barred. Be as specific as you can.

'Janis, at first we had fun together. I liked you. I asked you out. Then I drank too much and you took advantage. You raped me when I was unconscious. I have bitterly resented you for that. I have resented you for assaulting me when I was in a powerless state. I have resented you for the blood, bruises and pain I woke up to. I have resented you for how you seemed to take our prior contact as consent. I have resented you for the shame I held afterwards and the blame I laid at my own door. I have resented the secret I made of it and held for many years. I have resented the mistrust of men that this experience and my resentment about it instilled in me. I have resented "men" *per se* because of my resentment towards you. I particularly resented seeing you on your motorbike from the taxi that took me to the airport the following afternoon and the way you smugly winked, smiled and waved, as if it had been a great night for both of us – or perhaps as if to say, "I got away with it and there is fuck all you can do."'

Share the payoffs you have received from holding on to this resentment.

'Because of my resentment, I became victimised and bitter. I indulged in self-pity. Instead of taking any action about what happened, I became passive and, consequently, collusive. I may have played a small part in you doing it to someone else. Because of my resentment I distanced myself from other men. I made myself tough to protect myself from further attack. I got to justify being a workaholic instead of forging relationships. I became an even more self-righteous feminist instead of the brave, authentic, society-changing kind I really wanted to be. I got to judge "men" as emotionally incompetent and even pity them. Mostly, I got to hide my loneliness with the belief that I was better off without a man in my life. I got to avoid my pain.'

NB: I use the words, 'Because of my resentment' not 'Because of what you did'. This is very important.

When you feel an emotional shift, share the full cost of holding on to this resentment. (Please note that these costs were mostly experienced in my twenties and early thirties because I had done this process.)

NB: I use the words, 'My resentment cost me. . .' not 'what you did to me cost me. . .' Again, it takes ownership rather than blames. Blame is yet more victimised cost.

'All this cost me my ability to trust men again, my willingness to take risks with my heart, let alone my body. My resentment made what you did another reason to hate my body, to dissociate from it and punish it and focus on my intellect instead. I let it fuel and amplify my bulimia, which did long-term damage to my colon and may well have played a part in the cancer I was diagnosed with many years later. To some extent, it cost me my health.

'My resentment also cost me my sexual confidence and expression. It walked me into relationships with other men who wanted to put me down or who were "soft" and therefore "safe". But I didn't want soft without strong and I invariably walked away. My resentment closed my heart to the confident authoritative ones who really cared for me and loved me. It even cost me friendships because I threw myself into my work and neglected my social life. I didn't go home or call home as much as my parents wanted me to. I focused on what I could *do* instead of what my heart needed.

'In all these ways it cost me what I most wanted – intimacy, connection, being fully myself, having a sense of safety in my own skin.

'Mostly, I allowed it to weigh my spirit down, to dampen my connection with what sources me, to hold some aspects of Life Itself at bay. It cost me the compass that guides me through life's storms: my faith. And this was the biggest price of all.'

Ask for and offer forgiveness.

As I expressed these words, the tears fell just as they had when I first did this. Something in my chest opened and released some grief about the prices I have paid. To be clear, *I* did this to me. My resentment did all this to me. I deeply object to what happened. I wish I had been more proactive. He hurt me and took advantage. But I held on to the ill will for several years. It took me a while to get hold of it because I had been pretending the rape never happened and keeping it secret. *But the ill will cost me more than the experience itself.*

When we realise this we want to drop resentment like a heavy stone. We want to be free of it. We are ready to forgive. (If not, go back to the costs until you are.) We are even ready to ask for forgiveness for holding so much resentment. This may confound your mind! *But it is for us, not them.* It is another road out of personal hell. In this case:

'I am truly sorry for holding all this resentment. Will you forgive me for adding my aggression to yours?

'And I forgive you for what you did. I refuse to hold on to any ill will any more. I let it go.'

Again, I feel the relief I felt when I did this before. And it is not essential to use the word 'forgive' which is loaded with false meanings. It is enough to say, 'I refuse to hold on to the resentment. I let it go (or I lay it down)'.

As I have also mentioned, the idea of *asking for* forgiveness can seem abhorrent for some people who see it as a step too far, but this too is for our own healing. It is how we can drain the last drops of poison from our hearts and spirits. When I fully recognised the cost of my resentment towards 'men' – the knives I had left in my own wounds, the barricades I had built against *intimacy* (*in-to-me-you-see*, as someone wisely noted), the loneliness *I* created for fear of letting someone see me all the way through – I shed it like a snake sheds skin. Snakes do this to create space for further growth and to *remove the parasites that have attached to them*. This is what forgiveness – asking for it as well as giving it – did for me. I was very deliberate in this regard.

Choose what to do and how to be now.

When we let go of ill will new possibilities arise. We begin to see a path back to our lives. And we can make new choices:

'From now on I will not see you in all men. I will treat what happened as another opportunity for my awakening, for the reclamation of my value, femininity and self-expression, for the strengthening of my boundaries and self-respect. I will treat my body as the resilient vehicle it really is. I will leave this behind me. I will let love in again.'

And finally, you close your eyes and visualise yourself acting on choices. *The mind will not do what it cannot visualise.* This is the litmus test of your choices.

Now we can move on with our lives, lighter, freer, healthier, braver, more loving and more creative than before.

As I say, this is *not* a process to do face to face. The other person does not need to hear all this, especially if it is someone we are close to, like a parent or sibling. That said, I know of an exceptional case: a woman who was brutally raped, maimed and left for dead. First, she did this process as an internal conversation. Then she went to the prison and did it to her rapist's face. He had cut off both her legs, but she emerged saying that this encounter left her 'whole again'. And he collapsed on the floor in remorse when she asked for his forgiveness, which awakened his pure shame.

I have done this process many times, on all the men I have mentioned in this chapter (and a number of women too). I did one a week until it was done and made a commitment to let go of my ill will towards men whenever I noticed it. It became easier and easier. My spirit felt lighter and lighter. My relationships with men grew more trusting and intimate. And, when I forgave the ex-boyfriend who attempted suicide in my flat for mostly manipulative reasons, I sat at my kitchen table, alone but not lonely, and wrote these words at the end of a Clearing Process: *No less than man; no more than man; not given to man; not opposed to man; not competing with man; not proving anything to man; not resenting man. Man! What a relief!*

And it was. As far as I know, none of the men in question were aware of either my resentment (though a few may have picked this up from my passive-aggressive vibes) or my forgiveness. That was not the point. The point was to unburden my own soul.

Forgiving That Which Is

When we are resenting, we will receive many lifeshocks that draw our attention to it. Resentment is so slippery and invisible, it may take many wake-up calls just for us to admit it. And then we resent those too.

Through all of this, the 'betrayals' I have found hardest to forgive have come from one source, a source that many call 'God'. I doubt there is anyone or anything more resented on the planet. Every lifeshock we react against, every 'No, send it back!', every stroke of reality we give the finger to (because this obviously *should never have happened*) is – until reconciled – an expression of resentment towards 'God'.

I remain reluctant to use what is probably the most distorted and contaminated word in any language. The worst of human atrocities have also been done in that name. As Brad wisely said, 'God is a word that needs to be redefined anew by each generation for itself.' Jewish and Christian texts offer a plethora of names for G'D including, 'Lord,', 'Father', 'Saviour' and YHWH (Yaweh). Personally, I love the Muslim expression, 'Insha'Allah' (God willing), which has replaced 'health permitting' whenever I make commitments these days. I also love the Taoist text about the dharma which says, 'the name that can be named is not the Name'. Mostly, I prefer words like 'Source', 'Creator' and a phrase I have used in this book: 'That Which Is'.

For me, this encapsulates a saying that profoundly changed my relationship with the word 'G-O-D'. Attributed to the Sarmoung Brotherhood, an enigmatic esoteric school from Central Asia, it asserts, *'There is no God but reality. To seek him elsewhere is the action of the Fall.'* I love this. To me, it says God is Reality and Reality is God. Another way of saying this is that 'G-O-D' reveals Itself through lifeshocks (which is how we encounter Reality). As for 'the action of the Fall', Brad interpreted this through the story of *Adam and Eve*, which is told in both the Christian and Judaic traditions. In this story, the 'Fall' resulted from Eve listening to the serpent (mindtalk) and then convincing Adam to join her in eating from a forbidden tree in the Garden of Eden. This is often called 'the tree of knowledge', but was actually 'the tree of the knowledge *of good and evil*'. In other words, the tree of judgement, of believing we know what is *good* or *bad* and what *should* or *shouldn't* happen. This is how we fall from the innocence of our *humanity, authenticity and lovability* into the 'sin' (which simply means 'missing the mark') of *omnipotence, pretence and loveless-ness*. And thus 'reality' comes after us through *limiting, exposing* and *evoking* lifeshocks, calling us back into alignment with who we really are and what is really so.

I can't claim this interpretation as 'the truth' any more than I take the story of Adam and Eve literally, but I can testify to how it has manifested in my life. Nor can I wrap it in red ribbons, as if it makes reality any more palatable when it arrives in what seem to be cruel, brutal and unfathomable forms. If all the rape, murder, prejudice, torture, loneliness, starvation, neglect and deprivation in this world is 'God's will', then *fuck that and fuck Him* (says my reactive mind). *What kind of God would rain all this down on humanity? How can He betray us in such terrible ways?* And exactly how do we reconcile ourselves with living in a world where there is supposed to be a divine presence who is either screwing with us or abandoning us? Even Christ cried, 'My God, my God, why hast thou forsaken me?' before he finally surrendered to what was being asked of him. It is important to remember this and to acknowledge the amount of resentment we hold towards *That Which Is*. We store it up in every refusal of and every reaction against every lifeshock we don't like. And, just to be clear, this is as human and forgivable as it gets.

For me, these discoveries have given me what I set out

to find three decades ago – a way to find the divine in the paving cracks. I hadn't wanted to seek Something Greater on high mountains or in deep caves, to enter altered states of consciousness or transcend this earthly plane in order to live on another. Nor had I wanted to spend hours a day meditating or praying. I had longed to dive deep into the world's waters instead of rising above them; to find the heavenly in the earthly; to feel spirit *in* the body I loathed, not beyond it; to accept the shadows I cast as much as the light I shine. By becoming aware of lifeshocks and their guiding power, I found a very practical way of relating to the divine.

The first forgiveness process I did was on 'God'. We were instructed to do the process on one individual and I certainly recommend starting with the actual people in your life (this followed in my case), but I wanted to cut to the chase. I have made this a regular practice ever since. The payoffs for resenting *That Which Is* are epic: we can convince ourselves we are actually in control; we can blame our circumstances or lifeshocks for everything that goes wrong and for all our suffering; we can justify every decision we make, however cruel or irresponsible; we can become self-righteous iconoclasts who decry people's faith in the name of a superior rationale that 'God' couldn't possibly understand. Basically, we can step into His shoes and sit on His throne and declare that we know how the world and everyone in it *ought to be.*

But the costs are incalculable: we separate from what sources us and, in so doing, separate from our own essence; we close our eyes to whatever may live beyond the rational and close our hearts to a holy comfort in our darkest hours; we can see darkness and light, but not light *inside* darkness; we are cast into a loneliness in which 'we liveth to ourselves and dieth to ourselves' (Romans 14.7); we are aware of the universe outside us, but not of the universe *within* us; our agony has no meaning or purpose; our joy becomes random and inconsequential; we may manage to become 'true believers' of a particular doctrine, but we won't become *beholders* of What Is in all its inscrutable wonder. At least, these have been some of the costs and realisations for me.

Forgiving *That Which Is* can be tricky because it really helps to visualise *who* we are resenting when we do *The Cost Process*. However, there are a number of things we can visualise, depending on our beliefs and context: a prophet like Jesus, Buddha or Lord Krishna; something that symbolises 'The Source' to you, perhaps something in nature like a waterfall or the sun; a spiritual teacher who you see as an agent or even embodiment of 'The Source'. Sometimes I just close my eyes and see what image comes into my awareness. Once it was a whirling dervish. These are members of the Mevlevi Order founded by followers of the thirteenth-century Sufi poet, Jalaluddin Rumi, famous for performing a whirling dance known as the 'Sama'. The 'Sama' represents a spiritual ascent through the mind to 'The Perfect'. What matters is that we are *asking for and offering forgiveness for the resentment we have held against all the lifeshocks we rejected* – all the realities we have refused to accept and found so hard to bear.

I hesitated to share The Cost Process in this book. I was doubtful it could be fully grasped and experienced simply by seeing it in print. As with everything in these pages, the experience is what matters most, not the understanding. This is why I am offering up my own experience to what can seem like a deeply exposing and daunting extent. When it comes to forgiveness, I have needed skilled facilitators to hold my feet to the fire when my reactive mind is finding loopholes and snapping at my heels. *You don't need to do this. You don't really hold resentment. You're a good person. You have better things to do than this.* I have also needed assistance to let the full emotional impact of resenting and forgiving reverberate through my body. This is no intellectual exercise. It is a spiritual reckoning and a road out of purgatory. My hope is that this chapter will make that road more visible to more people and, if the words on their own are not enough to deliver the full healing experience of releasing ill will back into the ether, then readers will seek out this experience more fully.

When I was diagnosed with cancer, it had been some years since I needed to do this process on 'God'. I had worked that arsenal of resentments to the bone. I had found a way to keep reading the news that I once would have turned away from, sickened and weary, unwilling to open to that much reality. I had learned to stand *for* what I wanted to change instead of *against* what I hate, which just adds more separation to all the separating forces we are already dealing with. But the onslaught of lifeshocks relating to cancer, both personal and collective, tested my spiritual mettle. I saw it as another great betrayal. How could I be given what I had most wanted for such a long time – John and Gabriella – only to be denied a future with them, a *reaping of my just rewards*, as my mind framed it?

I didn't write about how I blamed and forgave 'God' in *The Cancer Whisperer*. It seemed too much to mention without the full context of this book underneath it. It felt too raw and private as well. But, in truth, it was what made me a 'whisperer'. It was what enabled me to own my part in how I got ill and what I was going to do about it. It transmuted the 'war on cancer', a long-running narrative that begs us to resent this disease at immense cost to our wellbeing, into an amnesty of awakening.

The One in the Mirror

Every accusation and judgement we level at ourselves adds to a stockpile of resentment that mounts in our hearts and psyches. Whatever mistakes we have made, however much harm we have done to ourselves or others, a time comes when we need to forgive the person in the mirror, to cast out the core beliefs that distort our reflection, to atone for how we have treated ourselves because of those beliefs and to release the resentment for which we have paid such a steep price. There is no one else we get up with every morning and go to bed with every night, from birth until death. Even when we direct judgements at others, we are distracting ourselves from what we most fear about ourselves. We are 100 per cent privy to our own cruelties and cock-ups and, arguably, there is no one we need to forgive more than ourselves.

As is likely very clear by now, this has been my nemesis for as long as I can remember. For many years, I was more familiar with the accusatory, discounting, undermining, spirit-dampening part of myself than I was with my basic decency as a human being. The *never-enough* part. The *too-much* part. The *whatever-you-do-is wrong* part. The *ugly-and-unlovable* part. Michelangelo famously said, 'I saw the angel in the marble and set him free.' Whatever self-regard I now display is the result of chipping away at my self-criticism, consciously and tenaciously, for several decades. While equivocal sometimes, it is robust and genuine. I know who I am and what I belong to. I accept my gifts as well as my flaws. I trust what I see and say it with confidence, not apology or hesitation. I could not write this book, in which I wear my insides on the outside, if I was not standing on the firm and abundant ground that is Sophie. My self-regard is not skin deep. It is as deep as a blue sky. It is a 'self' forgiven.

This does not mean I am all the way free. Some days I still need a rasp, the flat steel tool a sculptor uses to remove excess stone. But more often I need a riffler, which creates details like folds of clothing and locks of hair. Parts of me are fully carved and polished. Other parts are rough at the edges, and I never stop looking for what I have not yet forgiven or learned to love. My body has been the most difficult thing to forgive (first-world problem as this may be): the way it became a woman when I was still a child; its proclivity for weight gain; its ski-jump nose and Frieda Kahlo eyebrows (which require frequent plucking); its intolerance for most forms of travel (I once got seasick in a rocking chair); its lack of natural spring; its cancer marching through my cells.

Since I was diagnosed, I have attended to my mind and heart as vigilantly as I attend to my body. Clearing my mindtalk and all the suffering it generates has been a constant, like the primary drugs I am on. At times, I have also invested in therapeutic support for particular challenges I am facing. We all need support – other eyes to help us see ourselves – and this is especially true when our lives are under threat. I *might* have survived the last few years without this, but I would not have *thrived* or been transformed.

Recently, a man who has been supporting me since the third flurry of brain tumours was discovered, asked a beautifully lifeshocking question about the body I have found so hard to love: 'What would need to change for it to be safe for you to come home?' Two words thawed a chunk of ice in my chest I didn't know was there: *come home*. Lifeshock. I cried like a grown-up: freely, gratefully, with instant awareness of what had been touched and exposed. I thought of Brad who parted this world with the words, 'I want to *go home*.' I knew what he meant and, somewhere inside, shared that yearning. From my beginnings as an unwitting empathic toddler, through my early physical maturing into my addictions and eating disorders and, most recently, into living with a brutal disease, part of me has been trying to leave my body and 'go home'. And yet, all my lifeshocks have been pointing me in the opposite direction: to my humanness, my here-ness, my realness; to love in *this* realm; to the forgivable in my own being; to treating my body as a holy temple instead of an obstacle to the sacred; to the tantalising possibility that I could *come Home* instead of *going Home* if I just forgive myself enough to land here fully; and the possibility that my spirit could at last slip into some woolly socks and warm its feet in the glowing hearths of my flesh, blood, skin and bones.

The Visitor

I used to be allergic to the term 'self-love'. It seemed as out of place as 'self-help' in an interconnected universe, the epitome of what my mother calls 'navel gazing'. I still think it can be indulgent, even harmful, when it stands in isolation from love of others and love of life. But, recently, I read an article that said, 'there can be a dark side' to self-forgiveness because 'it can relieve feelings like guilt, but reduce empathy for others.' This is nonsense. If it lets us off a hook without *increasing* our capacity for empathy and love, it is not self-forgiveness. It is selfishness. The truth is that as long as we hold ourselves in ill will, our capacity to contribute and make a difference is thwarted. As Marianne Williamson, the American spiritual teacher, has said, 'The practice of forgiveness is our most important contribution to the healing of the world.' And that includes forgiving ourselves.

'The absolute refusal to hold ill will' is how we can do this. This is what Archbishop Tutu modelled so beautifully at the Truth and Reconciliation Commission in South Africa after Nelson Mandela, affectionately known as Madiba, ended Apartheid from a prison cell. When he left after twenty-seven years, Mandela said, 'As I walked out the door toward the gate that would lead to my freedom, I knew if I didn't leave my bitterness and hatred behind I would still be in prison.'

On 9/11 a Pakistani Muslim found himself on the ground a few blocks from the World Trade Centre when the South Tower fell. He was standing in stunned fear when a Hasidic Jewish man broke away from the fleeing mob, approached him and extended his hand, saying,

'Brother, if you don't mind, there is a cloud of glass coming at us. Grab my hand and let's get the hell out of here.' Then they ran together, hand in hand, free of the colossal ill will that divides their people, to safety. Afterwards, the Muslim, a man named Usman Farman, said, 'Regardless of who we are and where we come from, we only have each other.'

One of the victims of the 1984 Brighton bombing, where the entire Conservative Cabinet was targeted at the Grand Hotel (and where I assumed my own parents were staying when I first heard about it), was an MP called Sir Anthony Berry. Sixteen years later, when the man who planted the bomb was released from prison, Sir Anthony's daughter Jo arranged to meet him. His name is Patrick Magee and, together, he and Jo established a charity called 'Building Bridges for Peace' to better understand the roots of war, terrorism and violence. This unlikely friendship and their important work in countries like Palestine, Lebanon and Rwanda, as well as the UK, is the result of *forgiveness*: Jo's for Patrick and Patrick's for himself.

When a mother can forgive the man who shot her five-year-old son and a daughter can forgive a man who blew up her father, then what is possible for the rest of us when we exercise forgiveness? It requires a recognition of what resentment really costs us, and an emotional release, not merely a mental decision. Refusing to hold ill will is our work to do and our power to wield in the face of such a destructive force. Compassion is only possible when we forgive.

And. There is more. Forgiveness is more. It is both the act of releasing resentment and *what awaits us when we have done so*.

The first time I had multiple brain tumours ('too many to count'), which were found six weeks after my first scan, my head would start throbbing whenever I felt angry or resentful. The pain told me I could not hold the resentment and I moved into a continual flow of forgiving, lifeshock by lifeshock. This was less an act of will than a consistent attitude, without which the pain increased. For several weeks, perhaps a couple of months, forgiveness became a way of being. I didn't need to work at it. The cost was too immediate and tangible. When anger rose I took three breaths – in through my nose, down into my belly and out through my mouth – and let it go (something we can do anytime to shift our state). This flow of forgiveness was not sustainable once the tumours went away. Then I needed to do the work again. But, for a short time, I lived in a refined space where forgiveness was the status quo.

That experience seemed to open a portal which hadn't opened before and hasn't closed since. This is the portal through which forgiveness *visits*. It is nothing *I* have created or brought forth. Instead, it is mine to welcome in when it arrives with its basket of peace at my door. It is the same forgiveness that I enter when I drop my ill will, an ocean of mercy which is always there if I do what it takes to land on its shores. Sometimes, it is enough to stand at the water's edge and let the waves wash over my weary feet. Sometimes, I wade in up to my waist, arms aloft, as if I can only take so much at a time before diving under the surface. And these days, parts of that ocean flow into me, unbidden. I am not in it as much as it is *in me*. This does not excuse me from doing my part. A flare of resentment will block the flow and I need to unblock it, but the portal seems to remain open. Some days, forgiveness just enters and snuffs out the flare. Other days, it finds the unpardonable places carved out by the cruellest self-criticism. It reaches in where I have failed to reach out. It visits the homeless parts of me and offers them shelter. It urges me to come all the way home.

The Cost Process

This process is how to apply what I have written about in the 'Forgiveness' chapter. This is *how to forgive*.

To my knowledge, The Cost Process has never been published before. It comes late in the More to Life weekend because the mind needs to be awake enough to engage with resentment. Naturally, it is best learned experientially, as all these skills are, but it is also time to share these tools more widely. This one is worth its weight in gold. Don't worry if you don't get it or feel a shift or are unable to forgive. Be patient. You will only forgive when you *feel the weight of the cost*, not before.

Remember, *forgiveness is not to condone*. It is to release ill will for the sake of your own spirit and play your part in a systemic healing for the sake of humanity.

This doesn't work as an intellectual exercise. These are the basic steps:

Steps of The Cost Process

1. Close your eyes and bring to mind the person you have been resenting. Say their name. Then own the full extent of your resentments.

2. Share the payoffs you have received from holding on to this resentment.
3. When you feel a sense of sorrow, share the full cost of holding on to this resentment.
4. Ask for and offer forgiveness.
5. Choose what to do and how to be now.
6. Visualise yourself doing and being it.

For example

Here is a process which another of Brad's students did on his father *after his death*. We still live with the toxicity of resentment, even when the people we resent have gone. It is that tragic.

David's father was born in a Jewish family that had been uprooted many times, most recently by the Tsarist massacres of the late nineteenth century. They moved to Vienna only to encounter a new horror – the Nazi death camps. His father brought the manufacturing skills he acquired in pre-war Vienna to the UK, and David speaks of growing up in the safety of London as refugees with 'waves of persecution hovering around us like an unmentionable shroud.'

Brad Brown was himself a third generation Native American (Washoe tribe) with his own understanding of the impact of ethnic violence and mass killing. He helped David in his quest to find a way to relate to his

father and also, as he said, 'find myself along the way.'
The exercise below is part of what he did to make it
happen.

Owning the resentment:

'Dear Dad, I see your inscrutable, implacable face in my
mind's eye right now. I want to speak to you to own the
resentment I have held against you for most of my life
and claim my part in the emotional estrangement that
came between us.

It all began with the sudden outbursts of rage that
erupted toward me, my mother and sister during my
childhood years. You usually followed this up by stalking
out, slamming doors, and then there was nothing but
silence. You would stay stony-faced, closed off, as unmov-
able as a rock. You could stonewall us for days, weeks or
months at a time. More than your anger, I resented living
with your unreachable withdrawal.

Alone in my room everything seemed wrong, and it
was never made right, even when you started commu-
nicating again, because there was no exploration of what
had happened. Never any forgiveness to soften the heart,
never any new understanding that might redeem the
suffering – just an uneasy accommodation, until the next
sudden explosion.

I grew up fearing the noise of your rage, down to the
deadly vibrations I felt in my chest and arms if I was
standing too close to you. I resented your conviction,
your sense of invincible 'rightness' and your rock-like
indifference. I saw all this as unfairness that needed to
be condemned.

Owning the payoffs:

As I sat on my own for hours on end, the idea of making you wrong became a kind of survival strategy. If I could hate you then I had some kind of power, in spite of my obvious powerlessness. I could be strong in opposition to you, the patriarch, the bully, the tyrant.

I spent my childhood complaining and my adolescence rebelling. All my failures and any kind of self-indulgence could be excused, pardoned or justified by the wrongs that had been done to me. I felt righteous in my judgemental state, even if I also blamed myself for somehow making you turn away from me.

In my role as a rebel I could reject you in my turn, along with your faith, your so-called 'family values', your strange respect for 'strong leaders' and your curious support for the world's most repressive regimes. Everything you stood for fuelled my rage, as if I were fighting injustice itself.

Now I could become even more self-righteous than you. I could judge, bully and manipulate, because the world was hard like this, and I would be harder. I could avoid commitment and laugh at the self-delusion of those who had not yet figured this out. Coldness, betrayal, and suffering were waiting for them, but I had my very own exeat from life.

Naming the cost:

I repeated this pattern for years, never glimpsing my part in it, and it cost me most of the best things life has to offer: surrender, acceptance, inner peace that heals pain and restores the spirit. But my life contained no possibility of surrender. Just my own rage, my own withdrawals, my own brooding silences, which all those who professed to care for me were required to endure.

My long-held resentment cost me many relationships, especially with people who had the kind of authority or power that reminded me of you. It cost me my ability to stay close to male friends, girlfriends, teachers and bosses. I even resented my mother because she herself had not managed to resolve your struggle, or just get out and save herself.

Since the world had failed to deal with you, no relationship would ever be safe. But I was safe in my martyrdom, oblivious to my part in my suffering, with no inkling that resenting you was leading me to mirror your own way of being.

It was when I started this process work that I become aware of how much my state of mind was really my own creation. Up to then it was all about you. I blamed you for any failure in my life, and secretly reproached you for every hurt.

And the ultimate cost was the very intimacy I longed for and never had with you, until the very last years of your life. By then I had learned to stop and listen to you, the way I had demanded in vain that you did for me. I listened as your rage unfurled, I held my heart open until its energy was spent, and in this way I finally managed to be there, when your tightly held features softened before my eyes.

I am so grateful that instead of spending your last years hating you I was able to experience some of the connection I always wanted. Today I begin to see how your own experience of life might have affected you, and how perhaps some of the same patterns that had formed your reactions were affecting me in turn.

Asking for and offering forgiveness:
Now I apologise to you again, and lay my judgements down once more. You are the one who brought me into the world. You sustained me and worked for my sustenance every day of your working life. You did the best you could with what you were given. You followed your own path, and created your own destiny. You were proud of what you believed in, and you fought for it. I ask again for your forgiveness for the way I behaved and the way I treated you. And I refuse to hold ill will against you any more. As I say this, I feel very close to you.

Choose what to do and how to be now:
In future I choose to love and cherish the man you were – the dutiful son, father, husband, the one who sourced our family throughout our lives. I choose to honour your memory. And I choose to reach for the heights you saw things from. I want to use my life to challenge all that weighed down on our family and help others escape the hell we create on earth between us.

I choose to honour you as my father by living my life in the sight of the Father, whose justice is innately combined with mercy, and whose being is also very like a Rock.'

II

Grace

'What is grace?' I asked God.
And He said, 'All that happens.'

St John of the Cross

Bowled Over

Once, I was bowled over by 'grace'. It literally knocked
me down. I could not have been more closed to it
when it happened or more judgemental of the context
in which it happened. It was in my early twenties, before
I knew anything about Brad or his work.

I had fallen out with my mother earlier that year, the
details of which don't matter as much as the outcome.
That year a family Christmas abroad had been planned
to celebrate Mum's fiftieth birthday, but my stubborn
heels were still dug in about our argument and I had no
intention of apologising, even if it meant spending
Christmas alone. I was disinvited. This seemed deeply
unjust at the time, but I was yet to meet Brad or learn
any effective tools for dealing with my resentments. So
that was that. I was doomed to a spend Christmas alone
in my one-bedroom flat in Balham, South London, where
I lived at the time.

Instead my friend, Rosie, who had been my tutor at university, invited me to India. She was travelling to Meherabad, an ashram established by her spiritual master, Meher Baba, and wondered if I would like to join her. In truth, I didn't relish the prospect at all. Our friendship was quite new and it seemed risky to spend three weeks with her in a context I might want to run from as soon as I arrived. I was extremely wary of Indian gurus and anybody who followed one. It seemed like a fly-trap for lost souls – spurious and dangerous at once. I would need to have my wits about me and keep my guard up. At the same time, it was hard to ignore this chink of light in the Yuletide darkness and I had always wanted to visit India. I was gainfully employed and due some holiday time. It also seemed as if the universe had lined all this up with great precision and purpose that was beyond my seeing. I said yes.

It was everything I feared it would be: sleeping in a dormitory with devotees who seemed to love their Master without reason or question and assumed I felt the same; attending morning and evening 'Arti' (singing and praying as if in a church or synagogue); seeing suspiciously serene pilgrims line up silently outside his 'Samadhi' (tomb) before entering, one at a time, to bow down in deference. You see, he had died in 1969, but his followers described this as 'dropping his body', which disturbed me even more. The whole thing seemed both ludicrous and suspect, like a spiritual satire. I felt scared and lonely and wanted to go home.

At this time, I was in the throes of bulimia nervosa and my self-esteem was round my ankles. In that state, it was easier for me to judge everything and everyone around me than to admit the depth of judgements I levelled against myself. I had no love for Sophie, but I did have bulletproof defences. Or so I thought.

I tried to keep all this to myself, but Rosie sensed my discomfort and gently suggested I sit in the enclosed area outside Baba's tomb. The building is a simple structure of stone walls with a white dome-shaped roof, its corners decorated with symbols of the world's religions and a line of capital letters along the front edge that read 'Mastery in Servitude'. Attached to the building is a modest oblong area with a tiled roof and open sides. There are a few benches forming three sides of a rectangle where people sit in silence looking through the door on the fourth side into the small tomb, which is filled with murals painted by Swiss artist Helen Dahm, depicting the Master and his closest disciples. Nearby is an old water tower built by the British army, once part of the ashram, now a library and museum. The small collection of buildings sits on a parched hill in rural Maharashtra above a noisy railway line, and increasingly busy road, like a temple perched amidst the temporal world.

I sat in the open area before the Samadhi, watching as the person on duty handed out little orange sweets to people as they stepped out of the tomb area, having knelt down to pay their respects. This was called '*darshan*', which refers to an auspicious visit and blessing with a holy person. Only a few people could enter at one time, so I watched and waited, relieved there was no space for me, quietly judging the bowed heads resting on the foot of his marble tomb and assuming they would judge me in turn for not following suit.

Forty minutes passed before the tomb was empty and no one was queuing outside. I had no idea how rare this would be in the future and how many pilgrims would travel here from all over the world in their thousands for the chance to sit where I was sitting. Now, the way had been cleared, and my legs walked me to the door almost against my will. The foot of the tomb was covered in a perfectly smooth purple silk cloth, which I later discovered was changed at six a.m. each day. It was covered in petals and some carefully placed garlands. I was struck by the impeccable beauty of the place. Towards the head of the horizontal tomb, these words had been carved in large gold letters on the ivory marble: 'I HAVE COME NOT TO TEACH BUT TO AWAKEN'. I stood there for a few minutes, acutely self-conscious, my 'reactive mind' pulling me backwards and Something Else pulling me forwards.

Something Else won.

As one foot tentatively crossed the threshold, I neither wanted to be discourteous by not kneeling nor phoney by doing so. But I needn't have worried. No sooner had I planted my second foot inside the door than an invisible energy knocked me to the ground with astonishing force, even as the hard, slate floor somehow cushioned me as I landed. This energy, which was sublimely loving, laid me flat on my stomach with my face to the floor and my head touching the foot of the tomb, like a young tree prostrated by a great wind. For a few eternal minutes, I couldn't move. I felt the walls around my chest crumble like a sandcastle at the mercy of a single wave. As I lay there sobbing, I heard Rumi whispering over and over, 'There is some kiss we want with our whole lives, the touch of Spirit on the body.' *There is some kiss we want with our whole lives. The touch of Spirit on the body.*

And there Spirit touched my beleaguered body. Of this I was certain. It kissed all the hated places and pulled out the thorns.

I cried for days. I cried relief, gratitude and euphoric drops of awe. Afterwards, I felt a deep stillness as if a butterfly had landed on my soul. There are no adequate words to describe this experience. There is only a white crayon moving across a pale canvas. It was acceptance. It was the end of longing. It was Grace.

The Path Within the Path

There are some things we know that we can't un-know once we know them. I spent three weeks at Meherabad, mostly alone. Rosie, tormented by insomnia and missing her new husband whom she had married earlier that year, flew home after just a few days. It was as if her sole mission on that trip had been to deliver a package called Sophie. Spiritually speaking, I think it is fair to say I was dragged kicking and screaming to a place where something greater than I could conceive would bring down my concrete walls. I was such an angry, unhappy young woman: searching desperately, but truly lost. It would be twenty-six years before I returned.

I found it impossibly hard to integrate this experience into my Western, first-world life. I didn't know how to talk about it. I didn't want to deal with the raised eyebrows and anxious questions. And, as I explained in the introduction to this book, I didn't want an Indian guru, even one whose divinity had made itself so forcefully known.

Yet, it was Baba I prayed to on that Greek beach the morning after I was raped, asking for a flesh-and-blood teacher from a Western context who would show me how to touch grace in the here-and-now. Meher Baba was the most perceptible encounter with Spirit that I had ever known. Not a single visit to church on all those Sunday mornings as I was growing up gave me a glimpse of anything so real. It seemed to me that the church had been a very good idea once, but it had forgotten what the idea was. The Bible wasn't put together until AD 323, and very few people saw it until the Latin volume came out in the fifteenth century, when the printing press became available. That's several centuries for human interpretation to change and distort anything that had carried original truths.

I'm not suggesting there is no truth in the Bible, merely that it has been meddled with by the human mind, which is flawed and self-deceiving, as I know only too well. In parts, it also proposes too straight (which doesn't mean easy) a path to enlightenment for me to buy into. As Lao Tse, the founder of philosophical Taoism, said, 'The path that can be followed is not the Path.'

In the main, we are offered two choices in this regard. First, there is what Brad called 'the wide path'. This is the path most people travel, especially in the West. It leads towards the attainment of money, acceptance, prestige, power, success, beauty, happiness, security, family, belonging. *If we just work hard enough, if we are just good enough, obedient enough, clever enough, powerful enough, sexy enough, wealthy enough, special enough, THEN we will attain these things and all the rewards they pledge. We will ARRIVE.* This is psycho-logic. And even some branches of psychology (a discipline I value greatly and in which Brad trained me well) can perpetuate the illusions of this path to some extent. It too can sometimes appear to offer ultimate satisfaction, fulfilment and freedom, but these things rarely come because the reactive mind keeps barking at our ankles.

To be fair, this field has also been invaded by an army of self-help 'life coaches' who flood our Facebook walls with 'my life is perfect' messages. 'Just pay me lots of money and yours can be perfect too.' I prefer to see Life as the coach than myself as a 'life coach', and help my clients relate to it in a similar way. In my experience, psychology gives significant and valuable relief, sometimes shifting something at root that makes a lasting difference, but it is ultimately limited because its doors are often (though not always) closed to the unearned, unfathomable, bowl-us-over presence of pure grace. This is what I 'knew' and could not un-know when I returned from India. It was what shifted inside that never shifted back. I *experienced* 'grace', but couldn't define it. I didn't *understand* it. I couldn't explain it. And, however profoundly I ached for it, I didn't know how to find it again.

Second, there is what Brad called 'the narrow path'. This is the path of the true believers, the club-joiners, the religious flocks and spiritual sects, prescribed and definite, obeisant to certain laws, promising belonging and sometimes salvation, a straight line to paradise. The phrase 'straight and narrow' refers to the proper, honest and moral path of behaviour, which has a pejorative puritanical overlay that shows up in 'straight' versus 'gay' (or LBGTQ). Whether it relates to the Ten Commandments, strict religious rules or stringent morally driven vegetarianism (as an example), this path is all about following predetermined, formulaic rules that become hard-wired beliefs.

Somewhere along the line, life is likely to hit us with something that requires us to make our own moral choices and find another way to follow the underlying *principles* we adhere to. Until that happens, the narrow path is a highly attractive alternative when we recognise the horror of losing ourselves on 'the wide path', pursuing quick fixes of satisfaction only to feel wanting again: the path of *more, more and still yet more*. I have lost myself on this path many times. I have pursued beauty, success, wealth, prestige and belonging to my ultimate disappointment and detriment. I still value those things. I just don't want to attach myself to them and refuse to let them define me any more. This is an inestimable relief.

I am not saying anything new here. Most of us have an understanding of these paths, which are constantly on offer and highly seductive. Perhaps we even need to walk them in order to question them or qualify to step off them. Each of us, in our own way, is simply trying to do 'the right thing'. Nor is it new to speak of 'a road less travelled', as Scott Peck titled his first book; a way to be *in* this world but not *of* it, as the Sufis suggest – a path that has many forbears and has been offered since the beginning of time. Brad called this 'the path within the path'. The great philosopher and mystic, Gurdjieff, called it the 'Fourth Way', explaining that the mass of humanity live only in the first two stages of being: sleep and waking sleep, both of which are highly conditioned and subjective. In the third state, self-consciousness, we can know the truth about ourselves. In the fourth, objective consciousness, we can know the truth about 'the world as it is'. According to Gurdjieff, the Fourth Way differs from others in that 'it is not a permanent way. It has no specific form or institutions and comes and goes controlled by some particular laws of its own'.

This path within the path is counter-culture and confrontative of all powers and systems, but it is para-doxically inclusive. It exists within the body politic itself. It is not defined or prescribed. The sacred ('narrow' path) need not be separated from the secular ('wide' path). *In* the world but not *of* it once again. Instead, the sacred is *in* the secular and manifest in *everything that happens*: physically maturing at a very young age; a bomb being planted in my home; disappointing exam results; winning a speaking competition; being rejected by university peers; being raped when unconscious; arriving at an Indian ashram after a row with my mother; an 'cx' overdosing in my living room; a dear friend jumping off a bridge to his death; a mentor lying immobilised on the floor; marrying a man seven months after meeting him; the birth of a daughter against so many odds; a terminal cancer diagnosis; a best-selling book; a #MeToo hashtag; my determined seven-year-old being carried by her dad through the door this morning after climbing a snowy mountain that sang to her adventurous spirit, her feet turned to ice-blocks, wanting nothing but her mummy, screaming in pain.

It starts somewhere in our lives with the first 'lifeshock'. Then we notice another and another and another until we begin to heed Uncle Walt (Whitman)'s counsel to 're-examine everything you have been told and dismiss what insults your soul'. This is how reality comes to us, over and over, until we *notice* and *question* and *choose* anew. The path within the path is what Brad described as 'the apprehension of G-O-D in the midst of existence itself'. And *it is mapped by our lifeshocks*, moment by moment, person by person, each path untrodden by others and utterly unique. As my dearly beloved teacher wrote in his journals,

'A warrior's path is a path of destiny, waiting to lead us on. It's not a path you can trace on a map, or a formula you can write in a book. It's a path of what is next to happen in this evolving road-show that we're all part of, calling us to play our part in the picture. And, part of our part, especially if we are calling ourselves leaders, is to become a channel for that spirit so we can pass it on, and other people in turn may be inspired to face up to adverse circumstances, be raised up, to be of service, to challenge, to resist, to follow their inner vision and deepest purpose, to unify, to make things happen.'

I was *given* a body I struggled to inhabit, which led me into self-destructive behaviour, which led me into therapy, which led me to India, which led me to Brad, which put me on a trajectory to veracity and authenticity – which is where enduring beauty resides. I was *given* experiences of sexual assault, which led me to value my womanhood and live with firmer boundaries and hold out for a man who would honour me all the way through. I was *given* a privileged upbringing, which led me to question the world's disparities, which taught me humility, responsibility and gratitude, which called me to service, which carved out a vocation I could not have planned or envisioned. I was *given* friends who took their own lives, or attempted to, which taught me to empower rather than fix people, all of which compelled me to *choose life*. I was *given* cancer, which flushed out my clogged-up grief, propelled me into a life of writing, speaking and service to thousands of very ill human beings I would never otherwise have reached.

This path is circuitous indeed. There is no straight line to the goal because attainment is not *then,* but *now* and *now* and *now* and *now* and *now*. The moment is its own reward because it is imprinted with the origin from whence it came, an ambassador of That Which Is. This is how we experience the realness of life and, through it, the realness of ourselves. Each lifeshock provides exactly what we need in that moment to connect us with who we are, what we love and those we are here to serve. Lifeshocks challenge all the dogma and illusion. They mark a way that calls us into *connection* but cannot be institutionalised. They are also a sacred current on which we are carried towards revelation and destiny. And our transcendence of the reactive mind, our willingness to meet them with *yes*, is our rudder through waters that surge and swell with grace.

Take Off Your Shoes

The etymology of 'grace' is twofold. First, the noun is from the Old French *grâce* and Old Latin *gratia*, meaning, 'mercy, good will and God's unmerited favour'. Second, the verb is from the Old French *graciier*, 'to praise and give thanks'. As I understand this, grace is both 'God's *unmerited* favour', which comes to us just as it is because *it is*, and *gratitude*, which is how we can live grace-fully. This part is up to us.

There have been a few occasions in my life, besides India, when I have felt grace visit me, mystical and unbidden, as if I was being touched by 'God's favour' or a manifestation of another world. One was a couple of weeks after my friend, Nick, took his life. There was a period of time when we had his suicide note, but not his body. We were suspended in time, held between a written farewell and evidence of its achievement. We had gathered in Nick's home to support his wife as she clung to the belief that he would return, and put the rest of the world on hold. In private, I prayed for the safe passage of his soul.

One afternoon, about two weeks into this experience, I needed to escape the intensity of it all, to leave the house of delayed mourning and walk outside into the soft, broken sunlight of a cold winter's day. Filling my lungs with London, I headed for Starbucks, shoe shops and the solace of normality. I wanted the world to right itself and put me back to sleep. Being so *alive* each day was killing me. So was the relentless *now*.

I turned on to a busy high street, awash with early Christmas shoppers, when my legs started shaking uncontrollably. They almost buckled beneath me, but I made it to a doorstep to sit down. Tiredness crept through my veins like lava. I didn't care about the passers-by, some of whom stepped over me as they entered and exited the shop. I closed my eyes and asked for a sign from somewhere about what had become of my friend. Within what seemed like seconds, but may have been minutes, a strong stench made me open my eyes. Sitting next to me was a man I assumed to be homeless, offering me a polystyrene cup.

'You okay, love?' he asked me in an East London accent. 'Here, I got you a cuppa tea.'

This kindness ripped through me like a blade and my eyes brimmed over with grief. The man was filthy from head to toe, as accustomed to doorsteps as I was to a bed and hot water. I took the tea gratefully and drank it. He smiled with shocking generosity and yellow teeth. In that moment, I became as sure of Nick's death as I was of a grander, sweeter presence. My spiritual friend had killed himself. A homeless man had brought me tea. Reality always comes around. It announces itself, impersonal and impartial, but intimate as a suicide note and a yellow-toothed smile. A given; yet *given*. For a moment, I closed my eyes again and prayed that the waters had closed over Nick's tired mind like a blanket over a sleeping child. When I opened them, my friend with the warm tea had gone. So had the empty cup. To this day, I wonder if he was a figment of my imagination or an unexpected guest from another realm. But the gratitude this encounter left me with was very real. My anger with Nick subsided and I felt utterly thankful for who he had been in my life. A week later his body was found.

Seventeen years after his death, when I finally returned to the ashram in India, Nick's spirit seemed to visit me. I was sitting in the courtyard of the pilgrim centre, surrounded by bougainvillea trees in riotous flower, my face turned to the warm sun, when I felt his presence. At first, I doubted it and pushed it aside, but he persisted, almost pushing me off the wall on which I was perched. I asked if he needed something, but sensed him saying no. He was thanking me for praying for his soul when his wife had been busy praying for his safe return. 'Thank you. You helped me,' I heard him say. 'You're welcome,' I replied out loud. Then there was silence. But, along with an urge to discount this conversation as craziness, I also experienced a greater willingness to open to such moments of grace. I think that is when I finally laid Nick to rest in my own heart and let grief bring him close to me again.

Something similar happened when Brad died. I had known my last visit to California would be the final time I saw him. We both lingered on his doorstep as I was leaving to get into the taxi that was taking me to the airport. There were few words and surprisingly few tears. We rarely resisted letting tears flow in each other's presence, but that day they seemed to squeeze themselves from our ducts like sap from damaged birch trees. Sticky and reluctant to admit their *raison d'être*. Time slowed down and wrapped its shawl around our parting, eking itself out just long enough for us to observe these moments with due reverence. His wife, Anne, was standing a few feet behind him, having thanked me for coming and giving him another chance to serve. Her presence was comforting and limiting at once. For a moment, I felt awkward, as if my sadness was treading on turf that belonged to his family. *I am just his student and business partner. I am just one of his many friends.* But we were what we were to one another. And my love for him had no conditions, no end.

'Is that everything?' asked the taxi driver, having put my bags in his car.

'Yes, it is *everything*,' I replied without moving, my wet eyes giving the words to my beloved teacher before hugging him tight and closing the door behind me.

A few weeks later, when I was on holiday camping in a remote part of Africa with no phone signal, I dreamt Brad died and woke up knowing it to be so. Later that day, when a herd of wildebeest moved on to the plain, I felt his spirit pass like a warm wind. Two days later, a friend confirmed Brad had died the night of my dream.

'How do you know?!' she asked, amazed when I began the call by saying I knew he had gone.

'Because his spirit visited me,' I explained. 'He came to say goodbye.'

These experiences carried the same echoes of being bowled over by 'grace' that I had tasted when I was in India. They convinced me of the reality of a realm beyond the realm I walk in every day. Pyotr Ouspenskii, a Russian mathematician, esotericist and student of Gurdjieff, claimed to know as 'an undoubted fact that beyond the thin film of false reality there existed another reality from which, for some reason, something separated us.' He defined the miraculous as 'a penetration into this unknown reality'.

Brad defined the miraculous as 'a shift in perception' and, interestingly, 'miracle' is also an anagram of 'I'm clear'. One of the reasons he broke away from the therapeutic profession, as well as from the church (though never from the priesthood), is because he didn't want the ability to shift perceptions to seem his prerogative and power more than his patients' or congregation's. He didn't want to be the keeper of the keys to wisdom or hold 'miracles' out of other people's reach. He wanted to demystify his therapeutic and theological powers, to make them accessible to anyone who wanted to wake up from the deep sleep we call 'living'. He wanted to demonstrate that we don't need to wait for rare encounters with other realms to experience the divine. Nor do we need to wait years or decades for the 'defining moments' of our lives. We each have the power to shift our perception at will, to disarm the lies, to lift the veil of self-deception by challenging the thoughts that usually run rampant and unchecked through our minds. We don't need to wait to find 'God's unmerited favour' *there* and after when we can find it *here* and *now* in lifeshocks. Our part is to exercise *gratitude* even when the shit seems to hit the fan.

I am not grateful to have been sexually assaulted, but I *am* grateful for the self-regard those experiences propelled me to claim. I would give cancer back tomorrow if I could, but am *deeply* grateful for all the ways it has helped me inhabit my full self and the chance it gave me to fulfill my calling in new ways. I would even say that a divine red carpet seemed to roll out in front of me once I got my 'yes' to cancer, with all sorts of unsought and unforeseen guidance coming my way. Similarly, I still need to release flashes of envy for the naturally skinny and classically beautiful women I know, but I would not exchange what my own heavy-chested, weight-prone, cartwheel-deprived body has *given* me – psychological strength, emotional compassion, spiritual courage – for all the pearls in the sea. (Well, let's keep this real. Maybe I would exchange it for *all* the pearls.)

In some ways, gratitude is similar to forgiveness. Psychologists and spiritual teachers speak of its importance, it benefits and its healing power. We are encouraged to live gratefully. Sometimes we are urged to use prayer as a passage to forgiveness and thankfulness, which I am certain is effective for some. But not for all. It is not that simple. Gratitude is rarely something we can pull out of our boots at will. The way to an *authentic* 'yes' or 'thank you' is *through* an authentic 'no' or 'fuck this'. We need to release what *blocks* gratitude because it is less an intention or action than a river that needs to flow.

There is work to be done: to recap, the first four practices are *Noticing, Truth-telling, Choosing* and *Creating* in alignment with Life As It Is. Gratitude is *The Fifth Practice,* though the word 'practice' is somewhat misleading. More accurately, *Gratitude* is the unsought reward, a deep acceptance of the most painful experiences and appreciation for the growth, awakening, inner expansion, humility and open-heartedness that they ultimately bestow – *if* we allow it. It is both an act of will on our part, sourced by the disciplined effort of a spiritual warrior, and the gift that awaits us on the other side of suffering.

Many have testified to this: Viktor Frankl, Nelson Mandela, the Apostle Paul, Maya Angelou, to name a few. After surviving Auschwitz, Viktor Frankl said, 'I understand how a man who has nothing left in this world may still know bliss, be it only for a brief moment.' After serving twenty-seven years in prison, Mandela said, 'Deep down in every human heart there is gratitude and generosity' – as if it is an inner well from which we can all draw water. The Apostle Paul, whose suffering was extraordinary, was once beaten with rods, along with his co-worker Silas, and thrown into the dark, putrid, rat-infested prisons of that time. Bleeding – and in almost unbearable pain from the beating and the stocks in which their feet were clamped – they began singing hymns of *praise* and worship to the astonishment of other prisoners. And the title of Maya Angelou's autobiography (the first in a seven-volume series), says it all: *I Know Why the Caged Bird Sings.*

My dear friend, Catherine Rolt, can testify to this too, having lived with the brutal connective tissue disorder, Ehlers-Danlos syndrome her entire life. She has had *thirty-two* spinal surgeries, among many physical challenges, but shines with so much gratitude most people who meet her don't believe she is ill. Gratitude is how we embody grace.

I have also worked with literally thousands of students of Brad's work who have tapped deep gratitude at the most painful times in their lives. I am one among them, digging for grace in the most daunting moments of my life, finding the divine (not the devil) in the details, doing my best to come down from the mountain of my mind's illusions with an unwritten commandment ringing in my ears: *Take off your shoes. You are standing on holy ground.*

The Bottom Is Firm

My mother once told me that her greatest fear is to outlive her children. Losing Gabriella is the only heartbreak that could outrun the heartbreak of my leaving her. I cannot imagine greater anguish or more incapacitating grief. Perhaps that sounds contradictory. The grief I have written about in this book lifts us from the paralysis caused by denial, anger, depression and bargaining. But there is also a place and purpose for being stopped in our tracks, stunned into sorrow that surrenders all our claims on life until they sift through our fingers like sand. No, we were not built to lose our children without everything in the universe collapsing and being rearranged.

In May 2004, my dear friends, Elaine Alpert and Tom Colquitt, experienced this collapse in one of the worst possible ways. As Elaine wrote, 'Hijacked by a fit of anger and desperation on a dusky spring evening, my adolescent son, Rand, ended his own life.' Rand was sixteen years old and this happened on his brother's ninth birthday. His mother has asked me not to share too many details of how he did what he did, but the lifeshocks were intense, visceral and deeply harrowing:

'Horrific images from Rand's final act seized the night – feeling his weak pulse, urgently trying to revive him, Tom giving Rand CPR, police interrogating us as suspects, blaring ambulance sirens and lights – dozens of imprinted flashbacks. All while trying to shield our younger son from the mayhem. I never before knew the impact of full-blown post-traumatic stress. My whole system was on fire.'

And thus began a very long road through purgatory, awaking each morning to immovable dread, in search of cause and effect. 'Isn't it always, in some intrinsic way, the mother's fault?' She and Tom traced the multiple factors that accumulated into a perfect storm that led to their son's decision. As students of Brad's work, they faced the harshest of self-accusations and challenged them piece by agonising piece. They initially followed the inaccurately named 'Grief Cycle', unable to conceive how to go forwards, begging 'the powers-that-be for another chance to somehow make things right, for Rand to make a different decision, to love himself and us enough to stay.' For them, the tools Brad taught them were a saving grace. They knew they needed to rage and cry, to feel everything, to confront the lies that added suffering to their suffering, to voice their 'no' over and over, to empty it out. They knew that the only way out of the darkness was to move *through* it. As Elaine so eloquently writes, 'I was going to have to find a way to forgive Rand for leaving and to stop taking responsibility for what I could not change. Slowly wrestling free of the illusion that I was in control of much of anything, much less my own children, I began to accept that it was all so much bigger than me or Rand or any of us.'

Tom and Elaine were familiar with lifeshocks when all this happened. They were also aware of how few marriages survive something like this. They brought themselves to it consciously from the beginning. That very night their hands reached out to each other across Rand's body on a steel gurney. They looked into each other's eyes, pure love flowing between them, 'everything beyond the three of us hazy'. Shaking in the midst of their trauma, their hands sweating, 'saying yes and no and yes' to what they were seeing, they made an unequivocal commitment to do whatever was necessary to work through this together and still be together on the other side. Elaine says it felt 'sacred, like something opened up *inside* the horror of this moment.'

Even with all their wisdom about the gifts of lifeshocks, they resisted receiving them. They resisted hard. 'I have been afraid of discovering gifts too soon,' Elaine wrote six months after Rand's death, 'like a child sneaking to open presents under the tree before Christmas morning. Or much worse, afraid that it makes me a vulture, tearing at flesh still warm.'

But claim them she did: the pure love she has for her

son, which needed to be extracted like a diamond from the deep underground deposits of anger, regret and the stigma of losing a child to suicide; her gratitude for his life and all it taught her; the full recognition of her limitations as a mother and human being; the refined space in which she and Tom found themselves living, so close to everything vulnerable and precious and *real*. Now, thirteen years later, their other son is twenty-two and their marriage is rock solid. Tom has survived cancer, which struck one year after Rand's death, 'no doubt connected to thick and persistent grief.' And Elaine is offering transformational programmes to mothers who have lost children to suicide or overdoses (www. elainealpert.com), 'unwittingly in the centre of my dharma now, after many years of searching for my particular contribution' – which, in itself, required another surrender. They have been able to see the gifts 'beyond the manner of their delivery', gifts which many would have left to gather dust. They are certain they have been entrusted with something 'more mystical and beautiful' than they had ever imagined. Elaine recalls a turning-point conversation with Brad when she tearfully told him that she was somehow ever more grateful for her life in the wake of Rand's death.

'My dear,' he offered, 'You have been given a shortcut that most have to wait much longer, if ever, to know. You are living in grace.'

Brad knew what he was talking about. He had ground to stand on when he said this, having lost his firstborn son to a heroin overdose. As a young priest, he had also been profoundly moved by a formative lifeshock from his bishop, whose son died suddenly in a car accident.

Naturally, the bishop took time off and the congregation at their church were doubtful that he would return. But he did. And his first words from the pulpit were these:

'I have been to the bottom. And the bottom is *firm*.'

Kiss of Life

Last night, John, Gabriella and I returned home to Kent from Wales, where we spent the Christmas of 2017 with my entire family of origin: my parents; my brother, sister-in-law and their three now-adult children; my sister, brother-in-law and their two girls, aged eight and ten. My brother and his family recently moved into the house Dad built when we were children, which had been leased out to a tenant for several years. It was where I often felt hemmed in by the surrounding mountains and dark Welsh skies, but it was home. Its walls breathe with memories. The wooden floors creak with the formative lifeshocks of my childhood. My brother's bedroom, where the bomb was planted, is now his office. My nephew, a talented young musician, with 26 million plays on Spotify since he started out two years ago, is setting up a recording studio in a first-floor room looking out over the garden and the Gwyne Fawr river running through it. Something has come full circle and the circle is whole.

I can't remember the last time we all spent Christmas Day together under this roof. We crammed into the dining room, so many more of us these days, three generations of our clan. My 83-year-old dad, frail and resilient, needed help to cut up his food because he can't use his right hand since an operation a few months ago. He has mesothelioma, a form of lung cancer usually caused by asbestos and possibly, in his case, caused by the asbestos-riddled Houses of Parliament where he has worked for forty-seven years. Not that he would ever lay blame. Eighteen months ago, he had a third of one of his lungs removed, the entire pleura and several ribs. He insisted on doing this, against doctors' advice, instead of having palliative chemotherapy, and it gave him a new lease of life. Then the cancer returned. Again, he opted for more surgery because it was localised in one shoulder, but this has taken a serious toll. Nine weeks later, he is still in enormous pain and doped up on morphine to manage it. He bends like a willow from the excruciating discomfort in his neck, likely caused by damaged nerves during the operation. He shuffles more than walks, doggedly getting from A to B as independently as he can, but needing a carer 24/7. He is thin as a rake and keeps falling over, perhaps because of the drugs, perhaps because of a bleed in the brain from a previous fall, perhaps worse. As I write, he is being taken back to London in an ambulance for neurological tests to try to get to the bottom of it. He has a lot of cuts and bruises, including a few stitches in his head from one of the falls. Last time I spent the night at my parents' house in London, Mum and I needed to pick him up off the floor in the morning, where he had been lying for several hours having fallen in the night. Finding him there was the lifeshock moment when we realised he needed constant care.

But when the drugs wear off, Dad is sharp as a tack. I think he longs to go back to work and apply his alert mind to something other than how to lift a fork to his mouth. His dignity is impeccable. At my fiftieth birthday party, which happened a few weeks after his cancer was first detected, I acknowledged him in a speech and said how much we all wanted him to stay. I also said I hoped to outlive him so he didn't need to endure outliving me. Just six months ago, he was thriving, and I was the one who needed assistance to walk a few yards. He was so worried about me. He was relishing time with his grandchildren and still contributing to Select Committees in Parliament most days. He was, as poet Mary Oliver observed after her own experience of lung cancer, 'fiercely wanting. . .a little bit more of life'. Now the tables have turned. While I am thriving again, something in Dad is surrendering, turning towards death instead of away from it, planning his memorial service down to the last detail, basking in this Christmas Day with his entire family at the hearth of the home he built several decades ago. The losses we suffer at the hands of ageing and unrelenting diseases can soften the vista of dying. The *limiting* lifeshocks can help us yield to our mortality. The *exposing* lifeshocks can help us face our sealed-over fears. The *evoking* lifeshocks can bring everything back to love. They have been flowing thick and fast for all of us this week, but especially for him.

These three kinds of lifeshocks, about which I have shared examples throughout this book, proceed from three (not directly correlating) realms: *First Force, Second Force* and *Third Force. First Force* is all the energy and activity generated by the reactive mind. In many ways, this energy runs the world. What we say and do out of our 'no' to lifeshocks generates more lifeshocks from a reactive space, impacting those around us. To a large extent, reactivity begets reactivity and we call it 'normality'. Thus, the realm of First Force is the realm of 'Illusion', constructed by the mind's representations of reality rather than Reality itself.

On Christmas Eve, Dad started asking me about this book. He seemed to be anxious about it, concerned I might say negative things about my family and resistant to the level of exposure I might go to about myself (which is probably far worse than he fears!). This is just not what my parents do. His tone was wry; later he called it 'teasing'. But I reacted strongly to his suggestion that I might disclose the unhappy events of my childhood in such a way that would cast Mum and him in a poor light. 'How do you see me that you think I would do such a thing?' I retorted at my frail father. 'It insults me that you think I would.' He was sitting at a table in my sister's kitchen and I walked out, went to another room and burst into tears. First Force met First Force.

But these lifeshocks still awaken us. I recognised where his 'teasing' came from and was acutely aware of the glaring omission my deeply private family members are in these pages. I have sought to protect them and honour their wishes by not saying very much about them. And yet, I fear I dishonour them by saying so little. His words also exposed *my fear* of being this vulnerable with my friends and family, an unaddressed resistance to this book ever seeing the light of day. I am okay with it being read by strangers, but wonder what will happen to my personal relationships when friends and family see me this close up. In turn, my reaction got through to something in Dad. When I saw him the next day, he pulled me towards the chair he was sitting in and apologised unequivocally. He may not have dug into his lifeshocks the way I did, but something had opened his heart.

Something dissolved between us. Something was mutually forgiven that ran deeper than our encounter in the kitchen. Love prevailed.

Second Force is the energy and activity generated by the creative, transcending mind. What we say and do out of our 'yes' to lifeshocks delivers conscious, loving, well-intended lifeshocks to others. Oftentimes, though not always, these will evoke some kind of 'yes' from the people they impact. This is the realm of awareness, clarity and alignment with Life As It Is.

I went to see Dad the day before we drove back to London. Plans had been made to get him to a neurological hospital and then to a residential care facility, which he has been understandably resisting until now. Partly, he had one fall too many, but also a close family friend *happened* to call whose husband *happened* to be at a facility that *happens* to be a ten-minute walk from Dad's home in London and about which the friend had no complaints whatsoever. 'That was the Almighty,' my mum said in a rare nod to divine intervention. 'Indeed,' I agreed. Even so, Dad, who is also very deaf without his hearing aids, added, 'I know you think I can't hear you when you're all talking about me and making these plans, but I can you know. I hear it all.' We are not a family who express love very directly. My sister, Olivia (also a very private person), is probably the best at this among us, but on the whole it is more assumed and implied than stated. But Second Force took over on this occasion.

'That's because we love you, Dad. We are concerned about you. And we want to find a realistic solution that you are happy with. You are very *loved*.'

'Well yes,' he responded, his shoulders visibly relaxing and his face softening just a bit. 'Yes, I see that. It's love.'

My eyes tear up as I write these words. Dad's lifeshocks are penetrating deep. I have known and loved this man my entire life, but I have never seen his guard so down or his heart so accessible. He can be prickly, critical and quick to defend sometimes, but he has an incredibly generous spirit. He is a true public servant. And his devotion to his family cannot be faulted. Part of me wanted to tell him it is okay to go, that he has planted his heart in the people he loves and will always be held there. Instead, I listened to him express his pride in his artistic progeny: his musical grandson who is about to do a tour in the States and record some tracks in Spotify's New York studios; and his daughter, the published author, who won a public speaking competition at the age of fifteen 'which we didn't come to.' His voice was tinged with a melancholy that blew in from the seas of his past. I know that place, where the end drops in front of you like a cliff face and the sea birds swoop in squawking. But this was a space of receptivity not negativity, of his 'yes' shaking hands with my 'yes', a space where we are aligned with Life's intentions more than our own. This is the space of Second Force.

Third Force is any and *all* the energy that is present in any moment. It is *the* life force that uses First and Second Force activity to make itself known regardless, to awaken us through all of it – reactivity and creativity, hate and love, resentment and forgiveness, incursions and invitations. *Your* will and *my* will are employed by *Thy* will to lift the veils of illusion and bring us home to ourselves. As Rama Krishna declared, 'The winds of grace are always blowing, but you have to raise the sail.'

Whichever way the wind blows and whatever the tail-force of our lifeshocks, there are three fundamental constituents of inner freedom: *authenticity, lovability* and *humanity*. When we shed our false and feared selves to reveal our true selves; when we open our hearts instead of closing them; when we stop demanding how *life should be* and accept how *life really is*, we are spiritually free. There is nothing we need to prove any more. We replace protection with connection. We choose humility over arrogance. We bring down our guards and raise our spirits. Suddenly our lives take on a special radiance from within. We find the sacred here, there and everywhere. We serve. We pull fine threads of divinity from the fabric of daily life, of the mundane, the ordinary, the not-so-shocking after all.

Every lifeshock calls us, implores us back to this place in three essential ways, which I hope I have made clear: by *limiting* our omnipotence, *exposing* our pretences and *evoking* our longing *to* love, our longing *for* love, our merging *with* love. We can identify *omnipotence* in being controlling, demanding, fixing, bullying, having to have or do things on our terms, insisting on being right and believing we know how anything should be. We can identify *pretence* in dishonesty, deception, hiding, secrecy, phoniness, manipulating for effect, passive-aggression and false positivity. We can identify *loveless-ness* in withholding, distancing, indifference, cruelty, hard-heartedness, resentment, self-indulgence, exclusivity, prejudice and superiority. These are the cages we construct for ourselves and then wonder why we feel isolated, hopeless and disillusioned.

Similarly, we can recognise our *humanity* when we are acting and living with real limits, when we are open to all possibilities, when we are humble without being self-effacing, when we are willing to risk and be creative, even if it doesn't work out the way we want it to, when we are gloriously, even gladly vulnerable and when we experience serenity. We can recognise our *authenticity* in truthfulness, assertiveness, personal authority, emotional depth and congruence, self-awareness, integrity, steadfastness and a deep ease in our being. We can recognise *love-ability* in patience, attentive listening, mutuality, open-heartedness, empathy, co-operation, partnering, inclusivity, respect for diversity and our willingness to forgive. These are the qualities of being on offer in any moment that literally give us back to ourselves. These are drops of grace.

Some religions seem to have recognised these three levels of awakening. In the Christian tradition, these three kinds of lifeshocks can be seen to correlate with the Holy Trinity. First, God the Father, the Creator, who *limits* and humbles us, the Is-ness of it all (and therefore the biggest of these categories). Second, God the Son, the Redeemer, who *exposes* and reveals us, as he did the lies and corruption of the religious establishments of his time. But, in my view far more importantly, he was literally and ultimately *exposed* to the world as he died on the cross, arms stretched out in utter vulnerability, his heart centre wide open, willing to suffer to that extent *for the world* and *at its mercy*. He exposed the fullness of his humanity (as the Son of *Man*), including his own spiritual crisis when he publicly asked why his God had forsaken him. Third, God the Holy Ghost, the Sanctifier, who *evokes* and forgives us. The 'spirit' or 'ghost' is that which lives for ever, the breath of life (hence 'give up the ghost'), the essence of the Is-ness, ubiquitous, in the air, in everything, evoking connection, reminding us that we are One. At the same time, every manifestation of the Trinity limits, exposes and evokes us in some way because they are all ultimately of and through Third Force.

This trinity of lifeshocks also contains the 'self', which is *exposed*, relationships with 'others', which are *evoked* and the 'contexts' in which we move and meet external *limitations* beyond our control.

And therein lies our spiritual sobriety: *I am as I am, you are as you are, it is as it is. We Are One.* All else is drunkenness.

Most of my lifeshocks over this past week with my family have been both limiting and evoking. In past years, they were more exposing than anything else. Someone wise (possibly Ram Dass but I can't confirm) once said, 'We think we have got our lives sorted and then we go home for Christmas'. I have found this to be pointedly true, often retreating into a false self I thought I had long since dismantled and returning to the kindergarten of awakening when with my family of origin. But this year was different. My own illness has dissolved some barriers these past three years, evoking more love to flow between us and invoking more authenticity, especially from me. But it was Dad's presence which graced us all: the way his wife and children aligned behind a shared intention to meet his needs while upholding his dignity; being humbled by the courage he showed in attending every family gathering for several days in a row; feeling the poignancy of being together again in the home he built with his own hands; taking turns at slipping a hand under his elbow when he moved from one part of the room to another; seeing his left hand shake as it raised food to his mouth and performed tasks his right hand had discharged for over eighty years; seeing my beleaguered but dedicated mum adapt to each nuanced change in his condition; all of us surrendering to his inexorable mortality while holding space for another crescent of life to rise.

Sometimes we need to knuckle down and process our lifeshocks: clear our mindtalk, release our resentments, tell the truth and create anew until gratitude dawns. Other times, we can cut across the grass by discerning the nature of the lifeshocks – limiting, exposing or evoking – and claiming the *gifts of being* in real time.

Of course, not all religious traditions recognise a divine trinity. Indeed, it is antithetical to Islam's monotheistic assertion of God's absolute oneness. Similarly, the Jewish meaning of *Ehad* is that of Oneness itself. But even those who see a trinity of divine expression also acknowledge that which unifies them all. This oneness – that limits, exposes and evokes - is what Brad meant by Third Force, which comes to us from a space before and beyond everything while manifesting *in* everything that is Life Itself. And Dr Roy Whitten, who co-founded the More To Life programme with Brad, used to say, 'You can call it the Holy Spirit, the Source, the Creator, God, the One, Krishna Consciousness or M-I-C-K-E-Y M-O-U-S-E if you like! It's in *everything* and *every one of us*.'

Meher Baba called this presence 'the One behind the Many'. When I returned from that first unplanned, but apparently pre-ordained trip to India and fell back into the claws of my reactive mind, I dedicated myself to re-experiencing 'that kiss we want with our whole lives'. I had drunk from a sacred well that left me consciously, gratefully, thirsty for more. A year or so later, I experienced Brad's work for the first time. A year after that, I met him in person and knew him to be my human teacher, the one who could help me feel that kiss again. Nothing bowled me over with the same force as I had felt in the Samadhi, but I didn't need to walk across deserts or scale remote mountains to catch brief glimpses of the sacred with miles and miles in between. Instead, I entered the theatre of grace that is daily life. I learned to let my lifeshocks kiss me into consciousness. I learned to lift the veil of illusion and pull out my own thorns. Twenty-six years later, I returned to Meherabad in a state of deep gratitude for the downpour of answers to my earlier reluctant prayer and in the hope that Meister Eckhart, a Dominican monk and mystic of the Middle Ages, was exact in this wisdom:

'If the only prayer you ever say in your whole life is *thank you*, it will be enough.'

Part Three

Silence Roars

The only way to make sense out of a change is to plunge into it, move with it and join the dance.

Alan Watts

Keep Cleaning the Windows

The awakening process: I found it, I lost it, I found it again.
Then repeat.

K. Bradford Brown

Lead Us into Temptation

This morning John tripped over one too many Amazon packages from Christmas. The house is a tip: half-unpacked suitcases, Gabriella's new toys (the ones she's grown out of yet to be packed up for the charity shop), no room in the overflowing collection bins that won't be emptied until two days after New Year's Day 2018, which dawns tomorrow. We're all tired. The car had a puncture at eight p.m. on the M4 as we were heading home to Kent from Wales and is now sitting in the driveway, tyre still flat, where the AA recovery vehicle left it at two a.m.

John is a minimalist. I create clutter. Gabriella leaves disarray in her ebullient wake. John shouted first. I shouted second. Gabriella shouted third (with commensurate gusto). We are a shouty family when we're all below-the-line. Three blaming dramas under the same roof – although it is John's last line of defence (following avoiding and pleasing), my first. Gabriella is more like me when reactive

– quick to anger and comfortable expressing it. Within minutes the house was flooded with so much First Force energy that even the dog starting barking, which usually only happens when strangers come to the door. At which point, John took her for a two-hour walk in the pissing rain, Gabriella played with her new Scalextric and I finished drafting the chapter called 'Grace'.

The irony was not lost on me. When we are in danger of being struck by enlightenment, life swiftly knocks any lurking entitlement to that enlightenment on the head. Nearing the end of this book does not mean I'm nearing the end of reactivity or self-deception or falling asleep. Not a bit of it. I remain blessed by a nightmare neighbour living in my head and banging on the bloody floor every day: my 'reactive mind'. And as I have said, being awake is *never* automatic. The instant we stop *noticing* is the instant we forget ourselves and shack up with lies again. When John left the house, I took out my anxiety on Gabriella by saying, 'If you don't clear up those toys I won't buy you *anything* until your birthday (in four months' time).'

Technically, that would include food, clothes, toothpaste and stuff for school. To which she replied,

'Not even rocks and stones?!'

That girl of mine. That girl of Life's. I dissolved laughing, the lifeshock bursting my dramatic bubble and restoring me to my right mind – my conscious, creative, truth-seeing mind. Sometimes, we can shift our state with three conscious breaths. Other times, we just need one more lifeshock to snap us out of our slumber. Most times, we need to work to stay awake. As Brad often reminded me, 'Practise, practise, practise. I hated it then.

I hate it now, until I remember my last sonata.' And what better reason to get up in the morning? Staying asleep, moving through the world encased in a dramatic version of who we think we have to be because of who we fear we really are, is a very tiring business indeed. Every day, the reactive mind snaps at our heels and endeavours to reassert control. Be very clear about this. If you think you have banished it forever and transcended into a permanent above-the-line 'yes' to Life As It Is, look again. We just get more cunning at lying to ourselves.

I know this. For a while, after I married John, I took my eye off the ball because I was so happy in my new life. Lots of evoking lifeshocks and not quite enough suffering to keep me on my conscious toes! I did much less process work. I was less present for my relatively new business partner (and old friend), less awake to her fears and needs. I missed many lifeshocks about her declining confidence in my commitment to our company, until an email arrived, out of the blue, announcing her resignation. Effective immediately. She didn't warn me it was coming, but life tried to warn me in dozens of ways that I was too domestically content to notice or take seriously. Before I knew it, our clients and team had gone with her to a new partnership. My part was that I had gone back to sleep in some ways and the significant cost of all this, financial and emotional, woke me right back up.

But we can also be tricked into believing we just don't need to work at being awake any more because we have transcended into another realm of 'mastery'. I have seen this several times. The last time I saw Nick, he had said to me, 'Sophie, I'm no longer willing to engage with my reactive mind.' And one week later he was dead. Other times, I have simply seen people lose themselves while believing they are found.

The way the mind gets more sophisticated at lying is the 'bad news'. But there is so much more 'good news'. Firstly, it is all a Grand Design. Pearls are formed over time within oyster shells in response to an external irritant. Similarly, we create pearls of wisdom in response to lifeshocks entering our systems. We need this grit in our systems to grow.

We also *need* the lies to deliver us to the truths. They are not merely obstacles to overcome. They are gateways to pass through. I tapped into the beauty of my inner being *because* I had believed I was ugly, not in spite of it. I believed I was unlovable, which led me to an authentic self-acceptance and the true love of a true soul mate. As Brad used to say, '*Most love isn't.*' I believed I was 'too privileged', which led me to recognise the responsibilities my actual privilege bestowed on me and to count my many blessings. I believed I was an 'emotional fruitcake (a.k.a. crazy)', which birthed my emotional intelligence and took me on a deep inquiry into my empathic nature. I believed I was 'too much', which helped me embed a humility in my being before claiming my gifts and choosing to shine my light. I believed my personal power was 'dangerous', which ensured my vigilant awareness of the shadows that my light casts. I believed I was 'unworthy' of *the touch of Spirit on my body*, which put me on a path towards finding divinity *in* my humanity, not beyond it. In this sense, all roads lead to Rome, even the diversions. And most mistakes yield new information about things as they really are.

As a theologian, Brad saw this line of the Lord's Prayer

as highly questionable and likely subject to the mindtalk of someone who didn't get its original meaning: 'Lead us *not* into temptation, but deliver us from evil'. Look at the syntax. It doesn't work. If we are *not* being led into temptation in the first place, then what evil is there to deliver us from? Why the 'but'? What if it originally said, 'Lead us *into* temptation, but deliver us from evil'? A shudder went right through me as I wrote that. Amazingly, Pope Francis has also challenged the same line just this month, December 2017, and has proposed changing it. But his reasons are different. He believes it is inaccurate because it suggests that it is God, not the devil, who induces temptation.

But I think Brad, the spiritual maverick, was suggesting *exactly that*: temptation is a necessary part of the divine design. Because what if we need to be tested? What if we need to be walked into the desert for forty days and nights, to be taken to the brink of what we most fear we are, so that we know what the truth is delivering us *from*? What if the reactive mind leads us into the darkness precisely so that we can see what's on the other side, what's on the *inside*? Why would we seek what wasn't missing or pursue what we have not yearned for? And the best news of all is that, however far we disappear into unnecessary surplus suffering, lifeshocks will keep coming to deliver us to who we really are and the light we have forgotten.

When I apologised to Gabriella for shouting at Daddy (who apologised for shouting too) and for saying I wouldn't buy her *anything* before her birthday, I said, 'Sometimes, when I feel grumpy, I think and say things that I don't really mean.' She smiled and held my hand.

'It's not *you* who is grumpy, Mummy. Just like it's not

me who is rude. It's your *behaviour*.' And on we went with our day.

How to Love Lifeshocks

Everything in this book can be mapped on to this simple structure, which represents the 'I am' (the self) and its relationship with the 'I AM' (life itself):

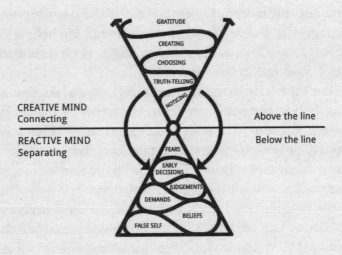

Heavens above

There are two profoundly different states of being: the reactive mind, which is *separating*, and the 'creative mind', which is *connecting*. The former is *below-the-line* and the latter is *above-the-line*, all of which I have explained in previous chapters. This line is the boundary between wakefulness and sleep, consciousness and unconsciousness, 'yes' to reality and 'no'. At any moment, we are in one state or another. There is no middle ground, just as there is no 'half-pregnant'.

In a *reactive, separating* state, we are run by fear and self-deception, entrenched core beliefs and inflated demands about how we, others and life *should be*. We inhabit our *false selves*, often calling them our *personalities*. This is the human ego in full control. It is also our automatic state of being, what we will revert to when we stop paying attention. This state bears some similarity to what the Sufis call 'The Commanding Self' (the *Nafs-i-Ammara* in classical literature). In *Learning How to Learn*, the Sufi author and teacher, Idries Shah, explains that this manifests in 'reactions, hopes (which I read as false expectations), fears and various opinions and preoccupations.' It is the egoic self on autopilot, following conditioned patterns.

In a *creative, connecting* state, we are aware of ourselves, others and the world around us. We feel open, free, loving, joyous, peaceful, awe-struck and grateful. This is where we feel grief and sadness too. This state is fuelled by clarity, truthfulness, insight, and a conscious commitment to align ourselves with Life As It Is, however antithetical to our personal desires. In this state, we inhabit our authority. We become authentic. We accept our flaws as well as our strengths. We access the heart's intelligence, which Sufis see as the gate to 'Divine Reality' and, as author and translator Kabir Helminski explains in *The Knowing Heart*, is the only part of us that is 'expansive enough to embrace the infinite qualities of the universe.' We unleash remarkable creativity in response to challenging situations. We forgive. We grow. We give thanks. We are fully, gloriously alive.

In several spiritual traditions, the reactive state of separation relates to *maya* (which literally means 'illusion' or 'magic', where 'things are not what they seem'), *samsara* (which means wandering circuitously in a cycle of 'endless drifting') or *hell*. In most religious and folkloric traditions, hell is an eternal destination located in the afterlife. However, the word reaches back to the Proto-Germanic *halja*, meaning 'one who covers up or hides something'. Existing below-the-line is a covering up of who we really are, a psychic underworld of resentment, victimisation and relentless suffering: a hell on earth.

By contrast, the creative state of connection corresponds with *nirvana* or *moksha, enlightenment* and *heaven*. 'Nirvana' is sometimes depicted as a place in the afterlife as well, but considered a state of consciousness 'above all others' in Buddhist traditions, the opposite of ignorance, greed and hatred, which 'cloud our minds, making us do stupid things.' In Hinduism, *moksha* refers to freedom from *samsara,* an emancipation from ignorance into self-realisation. *Enlightenment* is recognised in Western psychology as well as several spiritual traditions. It is sometimes said to be 'full comprehension of the situation', and relates to ignorance as 'a state of being in the dark'. It also points to insight, revelation and illumination. And the German philosopher, Immanuel Kant, described enlightenment as 'man's release from his self-incurred tutelage.'

Like 'hell', *heaven* is generally reserved for the afterlife, but what if 'the kingdom of Heaven' really is 'at hand'?

What if *heaven*'s *above* the line? What if it is on offer right now, here on earth, as Brad was certain it was; not at some future time that awaits us at the end of days, but as a state of being, of surrender to Life As It Is, as embodied truth, gratitude and grace?

This is why the top of the diagram is open, its arrows reaching into infinite possibilities and ever-expanding consciousness.

A path through the pathless path

The 'I Am' diagram shows five key practices for living above the line. The instant we *notice* (First Practice) our lifeshocks, feelings, mindtalk and/or behaviour, we move into the creative mind. We are not yet fully awake, but we are *aware*. Gurdjieff refers to this as 'self-remembering', whereby we become 'aware of the one who is thinking what we are thinking.' The circle at the centre of the diagram represents the eye of the needle, which we pass through as *noticing* shifts our state. This is the place of *recognition*, of seeing how we have missed the mark and taking responsibility for our self-crafted state of being, thus liberating our *ability to respond* instead of *react*. This passage can include the *pure shame* (as distinct from toxic shame) that I have written about earlier, especially when we are recognising our resentment or cruelty, how it has affected others and what it has cost us. At times, we may pass through this eye like a birth canal, but with commensurate relief and aliveness on the other side.

When we engage in *truth-telling* (Second Practice) by challenging our mindtalk, thus allowing the truth to make itself known, we transform our emotions and feel profoundly connected again. Fear dissolves and love blossoms. In other words, when we 'know the truth', it really does set us free.

When we are *choosing* (Third Practice) with discerning eyes, we are back in charge again. We don't just become more effective at implementing our own intentions. We begin to realise that life may have things in mind for us that we had never thought of. Instead of submitting to our false beliefs and circumstances we cannot control, we may look at the details of our lives and discern our life purpose – or what some might call 'destiny'. This is how we change our 'karma' and reside in our 'dharma', which Hinduism describes as behaving in accord with *rta*, the natural order that makes life and the universe possible. As my dear friend, David Templer (also a long-term student of Brad's and a senior trainer), says, 'Every conscious choice we make is another step forward on the pathless path of a just life.'

Out of conscious choosing flows the unbridled power of *creating* (Fourth Practice). In part, the creative imagination is liberated from the destructive imagination (mindtalk), allowing us to live more fluidly and boldly, to take more risks, to move un-self-consciously through the world, to open to higher realms and let them have their way with us. In this we *align with the creation that is going on all the time*, becoming part of it; less something we do than something that 'does' us. We become agents of creation, awakeners, conduits of conscious lifeshocks, open channels whose intuitive sixth sense is highly attuned to the ebb and flow of That Which Is. As Brad said, 'The unexamined mind slays the best in us while the best in us harnesses the powers of the mind to be aligned with the cosmos.'

As we harness this creative energy, we are often delivered to a state of awe, of a *gratitude* (Fifth Practice) which we cannot design or manufacture, an appreciation of our own value and sense of place, a fulfilment of purpose that goes way beyond the self-help notion of 'creating your own reality', because it kneels in wonder *at the reality that is creating us.* It relinquishes ambition to majesty and enfolds all the suffering, all the lacerating pain of cruelty and separation, into a faithful acceptance of everything that has happened and is yet to unfold. Here we meet loss as the poet Denise Riley eventually did after the death of her son, Jacob, and 'bear what can not be borne'. Everyone we have ever known, including our 'enemies', unveils themselves as the soul teachers they always were. We bow to them in recognition and forgiveness, crossing the gateway of gratitude into peace. We become the water, not the vessel that would contain it. We expand into the fullness of 'I Am' and we hear the silence roar.

Until we don't.

A constant companion

Living *above-the-line* does not end our engagement with the reactive mind. Perhaps some mystics and saints truly transcend it permanently, but the rest of us can learn to tame it and put a leash around its neck. We can be aware of it moment to moment. We can expect it to rise up in any way it can in order to reassert control. *Don't read this piffle. What does Sophie Sabbage know? This is too hard. Get a life! I can make you comfortable and happy. Facebook is much more interesting. Have a glass of wine.* It's like living with cancer. You need to keep a constant eye on it without making an enemy of it, prioritise your health and treatments, and ensure that *you have it* so that *it does not have you*.

'I Am' *all* that is depicted on the diagram, above and below, day and night, light as a feather and heavy as stone. I am a steward of truths because I have been a prisoner of lies. I am on to the lies quickly now. They pull me back into the cage often enough, but I don't let them lock it. I *notice* and go to work. The world trains us to be fearful, victimised and bitter, enslaved by the reactive mind. But inner freedom is negation not acquisition, a slow erasing of the false self through continued and resolute correction of our perceptions until we find increasing clarity, connection and peace. This has been my experience for many years.

Most importantly, when I am so blinded by fear that I can't claw my way back to clarity, as when I was first told of my 'incurable cancer', there is something in the universe that I can utterly count on: *lifeshocks*. Depicted by the downward pointing arrows on the diagram (but could easily be indicated by a series of arrows flowing in from the great beyond), there will be another and another and another, for as long as we walk this earth. No matter how many we miss, ignore, say no to and send back, they will keep on coming until we *notice* and WAKE THE HELL (OR HEAVENS) UP. I did not suspect what those gold words on white marble meant when I was a lost soul in India: *I have come not to teach, but to awaken*. The world is awash with 'teachers' who instruct, explain, preach and tell us how to be. Sometimes I wish I had another word to describe Brad, whose teaching vehicle was *awakening through lifeshocks*, perhaps our greatest and most persistent teacher of all. Because awakening is the *whole* darn point.

No matter how deep we wallow, how intensely we hate, how far we fall short, lifeshocks will keep offering us a way out of personal hell. This is the beneficence of the universe, an infinite generosity that we can tap at any moment, a perfect system of awakening and realignment. It is also how we can be sure we are not *alone* and remember that we are *all-one*. Lifeshocks are our constant companion, delivering exactly what we need to make the shift of perspective that produces miracles of being. It isn't that life is out to get us. It is that life is out to *help us get ourselves*. What can look like breaking down by saying 'yes' to lifeshocks that seem abhorrent is actually a spiritual surrender, an opening of our hearts to compassion, humility and gratitude, a breaking through to grace. Over and over, we are delivered to what Life has to offer, in all its unfathomable, but more discernible than we surmise, ways. This is faithfulness. Lifeshocks are such tangible harbingers of reality or, if you prefer, the divine. And *this* is what we can love in them.

Our part is to let the lifeshocks lead us to inner freedom and keep cleaning the windows so that we can appreciate the view.

Just Stay Alive

It's New Year's Day 2018. Dad just called from the hospital. They couldn't do an MRI scan of his brain because it was too agonising for him to lie on the hard couch that slides in and out of the machine, often with a 'catcher's mask' to hold the head in place. As such, we don't know if there is a bleed there or any brain tumours. But they did a CT scan of his body in search of clues as to why he keeps falling over and is now finding it hard to use one of his legs. The cancer has spread through his spinal column. His doctors are planning palliative radiotherapy and putting him on steroids. He called Mum first, then me, 'because you know what I am going through'. And I do, up to a point: the spinal tumours, the steroids, the radiotherapy to that which holds us upright and protects the primary pathway for connecting the brain with the peripheral nervous system. I even know what it is to be looking into 'that good night' and reaching for the inner surrender that lets us move into it like molten metal to take its shape.

But I don't know the grief of old age, the transition from leading a clan to needing them to sweep up your decaying leaves in the winter of your days. I don't know what this is like for *him*, how scared he is, how accepting. His voice sounded strong when he said, 'I won't be living long, darling', and I resisted the brief protective urge to suggest he may yet come back from this, which he yet might. The future is *always* unknown. Instead, I let a piece of my heart break.

I am inadequate. Truly. Not in the write-me-off-absolutely sense. But in the fact of my ultimate human inadequacy, the places beyond my reach, the ropes I can't let down to pull my dad out of these waters. There is such freedom in getting this and being okay with it. No need to fix or polish or save. Just a simple, clean impulse to be with my dad as he descends the mountain, whenever that time comes, and be with my grief along the way. If I can help him, even a little, to descend faithfully, to 'die before he dies' by releasing the part that still clings to the world, then this will be resplendent light for my sad but wide-open eyes. And this is *his* road Home, not mine.

It seems I am still being given the chance to *come home* instead of going home. My brain scan before Christmas showed further improvement, with just one 8-mm lesion remaining. This enabled me to take Gabriella ice-skating again over the Christmas holidays, which had seemed so impossible last summer. Meanwhile, cancer cells continue to circulate in my blood like microscopic lifeshocks I cannot see, but know are there. I like to think my healthy cells are meeting them as markers on *their* path within the path, learning to align and adapt and evolve no matter what. I try to assist the healthy ones with whatever interventions, medical and otherwise, may strengthen them for what lies ahead. I reject 'your cancer can't be cured' as an ironclad truth, while respecting the gravity of my situation and the brink it has taken me to already, more than once. I have planned my funeral, my next scans and a trip to South Africa in the spring to lead a course there. Then I slide back into *now* and wait for the next lifeshock to come.

I remember how easily I used to make New Year's Eve resolutions, at least five, carving them in confidence that there would be space and time for it all. Now, with cancer as a constant companion, my reactive mind tries to limit my intentions to this: *Stay alive, Sophie. Just stay alive.* But this is a mere nuance away from the intention I have held since my early twenties, and a radically different state of mind in which I aim, above all aims, to *stay* (fully, consciously, authentically, purposefully, creatively and gratefully) *ALIVE*. Insh'Allah, up to and including my last breath.

This afternoon, Gabriella and I started putting old toys into a box for refugee children. We took down the Christmas decorations and John burnt the rubbish in the garden while standing in the pouring rain.

'What would we do without him, Mummy?' Gabriella asked as she watched him through the clean kitchen windows, one of the many things John attends to in our home, either personally or by hiring some help.

I didn't answer. I didn't want to picture it or give my mind room to paint dark shadows on the walls. Instead, I picked up my daughter and pulled her into me, squeezing tight. Our golden cocker spaniel, Isla, stood on her hind legs and put her front paws on my thigh, wagging her tail enthusiastically as if asking to be picked up too. The memory of those long years of living alone with just a cat melted like breath on a mirror.

Then John left the bonfire to itself and started looking under the car seats for my prescription reading glasses. They're a purple Jimmy Choo design with a small rectangle of bling silver crystals on the sides, next to the hinges. I'd lost them somewhere between the puncture and crawling into bed when we got home. John knows they're my favourites and an investment in my ageing eyes. I popped Gabriella, who is getting heavier to hold, on to the kitchen counter and slipped an arm around her waist while we watched him search. As I stood there, I could feel my pores opening to these two great loves of mine and gratitude started humming in my cells like a hive of bees.

Lifeshocks Epilogue

My father died three months before this book was published in hardback. He never read it and for a while I regretted not having sent him the proofs so he could see the very high esteem in which I had come to hold him. Perhaps he did see. But I also knew there were experiences described in this book that would be painful for him to discover – not least the date rape in my twenties. He did not need to learn about that for the first time on his death-bed and I did not need him to know me that intimately. Still. It is the gaps we leave that cry out in the emptiness that follows, the unsaid, the unearthed, the unforgiven.

There were many lifeshocks in his final months – mostly limiting ones for him and evoking ones for me. He spent these months to-ing and fro-ing between his care home and the hospital in London. My brother was close at hand and spent a lot of time with him, making his own peace with this impending loss. My mother found it all increasingly distressing. My sister, who lives in Wales, longed to see him more than she was able to and I travelled to town from Kent as often as I could.

One such time was when he had been rushed to hospital again. My brother and his wife, Livvy, were away on a holiday planned several months previously, which I had urged them to go and enjoy despite the risk that Dad might die while they were away. He did. On the eve of his passing I left him on a ward in the hospital ICU as I headed home was feeling hopeless about getting him out of there. He wanted out badly. He begged me not to let him die in that cold, clinical, soulless place with strangers in neighbouring beds and sickness clinging to the sheets. It was a weekend and I had promised Gabriella a full dose of Mummy. I felt torn and tried to convince myself there was still time, that I could return on Monday and handle it all then. But deep down I knew differently and, as the last train to Kent rattled along the tracks that night, I called my dear friend Catherine to ask her to visit him first thing and call me with an update.

When I awoke on the following mid-March morning, snow was falling hard and the daffodils in our garden were bowed in defeat. I was already rearranging my day and promising Gabriella I would make up for it when a lifeshock arrived in the form of Catherine's text: 'You need to come as soon as you can.' As I drove through the snowstorm, stopping once to call my sister and update her, Catherine started advocating for my Dad to be released back to his care home despite the 'heart incident' which had occurred that night. She was told this was quite impossible and against all the rules, but a lifetime with Ehlers Danlos Syndrome has made her a master of plucking possibilities from seemingly impossible situations. She loved my Dad and love would not take no for an answer.

I was waiting in his care home bedroom when the

paramedics carried him in on a stretcher, ashen-grey, an oxygen mask on his mouth, which he removed as soon as he saw me. 'Sophie,' he gasped, his eyes wet with tears of relief, 'You are *here*.' Simultaneously, this lifeshock crushed my desire to rescue him from his suffering, insisted I surrender all control and implored me to love this man with all my might to the bitter-sweet end. He was considerate, appreciative and erudite up to and including the last words he spoke before slipping out of consciousness: 'I am grateful to you all. And now may flights of angels sing me to my rest.' A few hours later, having been joined by my niece and nephew, it became my privilege to feel Dad's paralysed right hand relax between mine as he took his last breath. That lifeshock was one of the most brutally exquisite moments of my life.

We buried him at his beloved church on the side of a Welsh mountain. It bucketed rain through the entire service, an intimate family gathering, but the clouds suddenly parted as his coffin was lowered into the ground. The sun shone down on us and a red kite circled directly overhead. I see them frequently these days, like John sees herons, and feel Dad's spirit soaring on their majestic wings.

Six months after the gentle funeral, a thanksgiving service was held at St. Margaret's Westminster, attended by over six hundred people including representatives of the Queen and numerous colleagues from the House of Lords. As I stood at the pulpit to give a tribute and looked out across the packed church, I felt immensely proud to have been his daughter and to have owned my pride in him so publicly in this book. I spoke of him without notes or concern about the various dignitaries who were listening. It was more *for* him than about him and I painted his shadows as luminously as I depicted his light: his cantankerous, hyper-critical, highly impatient character, beneath which resided a peace-maker, an adored father and grandfather, and a true public servant who made an indelible mark on the world. At times he had been desperate not to die but, in those last months, his suffering carried him to that point of acceptance where he could plan this entire service meticulously and say to my brother, 'I just want to enjoy my memorial now!' as if he would be sitting in the front pew. I felt certain that he was.

It was his birthday a few weeks ago and Gabriella and I were playing her current favourite game in the garden of the new home we moved into recently. I throw a football over the high netting of her trampoline and she bounces to catch it before throwing it back over. We count how many catches we can do without dropping it and she somersaults with delight whenever we exceed our target. On this occasion, she suddenly sat down and cried.

'I miss Papa, Mum,' she confided, 'I wish we could take him a cake with candles to blow out. That was the last time I saw him. On his birthday, blowing out candles. Do you think he will hear us if we sing "Happy Birthday" to him now?'

It was hard to believe, but in that moment a red kite flew low into the garden, momentarily so close she might have bounced high enough to touch it. 'There he is,' I exclaimed at this impeccable lifeshock. 'This is how Papa visits us these days. Sing, darling sing!' It soared higher and higher with each note until it had disappeared into the Mystery and left us doused in delight.

Dad's death did not cast me adrift. I have touched my own death twice in the past few years and was as ready for his as my own. But losing a parent is a major milestone, even in adult life when they are old and it is expected and people say, 'Well he had a good innings' as if sorrow is less relevant somehow. I have since learned there is a term for unrecognised mourning in society: 'disenfranchised grief'. How very skilled we have become at this in so many ways. We disenfranchise great swathes of the human experience until those daily imprints of Something Greater – lifeshocks – pound hard enough for us to pay attention, to feel what needs to be felt and honour what needs to be honoured, to become ever more integrated and aligned and free.

It is now, two days before the first anniversary of his death, when the sorrow is no longer acute and an emotional equilibrium has returned, that I miss him most. I miss telling him what I'm up to. I miss him liking my Facebook posts, tracking my media appearances, attending my talks, showing such complete interest and pride in my life. I miss him phoning to tell me off for not phoning him more often. I miss the way he loved Gabriella and our dog.

Ten months after his death I gave a TEDx talk entitled, 'How grief can help us win when we lose' and received an instant standing ovation from the entire theatre audience. It was a peak experience in my life and the moment I realised I was fatherless. With the exception of John, Dad was the person I most wanted to bear witness to the soothing truths his death had helped me embed in my heart: that we can be expanded by loss not diminished and that when we grieve well those whom we have lost somehow stay with us. Their essence lies seconds beneath the surface and red kites circle in our skies.

Appendix

Origins and Application

While I have placed these teachings in relevant contexts at different times in this book, the emphasis on real experience rather than academic argument has been deliberate. Essentially, this work is rooted in existential philosophy and the work of existential therapists, including one of Brad's teachers, Viktor Frankl.

The whole point of existential psychology is to get away from the theoretical framework and focus on the individual's personal encounter with existence. When, in the More To Life programme and my own courses, we ask people to identify a lifeshock moment, we are inviting them into an *existential encounter*. They are being asked to re-experience a moment in time in such a way that sensory data can be separated from interpretations of that data and the feelings those interpretations generate. A complex experience is broken down into its accurate parts.

In the late twentieth century, research by David Eagleman of the Baylor College of Medicine demonstrated that our consciousness lags 80 milliseconds (which equates to one-twelfth of a second) behind actual events. Dr Brown recognised that this twelfth of a second exists between the existential moment and the mental interpretation that arises *afterwards*. And this is precisely what Frankl refers to in his famous observation,

'Between stimulus and response there is a space. In that space is our power to choose our response. In our response lies our growth and freedom.'

Frankl and his wife, Tilly, were transported from a Nazi ghetto to the Auschwitz concentration camp in 1944 and he was later moved to Kaufering, a camp affiliated to Dachau, where he spent five months working as a slave labourer. As a psychologist, Frankl was aware that we are the ones who give meaning to our experiences and, since we are the meaning-givers, we get to choose our response to the hands we are dealt – even in a context of severe suffering.

Following in this tradition, Brad never came up with a theory and tested it out. Everything he created was drawn from personal experience, as well as the experiences of his clients and students. In this, he joined existential therapists in offering practices, tools and methods designed to help people engage directly with their lived experience.

This began with his work as a clinical psychologist. He founded the Institute for Family and Human Relations in Los Gatos CA with his wife Dr Anne Brown (a psychotherapist specialising in family therapy) and the two of them personally trained therapists there for over twenty years. The methodology described in this book was first developed in that setting. He was also an active church minster throughout this period, supporting parishioners with their deepest fears and highest hopes.

His early insight and innovation was the particular work he did with lifeshock moments, which unlocked the unconscious mind with remarkable ease and at far greater speed than most therapeutic practices. While separating events from interpretations is certainly not original, I have not come across the same way of working with lifeshock moments, even in related work such as Cognitive Behavioural Therapy or Rational Emotive Therapy.

His second significant insight was to observe the way lifeshocks wake us up to our own conditioning and help us recognise behavioural patterns and belief systems that limit growth, potential and evolution. He described them as 'shocks to the system' – the unconscious matrix of received meanings and conditioned responses that society has taught us growing up. Lifeshocks come, not to make us more comfortable, but to wake us up to what we don't want to see: our complacency, resignation, bad faith, avoidance, controlling, bullying, cold-heartedness and manipulation.

Again, this has echoes of some other teachings. But Brad's greatest breakthrough was to identify another 'system' at work, a pattern in the apparently random that manifests as three specific categories or qualities of lifeshock which we all receive: *limiting, exposing* and *evoking*. I have described these in detail in these pages – what they challenge in us and what they restore in us. In the acceptance of our *humanity*, the expression of our *authenticity* and in our ability to *love* and *be loved*, we become integrated, aligned and free. The universe is delivering us back to ourselves in these three ways, lifeshock by lifeshock by lifeshock. These types of lifeshock also relate to three existential categories: I AM, YOU ARE, IT IS. In other words:

I am as I am (not as I think or fear). *You are as you are* (not as I imagine you to be). *It is as it is* (not as I think it should be). *We are one* (interconnected and inter-dependent, not the separated entirely independent entities the ego wishes us to be).

This is the same creative acceptance of *What Is* that Nietzsche recognised:

'My formula for what is great in mankind is not to wish for anything other than that which is; whether behind, ahead or for all eternity. Not just to put up with the inevitable – much less to hide it from oneself – but *to love it.*'

To love it.

Yes, but how?

By receiving the three great gifts of lifeshocks and loving them, one by one by one.

Case Studies

These principles have been tried and tested in diverse context for several decades. These are just a few examples:

1. A study of the More To Life self-esteem course showed it produced higher, more robust and longer-lasting results for the ordinary people who participated in the course than the trainee counsellors who formed the control group in the study.
2. The Mandela Rhodes Foundation used our material as the basis of its training for young black leaders and co-opted one of our teachers as a mentor for its students for over ten years in South Africa. I personally trained some of these scholars during a week-long course on Robben Island.
3. Our methodology was used by inmates at Bastrop

Prison, Texas, which was one of many penal institutions that have used it. There it was part of a ten-year federally funded drug treatment programme which had outstanding ongoing results.

4. A Canadian physics professor taught one of our courses ('People on Purpose') to his class. His students did so much better than their colleagues in exams that the college called for an investigation to see if they had been cheating.

5. In my own consulting business, I delivered these practices to leading organisations for over twenty years, from British Airways, HBoS, Unilever and lastminute.com to the NHS and local education authorities and many more. My business won the award for Best Culture Change Programme one year. While we did not go into the more spiritual aspects of this book or even use the term lifeshocks in those settings, we taught tens, perhaps hundreds, of thousands of leaders and employees to work with their corporate lifeshocks to improve performance, creativity, service, leadership and employee engagement.

6. I have been delivering workshops to cancer patients since my diagnosis to empower them to direct their own treatment and listen to the lifeshocks this brutal disease can deliver in ways that bring healing, transformation and peace.

7. The More To Life global educational charity has been delivering this work to many thousands of individuals since 1981, with centres in the UK, the USA, South Africa, New Zealand, Australia and Spain. It has also been taught in a number of

countries and in some other languages. Several core courses are CPD accredited in the UK. Our training rooms function as highly supportive environments with skilled emotional support, leaders who walk their talk and trainers who have become masters of these practices by engaging with lifeshocks to transform their own lives. Outside the training room, more support is available in various forms.

Dr K. Bradford Brown

Dr Kenneth Bradford Brown, informally known as Brad, was my beloved teacher from 1992 until his death in 2007. Brad was born of humble origins in Nevada, USA. After graduating from high school, he started a dry-cleaning business near Oakland, California, married and became a jazz band leader. Called to the ministry following a spiritual awakening, he attended the University of California before continuing on to seminary. He was ordained as an Episcopalian priest, immersing himself in the Civil Rights movement and anti-war activism while serving in two parishes. While he eventually stopped working as a parish priest, he remained an ordained priest until his death.

Brad studied directly under Carl Rogers, Viktor Frankl and Alan Watts, three major contributors to the philosophy and practice of psychology in the last century. He was also highly influenced by Dr Aaron Beck's *Cognitive Therapy*, the social psychologist Erich Fromm, as well as the ideas of George Ivanovich Gurdjieff and P. D. Ouspensky's *Fourth*

Way philosophy. Frankl, who survived Auschwitz said, 'The last of the human freedoms is to choose your own attitude in any given situation, to choose your own way.' This simple, profound truth underpins the methodology that became Brad Brown's life's work. His mission was to advance and modernise transformative learning, making it accessible to anyone who wanted to change their lives and enabling them to walk a conscious, courageous and sacred life path through an asleep, fearful and secular world.

In the mid-1970s Brad founded the Institute for Family and Human Relations in Los Gatos, California, with his wife Dr Anne Brown. By 1979 he had evolved a new methodology that he called 'the work' (a name later chosen, coincidentally, by Byron Katie), but never wrote a book about it. He believed transformation could not be understood, only experienced, so he co-founded, with Dr Roy Whitten, an educational programme in 1981 (originally called The Life Training and now called More To Life), which has touched the lives of thousands of people across four continents.

In the 1990s, Brad teamed up with Janet Jones and Sophie Sabbage to take his work into the corporate world through their company, Interaction. As a result, his work has reached top retailers, banks, airlines, penal institutions, domestic violence shelters and pioneering educational and charitable institutions – from the Mandela Rhodes Foundation in South Africa to the Prince's Trust in the UK, and in school and university programmes on both sides of the Atlantic. Brad and Sophie conducted his last Board meeting at his home in California three months before he died.

A servant leader in every way, Brad grew a cadre of

other leaders to take the work forward. He resisted being in the limelight or hailed as a guru. He was an avid sailor who travelled widely and a prolific journal writer. Brad died on 10 August 2007, survived by his wife Anne, five of his six children and a growing number of grandchildren and great-grandchildren.

Acknowledgements

Dr Rosie Jackson, author of *The Glass Mother* and *The Light Box*, for your adept hands in these pages, your piercingly accurate feedback (especially your utter truthfulness about aligning my being with my words), your long friendship in my life and all you have taught me about how to write, not to mention how to love the Source of It All.

David Templer, More To Life senior trainer and dear friend, for the generosity with which you helped me discern the nuances of Brad's work over several 'Zoom' calls, the research you did for me without my needing to ask, your contribution to the appendix and all you do to sustain Brad's legacy. You are an oracle of wisdom.

Dr Roy Whitten, who co-founded the More To Life programme with Brad, co-created the core entry-level course, played an important role in shaping some of the material, and whose contribution for many years made a lasting difference. Brad was my teacher, but Roy touched my heart and inspired my living too. He also officiated my multi-faith marriage to John. Together he and Brad birthed what has changed the lives of thousands.

My brother, Rupert Edwards, for literally saving my life in the autumn of 2017. You may not like me saying that publicly, but some gratitude is to be shouted out loud.

Anne Brown, Brad Brown's widow, for trusting me to write this book and to honour the legacy of a man we loved in different ways and miss so acutely.

Professor William Torbert, creator of *Action Inquiry* and author of *The Power of Balance*, for all you have taught me about living in inquiry, moment to moment.

John Hoover PhD, author of *The Uniting Power of Conflict*, for your valuable contribution to Brad's body of work, some of which is reflected in these pages.

The people who have supported me emotionally and spiritually in these recent challenging years: especially Catherine Rolt, Stuart Camp, Dr Kim Jobst, Peggy Jarrett.

Mark Booth, my awesome editor, for your patience and brilliance, for caring about my wellbeing more than my deadlines, and for seeing my value as an author.

And finally, but most importantly, my husband John Sabbage. Because of you, this book exists. Because of you, I know peace.

In addition, I wish to thank:

My parents, Nick and Anne Crickhowell, who would prefer me to keep my inner life to myself, but who have supported me anyway. Especially my darling father who died before this book was published and who I miss immeasurably.

All the members of Brad's immediate family, including those I am privileged to know: Sara Marks-Brown, Joel Brown and Kai Brown.

My publishing team at Hodder & Stoughton, especially

my funny, professional and dedicated publicist, Karen Geary.

My literary agent: Valeria Huerta, who has championed me as a writer from the beginning and ensured I became an international author. She is a shining spirit.

Peter Lurie, for producing all the graphics, changing them several times and being good at many things I am pants at.

Sue Oldham, the More To Life trainer who first taught me about lifeshocks and mindtalk and who first showed me what a powerful woman really looks like. Sadly, she died a few months before the publication of this book.

My sister, Olivia Clarke, for showing up when the shit hits the fan – not just for me, but for our father and my daughter.

All those who have contributed their very personal stories to this book, whether anonymously or under their real names.

Life Itself, for every lifeshock and every awakening.

Photographic Acknowledgements

The author and publisher would like to thank Ranald Mackechnie for his permission to use the photograph on page xiii.

Resources

Sophie Sabbage

To find out more about Sophie's talks, workshops and writings, go to:
https://www.sophiesabbage.com/

Sophie's TED x talk,
'How grief can help us win when we lose' can be found on YouTube

To follow Sophie on social media, go to:
Facebook
facebook.com/sophie.sabbage.1
facebook.com/thecancerwhisperer
facebook.com/sophiesabbagelifeshocks
Twitter – @sophiesabbage
Instagram – @sophiesabbage

More To Life

The More To Life Programme

To find out more about this non-profit educational organisation and to participate in courses where you can experience these teachings (and much more) go to:

https://www.moretolife.org/

There are centres in the UK, USA, New Zealand, Australia, South Africa and Spain. All these links can be found at the above site.

Facebook:

Life@MoreToLife.org

Legal Page

References

Dr K. Bradford Brown, *Touchstones for an Inner Journey*, Lifetimes Press 1988
This is no longer in print but similar publications are available from lifetimespress.com.

Anna Sewell, *Black Beauty*, Penguin Books 2008, originally published in 1877

Harper Lee, *To Kill A Mockingbird*, Warner Books 1960

Viktor Frankl, *Man's Search for Meaning*, Beacon Press 1946, revised edition 2014

Jeanette Winterson, *Gut Symmetries*, Ipso Books 2016

Elizabeth Gilbert, *Big Magic*, Penguin Books 2015

Maya Angelou, *I Know Why The Caged Bird Sings*, Ballantine Books 2009, originally published in 1969

Daniel Ladinsky, *The Gift – Poems by Hafiz the Great Sufi Master*, Penguin 1999

Daniel Ladinsky, *Love Poems from God*, Penguin 2002

Pablo Neruda, *Twenty Love Poems: And A Song of Despair*, Jonathan Cape 2004

Walt Whitman, *The Complete Poems*, Penguin Classics new edition 2004

Elizabeth Kübler-Ross and David Kessler, *On Grief and Grieving*, Simon and Schuster UK reissue 2014

M.K. Gandhi, *An Autobiography: The Story of My*

Experiments with Truth, Penguin Classics new edition 2001

Ram Dass, *ramdass.org*

Brené Brown, *The Power of Vulnerability*, Sounds True 2012

Denise Riley, *Say Something Back*, Picador 2016

Pyotr Ouspenskii, *The Fourth Way*, Knopf 1957

Idries Shah, *Learning How to Learn*, first published by Octagon Press 1978

Kabir Helminski, *The Knowing Heart*, Shambala Publications 2000

Professor William Torbert, *Action Inquiry, The Secret of Timely and Transforming Leadership*, Berrett-Koehler 2004

Rupert Sheldrake, *The Science Delusion*, Coronet 2012

Nelson Mandela, *The Long Walk to Freedom*, Abacus 1995

Lao Tze, *Tao Te Ching*, Dover Publications 2000

Friedrich Nietzsche, *Ecco Homo: How One Becomes What One Is*, Penguin Classics new edition 1992

Extracted Wisdom of Alan Watts, Amazon Media

U2, *Achtung Baby*, Island Records 1991

Harry Nilsson, *Without You: The Best of Harry Nilsson*, Sony Music 2011

Various Artists (including Liza Minnelli), *Cabaret*, Universal Island Records 1972

Paramore, *Misery Business*, Fueled by Raman

Irene Cara, *Fame: The Original Soundtrack from the Motion Picture Fame*, Sandrew Metronome 2016

Bonnie Tyler, *Total Eclipse of the Heart*, Collectables Records 2011

Read on for an exclusive extract from
Sophie Sabbage's bestselling

The Cancer Whisperer

Finding courage,
direction and the
unlikely gifts of
cancer

'A brilliant book, for anybody
who is living with cancer...
this is invaluable'.
– *Lorraine Kelly*, ITV

The Cancer Whisperer

Sophie Sabbage

When your life is on the line and every decision seems potentially perilous, a lot of cancer patients want the doctors to make their decisions for them. I understand that. And if that's how you want to navigate your journey, then this book may not be for you. But if you have some sense that directing your own treatment, trusting your own wisdom and taking charge of your own care is treatment in its own right – psychological medicine for your cells, medicine that may matter as much as the drugs you are taking and the food you are eating – then I am writing this for you.

This book is for the cancer patient who wants to remain a dignified, empowered human being when your doctors and diagnosis are scaring the shit out of you, you're so shocked you can hardly put your shoes on in the morning, you're caught in the cross-fire between orthodox and complementary medicine and, disturbingly, the medical system treats you like a disease, not a human being. It is also for the cancer patient who has a hunch that there is something for them to learn, gain or even be transformed by – if they just knew how to relate to this disease differently to the way most of society does. It is for the cancer patient, perhaps any patient, who is looking for another way.

This is part memoir and part self-help book. I'm writing it to help you author your own story with wisdom, realism, creativity and courage. I want to share with you how I am navigating my own way through shock, terror, grief, other people's awkwardness in the face of my prognosis – and how I'm sustaining an ongoing inquiry into the nature, causes, lessons and gifts of this devastating but illuminating disease.

I started writing this book ten months after my initial diagnosis. I am living with cancer, but almost all my metastases have gone. I still have a primary tumour in my lung and the ever-present possibility that my cancer will mutate and march like an army through my body again. My cancer is systemic and "incurable", but I am living with it. No, I'm thriving with it. I listen to my doctors, to whom I am grateful beyond measure, and I attend all my appointments. But now I receive phone calls to ask me when I'm available and my doctors *suggest* rather than *tell* me what to do. We have become collaborative partners on my journey, instead of staying caught in the top-down doctor-patient dynamic that still prevails in so much of our medical culture.

The fact is, my disease may well still kill me. Indeed, if I line up behind all the statistics, predictions and likelihoods of having stage four lung cancer, I am a certain goner. At the same time I choose not to line up behind those things. I listen to them, yes, keenly and humbly enough to pare back the crusted layers of denial that shield us from words like 'terminal' and 'incurable' until we can hear them without breaking like glass. But I choose to get it without giving in to it, to surrender without succumbing, to shout my name over the rooftops of statistics before my identity is submerged in the cold anonymity of numbers. I am under no illusion as to the gravity of my condition, but I am now able to lean ever so gently into tomorrow without fear of falling or drowning or bursting into flames.

I want to live almost more than anything. *Almost.* I dedicate my days, hours and minutes to extending my life, with a fierce and unwavering intention to raise my daughter into adulthood, grow old with my beloved husband and make the difference I like to think I came into the world to make. But the biggest win is not surviving cancer, as epic as that would be, and as huge as my purpose is to do so. The bigger win is in preserving my personhood, whatever the outcome – that hard-won "I" that neither belongs to my body nor will disintegrate with my body – and knowing that I let it blossom in the face of cancer, even if my flesh withers. The only way I know how to do that is to notice the eagle across the water and the field of possibility on the windblown shore of another country as I steer my ship through this experience, making one brave, faithful and dignified choice at a time.

At the start of this journey my diagnostician, the doctor who reviewed my first CT scan and conducted my bronchoscopy (a procedure that is not for the faint of heart), said an extraordinary thing to me before passing me on to the oncologist:

'Don't become a patient, Mrs Sabbage. Live your life.'

I took what he said deeply to heart. It empowered me to reach for more than outrunning my prognosis – or dying bravely because I believed it. When I was in deep, fresh, hot-off-the-press shock – about to disappear into that starless night where you cannot see or hear or speak for wishing something different – that doctor awakened the best part of me. It was the part that knows the future is never written, that everything happens for a purpose greater than my seeing, and that when the shit hits the fan I can either fall to my fate or rise to my destiny. I think I have been rising ever since.

In this book, I will share some of the research I've done, the treatments I've chosen, the diet I follow and the resources that have made the biggest differences for me. I hope this information will help you find shortcuts through the mass of information out there about cancer, much of it conflicting. I also recommend specific books and films I consider essential reading and viewing for anyone diagnosed with this disease.

However, I am not a doctor or medical expert of any kind. I am a cancer patient and a facilitator of human transformation. I'm not qualified to help you overcome your condition. I am qualified to help you overcome your *conditioning*, which I believe is also fundamental to the healing process. I can help you *be* well, even when you *feel* ill, and release yourself from emotional factors that may have contributed to your *dis-ease*.

I don't need to add to the library of books already out there about diet, wellness and treatment protocols. However, I *can* assist you in charting your way through all that data with a clear mind, attuned intuition and robust sense of self. Whether or not you become clear of cancer, you can still become free of cancer. That is, free of the fear it feeds on; free of the deadline it imposes; free of the power it can wield over your choices; free of the toxic beliefs that contaminate your healing process;

free of the perception of inevitability marching you to your fate.

Though I can't offer magic cures or miracles, I hope this book will enable you to find healing you may not otherwise have found. Out of my own experience with cancer, and twenty years of experience of working with people to awaken their minds and free their spirits, I have designed a practical and, hopefully, transformative process that will support you to take radical responsibility for your treatment and unlock the wisdom of your disease. *My main aim is to help cancer patients transform their relationship with cancer such that they are transformed by having cancer, whatever the outcome, live or die.* So I hope this book will help you experience the vibrancy of vulnerability, the power of purpose, the freedom of authenticity, and the wonder of forging your own path through a dense, dark forest that sometimes seems to offer no respite or escape. Mostly, I hope it will help you listen to your hunch that cancer has something to teach you, if you only knew how to listen to what it is trying to say.

This is what horse whisperers learnt to do with horses – understand their language and communicate with them on a whole new level. They tested the limited levels of understanding and took it to a new horizon, working in sympathy with the horse to gain co-operation instead of trying to "break" it through dominance and control. Through the whispering process, the horse "joins up" with the human, willingly accepting his or her leadership and choosing to be guided by them from that point on.

Similarly, we have been trying to break cancer for decades, even centuries, to little avail compared to the progress medicine has made with other diseases. We are in a hostile and adversarial relationship with a condition there is still no reliable cure for. We are aware of contributory factors that lead to cancer, but few irrefutable causes, while the number of people being diagnosed is increasing exponentially. So perhaps it is time to communicate with this disease on a whole new level and take our relationship with it to a new horizon by working in sympathy with it to gain its cooperation. Perhaps it is time to take it off the battlefield and into the classroom. Perhaps it is time to ask not only how we can heal the cancer in our bodies, but also what our cancer is telling us about how to heal our lives.

This is my inquiry. I am a fellow cancer patient doing all I can to learn from my disease and change my life because of it. I am gravely ill, yet weirdly well. More grateful to my cancer than afraid of it. Inhabiting a rarefied space between my fierce will to live and my necessary willingness to die. Witnessing the way a bird sings its way towards nightfall and gives itself to the world until its very last note in a flight of perfect authenticity. Wanting to live the exact same way. Inviting you to live the exact same way, however our stories end.